Hostile

"Today's Israel and Modi's India are natural partners, sharing values of racist ethnocracy and illegal annexation, and, for Israel, offering a market for military and other advanced technology. This valuable study traces the complex evolution of their relationship from their independence to its recent blossoming as the societies and the international context changed, providing particularly rich insights into India's development through this period."

—Noam Chomsky

"This is a brilliantly written book and a call for global solidarity. Essa reveals the mutual agenda of the unholy India-Israeli ethno-nationalistic alliance, showing just why both those states are a danger to progressive internationalism. In dealing with the rise of Zionism, along with Modi's capture of state power in India, he deals with their ramifications on Kashmir and Palestine, on Indian diaspora and Israel's role in Africa."

—Ronnie Kasrils, former South African Intelligence Minister, author and activist

"For decades, India's leaders spoke in hushed tones about their relationship with Israel. Azad Essa's thoroughly-researched and crisply-written *Hostile Homelands* reveals the long history of their alliance and shows how it is built on shared supremacist ideological projects whose devastating and inhumane consequences are borne by Palestinians and Kashmiris living under occupations. This is an essential, must-read book."

—Mohamad Junaid, anthropologist and Kashmiri writer

"Azad Essa's brilliant and courageous book is the definitive treatment of the overlooked alliance between the far-right wing governments of India and Israel. This text is essential reading for the escalating neo-fascist forces in our turbulent times."

—Cornel West

"A necessary and urgent account."

—Siddhartha Deb, author of *The Beautiful and The Damned: New Life in India*

"*Hostile Homelands* is an authoritative study of the past and present of India-Israel relations. It reveals a troubling convergence of Hindu nationalist and Zionist worldviews. Equally, the book is a useful primer for thinking about how and why illiberal, authoritarian and Islamophobic forces are building alliances, globally."

—Somdeep Sen, Associate Professor and Head of Studies, Global & Development Studies, Roskilde University, Denmark

"A revealing exposé of the complex history behind the current Israeli-Indian relationship. *Hostile Homelands* traces the current Zionist-Hindu Nationalism alliance throughout the years, deconstructing the relationship between Delhi and Tel Aviv starting from the time of seeming hostility and political expediency following India's independence, to the gradual and, eventually, complete affinity between both countries. Essa's book provides a critical reading of an involved and rarely covered subject that spans far-right nationalist ideologies, powerful financial and military interests, as well as human solidarity. This book is an essential read that challenges the typical understanding of Zionism as an exclusively European phenomenon and Hindu nationalism as a provisional Indian experience."

—Ramzy Baroud, author of *Our Vision for Liberation: Engaged Palestinian Leaders & Intellectuals Speak Out*

"*Hostile Homelands*' quest is formidable and timely. Azad Essa lays bare the historically malignant roots of an often overlooked and underestimated kinship between two ideologies—Zionism and Hindutva—hungry for land and hungrier for dominance."

—Mohammed El-Kurd, author of *Rifqa*

"In this volume, Essa forces us to confront the grotesque end-game of colonial violence— Modi's India and Zionist Israel. The enduring and shape-shifting connections between these ethnonationalist entities offer a profound wake-up call, a realization that today, the most vocal among the world's purported democracies are, at their core, the most profoundly anti-democratic."

—Nazia Kazi, Ph.D. Associate Professor of Anthropology, Stockton University, NJ

"A meticulously researched and well-crafted book on the under-covered subject of the ever-evolving relationship between India and Israel. If there is any authority on the topic today, it is Azad Essa, who delivers a comprehensive and detailed account of a 'special relationship' in need of examination and critique. As he takes readers through the history of the diplomatic, military and economic ties between India and Israel, Essa insightfully explores what happens when a nation negotiates the tension between principles and interests— and what happens when, particularly under the ethnonationalism of Narendra Modi, they converge."

—Laila Al-Arian, *Al Jazeera English*

"This is the definitive book on Indian-Israel relations that we have been waiting for. *Hostile Homelands* is not only an intellectual tour de force; just as importantly it will also foster new solidarities and anti-imperialist organizing."

—Jasbir Puar, author of *The Right to Maim: Debility, Capacity, Debility*

Hostile Homelands

The New Alliance Between India and Israel

Azad Essa

Foreword by Linah Alsaafin

PLUTO PRESS

First published 2023 by Pluto Press
New Wing, Somerset House, Strand, London WC2R 1LA
and Pluto Press Inc.
1930 Village Center Circle, 3-834, Las Vegas, NV 89134

www.plutobooks.com

British Library Cataloguing in Publication Data
A catalogue record for this book is available from the British Library

ISBN 978 0 7453 4501 7 Paperback
ISBN 978 0 7453 4505 5 PDF
ISBN 978 0 7453 4503 1 EPUB

This book is printed on paper suitable for recycling and made from fully managed and sustained forest sources. Logging, pulping and manufacturing processes are expected to conform to the environmental standards of the country of origin.

Typeset by Stanford DTP Services, Northampton, England

Simultaneously printed in the United Kingdom and United States of America

For my Hafsa

We were mistaken when we thought the homeland was only the past . . . the homeland is the future.

—Ghassan Kanafani, *Palestine's children: returning to Haifa and other stories*

Contents

Foreword

Linah Alsaafin

It's been 10 years since Azad Essa visited Palestine. In the decade since, we struck a friendship that tipped into mentorship, and later on—for a brief period of time—became colleagues working for the same media company. I met him in Ramallah, after my brother—who couldn't come back to the occupied West Bank because unlike most of my family, he did not have a West Bank ID—called to ask if I could show his friend around in order to avoid the trappings of "conflict tourism." For a week, Azad and I traipsed around the different cities and villages in the West Bank, which is saturated with checkpoints, inaccessible Jewish-only settlements, and Israeli soldiers. Beyond that ugly facade, he was introduced to the rich history of Nablus and its shopkeepers, the alleyways and ancient churches of Bethlehem, and the gritty hardiness of Hebron's Old City.

At my insistence, since my Israeli military-issued ID restricts me to one territory, he visited Jerusalem and Yafa—once called the Bride of the Sea before 1948 but now a neglected southern suburb of Tel Aviv, a city that itself is built upon the remains of six ethnically cleansed Palestinian villages. Inevitably, his visit resulted in a determination on his part not just to study the cruelty meted out by a state against a colonized population, but a resolve for placing such power in relation to the support and facilitation awarded to it by other countries.

One such country, already at the time shooting at an upwards trajectory with Israel, was India. It seems odd that despite having relations—both covert and official—that span almost the entirety of Israel's existence, there has been a shortage of literature written on the subject matter.

India, the so-called largest democracy in the world, has often expressed its support for Palestine. But as this book deftly illustrates, its purported support for the Palestinian cause was in reality contingent on Indian interests. The deep connections between the ethnonationalist ideologies of Zionism and Hindutva, the predominant form of Hindu nationalism that has taken root in India, was always likely to ultimately culminate in a shift in India's foreign policy.

The sister ideologies go way back. In the 1920s, the man who furthered the concept of Hindutva, Vinayak Savarkar, wrote that "If the Zionists' dreams are ever realized—if Palestine becomes a Jewish state—it will gladden us almost as much as our Jewish friends." To pare it down to the basics, Zionism and Hindutva are both predicated on creating a supremacist nation built upon a single, united identity. Israel, according to its own law, is the state for its Jewish citizens, "in which it exercises its natural, cultural, and historic right to self-determination."

So how did India, which once considered Zionism a form of racism, become Israel's number one weapons trade buyer, accounting for 42% of Israel's arms exports since Modi came to power in 2014?* How did India, the first non-Arab state to recognize the Palestinian Liberation Organization (PLO) and one of the leaders of the Non-Aligned Movement that opposed colonialism and apartheid, simultaneously maintain its colonial occupation of Kashmir since 1947 and metamorphose into extolling Israel's settlements as a model to colonize Kashmir with its own Indian settlers?

* https://middleeasteye.net/news/india-israel-arms-trade-numbers (last accessed July 2022).

The answer can be surmised from the contradictions of Indian nationalism and the larger myths of Indian-state formation in which its foreign policy was used as a cover for its colonization of Kashmir. It can also be analyzed from the mix of a deadly ideology inspired early on by European fascism, one that has reached dizzying heights under Narendra Modi, and seismic changes to the geopolitical order. This book traces the history of Hindutva and how it came to be seen by Indian officials as a "civilizational tie" to Israel's supposed success story of being. It also traces a chronicled study of the transposition of India's relations with Israel, beginning with Jawaharlal Nehru's recognition of the state in 1950, the secret collaboration between the RAW and Mossad intelligence, the burgeoning development of the military industrial complex, to the official normalization of ties.

The relations represent a "moral-political degeneration," as described by writer and social activist Achin Vanaik. But for others, such as Egyptian researcher Mustafa Shalash, India has embraced a realist approach and sees Israel not only as a gateway to Washington, but also as an effective and powerful technology mediator and supporter on the international stage. Shalash refers to how the privatization of India's economy in the 1980s opened the door to neoliberalism, leading to an alliance with the United States. A direct consequence of neoliberalism was presented in the cache of opportunities across the sectors of agriculture, technology, and security, which Israel gradually invested in, resulting in $5bn worth of trade deals per year between the two countries.

Under the rule of the far-right wing BJP party, India has sought to emulate Israel on several fronts. It has adopted "homeland security methods" and counter-terrorism as a response to popular mobilizations and resistance. It signed into law the 2019 Citizenship Act—similar to Israel's return law which affords any Jew from around the world the right to relocate and gain automatic citizenship. (The BJP's version fast-tracks the naturalization of non-Muslim minorities who come from three Muslim-majority neighboring countries.)

Thirdly, its complete annexation of Kashmir increasingly resembles Israel's settler-colonialism in Palestine. The situation in Kashmir, one of the most militarized regions in the world, is becoming even more untenable after Modi revoked its semi-autonomous status in 2019. Visiting it a year earlier, I was rattled by the sheer amount of heavily armed soldiers stationed every few hundred meters or so. Some of the buildings in downtown Srinagar were pockmarked with bullet holes, others completely shuttered. The atmosphere was one of tension and normality, and carried undertones of apprehension and a brittle business-as-usual demeanor—something I recognized in Palestinian cities after an Israeli raid, an arrest spree, or targeted assassination.

The word resilience has been overused to the point of becoming a cliche when describing the spirit of an occupied people, but it was evident in the Srinagar storefronts whose businesses remained open despite the odds, in the body movements of the teenagers playing cricket, in the homes that begrudgingly went about life with the gaping absence of a father, a son, or a brother. Now, the government is preparing to send an influx of Indian settlers, a recipe for engineering demographic change at the expense of Kashmiri Muslims and which may lead to widespread forced displacement.

It rings too close to comfort, and funnily enough, brings me back to Azad's Palestine trip. He anticipated the sinister connections and similarities and decided to do more digging, uncovering the reasons Modi's India desperately wants to be like Israel. His trip in 2012 left an indelible mark on him, and I remember badgering him to write his impressions about Palestine. *Hostile Homelands* takes it full circle. Its importance goes beyond gaining awareness of the political developments in Palestine, Kashmir, India, and Israel. Its significance lies at the heart of how such colonial connectivities take shape and materialize, and it provides an urgent context for the importance of transnational solidarity against movements of settler-colonialism, occupation, and apartheid. It also allows us to see how our struggles are connected, and to wield this power of knowledge as a weapon in the fight for justice and against the very mechanisms of bigotry, intolerance, and repression.

In the time that I've known Azad, he has gone from coaching, editing, and encouraging my first published news articles—done with the gratifying mix of humor and down-to-earthness—to becoming an award-winning journalist, co-founder of an alternative news website in his home country of South Africa, and now, even a children's book publisher. His tenaciousness in pursuing subjects for his stories, as well as his acumen, has helped him navigate elections, droughts, refugee crises, and economic issues in sub-Saharan Africa.

Using a detailed methodology that spans archival documents, commemorated speeches and statements, evolving policies and the rise of certain ideologies, *Hostile Homelands* reevaluates the lens of the historical relations between India and Israel, as well as India's alleged commitment to Palestine, and how that has done more harm than good to the Palestinians. With India and Israel charting a new unprecedented apex in their relations and with the occupation and persecution of Kashmiri Muslims, Indian Muslims, and Palestinians becoming more deep-seated, this book is as timely as ever, and will force the reader to not only question the nature of such alliances, but to recognize the consequences and limits of this affiliation on solidarity and justice worldwide.

Linah Alsaafin is a Palestinian journalist and writer.

1
A Story of Two Partitions

> The fight between the Arabs and the Jews in Palestine is a creation of British imperialism. I have every sympathy for the Jews, but they have adopted a wrong policy in looking toward the British government and in not coming to amicable terms with the Arabs and making Palestine free. —Mohandas Karamchand (Mahatma) Gandhi[1]

> The creation of a Jewish national home in Palestine was unacceptable because Palestine was not a wilderness, or an empty uninhabited place. It was already somebody else's home . . . this generous gesture of the British government [the Balfour Declaration] was really at the expense of the people who already lived in Palestine. —Jawaharlal Nehru[2]

On September 27, 1936, as the Indian struggle for independence against British rule was reaching its apex and Europe continued to hurtle toward a new war, the leader of the Indian National Congress (INC), Jawaharlal Nehru, spoke about Palestine. In his speech in the historic city of Allahabad, Nehru drew a direct connection between the Indian and Palestinian struggles against the British.

> We meet today especially to think of the little country of Palestine and of its troubles. In a world view this problem of Palestine has relatively little importance for bigger things are happening elsewhere. And yet it has an intrinsic impor-

> tance of its own and it throws a light on the working of imperialism from which we ourselves suffer.[3]

At the time, Palestine was in the throes of a revolt against British rule and endless Jewish migration from fascist and anti-Semitic Europe. In his speech, Nehru traced the crisis in Palestine, between "the Arabs and Jews" to the hand of British imperialism. "British imperialism, as in India, has tried to play off one community against the other and set the Jews against the Arabs," Nehru said.[4] He added that whereas Jews in Europe were victims of fascism, they had nonetheless allowed themselves to be "exploited" by the British. He placed the burden on Zionists to come to terms with Palestine as an Arab country and bid them to "cooperate"; his sympathies remained with the Arabs who faced "a fresh determination" from the British to crush their movement for self-determination. There was no reason they could not get along, he argued. Nehru's comments in 1936 were not uncharacteristic for the INC. As an organization formed in 1885, the INC had followed decades of pursuing liberation for India from the British through an engagement in international issues and liberation movements around the world, including Egypt, Syria and Iraq.[5] "It was through common opposition to British imperialism that the first real political ties between India and the Arab world were forged," academic Arthur G. Rubinoff writes.[6] On the matter of Palestine, the INC had put out its first statement as early as 1922. Mohandas Karamchand Gandhi, also known as the Mahatma, lent his support to the Khilafat movement. The Hindu-dominated Indian nationalist movement supported the restoration of the Ottoman Empire as a means of integrating the Indian Muslim elite under its wing.

Given their sphere of influence, it was inevitable that the Zionist movement was also determined to gain the approval and support of the Indian Congress. So convinced that their cause for national liberation was genuine, Zionists looked to Nehru and Gandhi to gather testimonials. Gandhi's theatrics of a semi-naked, semi-starved, Holy Seer leading a non-violent and civil disobedience campaign against the world's greatest Empire stood in contrast to Zionism, but it appealed to the liberal sensibilities of the international media, and captivated Western publics, too, including European Zionists, enamored by the soft power of the East. This is not to imply that Indian approval was seen as paramount to the Zionist project. David Ben Gurion, Israel's first prime minister, even admitted that outreach to India and China were limited.[7] But India, as the Jewel of the British Empire, carried a certain prestige alongside the moral heavy weights, Gandhi and Nehru, and the literary mysticism of Rabindranath Tagore.

Gandhi was, as Mosher Sharett, a Ukrainian Jew who would become Israel's second prime minister, described him: "the greatest of the living Hindus."[8] And Nehru was deemed the leader of "undivided India", home to the largest population of Muslims on the planet. The Jewish Agency sent Immanuel Olsvanger (1888–1961) to India to try to persuade Nehru and Gandhi to support the Zionist movement. He failed. Martin Buber, Judah L. Magnes, Albert Einstein, and many others, wrote to Gandhi and Nehru, on their own accord. They mostly failed, too. Following years of overtures and requests, Gandhi expressed his views in an editorial in his weekly newspaper, *Harijan*, in November 1938, which disappointed proponents of the Jewish state:

> My sympathies are all with the Jews. But my sympathy does not blind me to the requirements of justice. The cry for a national home for the Jews does not make much appeal to me . . . it is wrong and inhuman to impose the Jews on the

> Arabs. What is going on in Palestine today cannot be justified by any moral code of conduct.[9]

But the story of Gandhi's rejection of the Jewish state is not as straightforward as it first appears. Gandhi's decision to refuse to support the state was partially driven by a thirst to bridge a gap between the Hindu-dominated Congress party that proposed a strong, ostensibly secular central government and the nascent gathering of Muslim elites who, concerned by their minority status under Hindu majoritarian rule, were hankering for self-determination and greater autonomy within a more federal India. Gandhi was initially categorical in his support for the Palestinian cause. The Jews, Gandhi said, could settle in Palestine "only by the goodwill of the Arabs."

Later, however, his position appeared to change. In 1946, he told an American journalist, "The Jews have a good cause . . . if the Arabs have a claim to Palestine, the Jews have a prior claim."[10] It is Indian author P.R. Kumaraswamy's contention that once Gandhi's famous 1938 comments in *Harijan* had been used to formulate the backbone of India's foreign policy, his later hesitation to fully support Palestinians was in contradiction to Indian interests and was therefore buried. In Kumaraswamy's words, to change course and follow Gandhi's altered approach would "have eroded, if not destroyed, the 'moral' content of India's pro-Palestine policy."[11]

Nehru, too, looked to Palestine as a way to cement the Congress' brand of international solidarity with anti-colonial movements worldwide. It was his firm belief that Britain was the source of all division in Palestine and therefore the Zionist collusion with the British to wrest control of Palestine made the prospect of his support for that project untenable. Moreover, he was averse to religious nationalism. At the time, the INC itself was battling against a demand by the Muslim League for increased autonomy and then later a separate state for India's Muslims.[12] In October 1937, the All India Congress Committee (AICC)[13] rejected the Peel Commission's proposal of a partition plan in Palestine, and pledged the solidarity "of the Indian people . . . in their struggle for national freedom."[14] Months later, in February 1938, Congress condemned Great Britain and expressed its "emphatic protest against the continuation of the reign of terror . . . maintained in Palestine to force (partition) upon the unwilling Arabs."[15] In September 1938, the AICC, again, urged Jews not to take shelter behind British imperialism.[16]

Many of these decisive statements from the INC have their origins in the speech delivered by Nehru on Palestine Day, September 27, 1936 in the city of Allahabad. In this address, Nehru had located India's fight for independence as "part of a world struggle against imperialism and fascism [including] the struggle that is going on against British imperialism in Palestine."[17] He then blamed the strife between Palestinians and the in-coming Jewish migrants as one primarily created by the British. "It is a misfortune they should allow themselves to be exploited in Palestine by British imperialism."[18] In so doing, Nehru, the key shaper of the Congress party's and ultimately India's foreign policy, reduced the conflict between communities in Palestine and in British India to "an imperialist diversion."[19] In 1938, he wrote that "there is no religious or cultural conflict in India . . . the tremendous and fundamental fact of India is her essential unity through the ages."[20]

Nehru had thus concluded that both Zionists and Muslims on the Indian subcontinent had fallen prey to divisive British tactics and were effectively undermining Arab and Indian aspirations for independence. Parallel to these efforts, Nehru and the Congress continued to instrumentalize Palestine to woo Indian Muslims away from the Muslim League. The incorporation of Palestine as a policy matter for the INC would become known to the Hindu right wing as one example of Congress' "appeasement of Muslims" they argued came at the expense of the needs of the nation. Though there was a surge of pan-Islamism in India, it is more conceivable that Congress saw hedging their bets with economic, political and social ties with the Arab world as more lucrative than with the prospect of a small Jewish state. Rubinoff argues that Muslims were subsequently used as "justification" for their hesitation to become closer allies with what then became the state of Israel. "It's what the Indian diplomatic establishment uses and used as an excuse for not acting [to improve ties with Israel]," Rubinoff told me.[21]

India's position on Palestine also helped accentuate Delhi's credibility as a leader of the anti-imperial movement. "Conscious of the implications that partition on the basis of religion would have in each other's own geographic regions, the Arabs cooperated with the INC rather than the Muslim League," Rubinoff writes.[22] The Independence party, a nationalist Palestinian party, adopted a boycott of the British in 1939 in the same mold as the INC.[23] The Zionist movement, once the benefactors of British imperialism, now in revolt against the British, also looked to the Indian National Congress as comrades-in-arms. From the United States, Emanuel Celler, U.S. representative of New York's 15th district, wrote to Nehru in April 1947 expressing his regret that the Indian leader had decided to align "with the Arab League in the matter of Palestine." Celler claimed he understood Nehru's dilemma given the "factional and religious strife" in India before suggesting that Nehru had sacrificed principle for political expediency. "I realize that peace in India is difficult without the goodwill of 90 million Moslems, but I assure you that your statement on Palestine would make no difference to Mohammed Ali Jinnah [leader of the Indian Muslim League]. I am sure your statement is of political expedience."[24]

As head of the Congress party and its director of foreign affairs from 1928, Nehru's directives informed the nascent policies of the government-in-waiting ahead of India's independence in 1947. Nehru saw Zionism as an innovation; an invented nationalism that threatened his idea of India itself.[25]

The Federal Plan and Partition

In 1947, on the eve of the partition of the Indian subcontinent, the incoming Indian government became part of the United Nations Special Committee on Palestine (UNSCOP), an eleven-member committee tasked with finding a solution to the Palestine question. Under Nehru's directives, India opposed partition and along with Iran, and the former Yugoslavia, suggested a federal solution in which all citizens would enjoy equal rights. Under this plan, Arabs would gain 56% of the territory and Jews would be granted 44% in what would be known as national states. The federal government would control immigration, defense, and foreign policy, while the national government would decide on education, land, and housing. "The objective of a federal-state solution would be to give the most feasible recognition to the nationalistic aspirations of both Arabs and Jews, and to merge them into a single loyalty and patriotism which would find expression in an independent Palestine," the minority proposal stated. It also concluded:

> it is a fact of great significance that very few, if any, Arabs, are in favor of partition as a solution. On the other hand, a substantial number of Jews, backed by influential Jewish leaders and organizations, are strongly opposed to partition. Partition both in principle and in substance can only be regarded as an anti-Arab solution.[26]

Moreover, it argued that "the constitution shall forbid any discriminatory legislation, whether by federal or state governments, against Arabs, Jews or other population groups, or against either of the states; and shall guarantee equal rights and privileges for all minorities, irrespective of race or religion."

India's representative at UNSCOP lamented the passing of the 1917 Balfour Declaration that had created the impetus for a Jewish state without the consent of the existing residents.[27] The Federal Plan was dismissed by the Arab bloc as well as the Jewish Agency. The Arabs felt that the plan gave too much away, while the Zionists believed that it did not go nearly far enough in fulfilling their demands for a Jewish state.[28] At the heart of the Jewish opposition of the federal plan was the question of Aliyah, or migration to Israel. Zionists of all persuasions, from liberal and labor to the right wing were "unanimous on unrestricted Jewish immigration [which made the plan] unrealistic to expect the Zionists to subject this core issue to an Arab veto."[29]

Parallel to efforts to secure Nehru's support for the Jewish project, Indian supporters of the Jewish state wrote to the Zionists abroad urging them to remain steadfast to the larger state project.[30] In November 1947, the UN General Assembly finally adopted the partition of Palestine. The newly independent states of India and Pakistan, along with the Arab bloc, voted against it. Thousands of Palestinians were arbitrarily arrested, pushed off their land or killed. When partition came in 1948, it gave way to further catastrophe. Known as the Nakba, around 720,000 out of 1.3 million Palestinians had become refugees from mid-1949.[31]

Concomitant to the developments in Palestine, was the partition of the Indian subcontinent under British stewardship. During colonial India, Britain ruled over parts of the subcontinent directly—the areas that were termed "British India"; in addition, over 500 small and large territories were indirectly ruled by Britain—they were under the control of regional princely rulers. They each exercised different levels of control and subservience to the British. India, then, was by no means a nation. And as Sunil Parushotham writes, India was not "destined to be a Republic. It had to be made into one."[32]

British colonial rule was instrumental in exacerbating tensions between communities in India. The British census of 1871–2 for instance, in which Indians were classified by age, caste, religion, and occupation, had several administrative and political consequences. First, it collapsed identities into distinct categories, for instance Hindu and Muslim. Second, it also created the specter of a Hindu majority, leaving Muslims acutely aware and now fearful for their future as a minority.[33] "It seems that the projection of cleavages within colonial society was essential for sustaining colonial rule, which used a variety of texts, forms, and methods to continue and promote their rule even at the cost of strained communal relationships in India," R.B. Bhagat writes.[34] "At this juncture of history, the census counts first tried out in 1872 aided in the articulation of the cleavages of majority and minority, a handmaiden in creating communal consciousness in the early twentieth century," Bhagat adds.[35] (More in Chapter 3).

As a result, Muslim leaders like Muhammad Iqbal and the leader of the Muslim League, Muhammad Ali Jinnah, knew that Muslims were a majority in the northwest and eastern portions of the subcontinent, and began to articulate a demand for greater autonomy for these regions. Given that Nehru was insistent on a centralized Indian state, in which the Congress party would replace the British as the keeper of the vast subcontinent, he categorically refused Muhammad Ali Jinnah's demands for autonomous Muslim regions inside a larger federal state.

This insistence came at the cost of so-called unity as the subcontinent was carved into the image of its two biggest religious identities. Partition of the two primary regions—Punjab and Bengal—occurred, as British officials used outdated census reports to mark the boundaries that would divide the two new nations. Immense violence, displacement, dispute, and later annexation followed. It stirred one of the largest migrations known to mankind as 17.9 million people moved between newly formed Muslim and Hindu majority homelands.[36] Between March 1947 and January 1948, the bloodletting left around a million Hindus and Muslims dead across the subcontinent. "Having lit the fuse, Mountbatten handed over the buildings to their new owners hours before they blew up, in what has a good claim to be the most contemptible single act in the annals of the Empire," Perry Anderson wrote.[37]

On September 17, 1950, more than two years after its creation, the Indian government recognized the state of Israel. There were no exchanges of diplomats or envoys, no promise of trade or joint projects. Instead, India allowed Israel to open a single "immigration" office in Bombay (now Mumbai) more than 1,000 km away from the political class in New Delhi. For the next 40 years, it would be a relationship marked by ambivalence and indifference and most crucially, the struggle of perceptions.

In the weeks prior to its recognition of Israel, the Indian government labored tirelessly over the pros and cons of altering its position on Israel. Delhi's concerns revolved around three issues: India's image, the country's economy, and the specter of Pakistan. As part of the process, three envoys who represented India across much of the Middle East (Egypt, Lebanon, Iraq, Iran, and Jordan) were tasked with compiling their opinion on whether India ought to move ahead with recognition. In their individual assessments, the extent to which India's decisions were predicated on its own self-interest becomes clear. Dr. Fyzee, the ambassador to Egypt wrote that should India recognize Israel, "the Jewish controlled press in both Britain and America is likely to take a more favorable attitude to India."[38] Ali Zahir, the envoy to Tehran added that given Iran (and Turkey) had already recognized Israel, India was unlikely to face censure in that country. In none of the arguments posited by the envoys was the fate of the Palestinians even mentioned.[39]

In a letter written to Nehru in April 1950, BV Keskar, a deputy minister in the Ministry of External Affairs, argued that "the main question is to decide whether we get any benefit in one form or the other from the Arab countries because of non-recognition."[40] Rubinoff told me that India "looked at the Middle East and saw three million Israelis and 120 million Arabs. They thought about their energy needs and they considered their place in the international order."[41] In the years following Indian independence, more than 70% of both its imports and exports traveled through the Suez Canal.[42]

However, partition had left a gaping hole in the Indian project and represented a moral failure of the Indian National Congress. To embrace Israel meant validating the two-nation theory as well as Pakistan. Moreover, India now felt the need to compete with Pakistan for attention in the Arab world.[43] "Pakistan forced the Indians to be more critical of Tel Aviv than otherwise might have been the case," Rubinoff says.[44] It was this failure of the partition, then, that helped energize the Hindu right's ambition of "uniting" all of India and correcting, as they saw it, a historic wrong. Likewise, Dr. Fyzee warned that if India recognized Israel, India might lose votes at the UN, and Pakistan would be able to exercise greater anti-India propaganda. Keskar, in his letter, said that wooing the Arab world hadn't yielded dividends in India's dispute with Pakistan, an accusation that would become a regular refrain among Hindu nationalists in later years. The possibility of the Arab world taking Pakistan's side over the disputed territory of Kashmir also loomed large. Nehru knew "he could not afford to alienate the Arabs and Muslims . . . especially on the Kashmir issue," Punyapriya Dasgupta wrote.[45]

In a communique justifying its eventual recognition of Israel, the Indian government referred to Israel as "an established fact" and claimed that non-recognition would hamper its ability to wield influence in solving the crisis. At a press conference, Nehru said:

> After careful thought we felt that while recognizing Israel as an entity, we need not at this stage, exchange diplomatic personnel . . . it is not a matter of principle, it is not a matter on which two opinions cannot be held. That, in the balance, is the decision we arrived at and, we think, is a correct decision.[46]

Consolidation with the Arab World

With the introduction of the new Egyptian president, Gamal Abdul Nasser, in 1954, Nehru's pursuit of closer ties with the Arab world took on new meaning. Nasser's and Nehru's anti-colonial sentimentalism fed off one another, as both looked to create a rampart between cold war hostilities of the superpowers and the nascent African and Asian states-in-building.

But Nehru was typically indecisive. Take the events in the days prior to the Bandung Conference in 1955. The conference was billed as the largest ever gathering of movements on the precipice of liberation. Israel, through its repeated acts of settler-colonialism, attachment to the imperial powers (Britain, U.S., and France) and ethnic cleansing of the Palestinian population, had no place at Bandung. Nehru was open to inviting Israel to the conference, only choosing to exclude Tel Aviv to avoid upsetting his Arab comrades. But even at Bandung, where a pro-Palestine resolution was passed, Nehru called for moderation when searching for a solution to Israeli aggression.

The launch of the Non-Aligned Movement (NAM) in 1961, a grouping of ultimately around 120 countries, officially opposed to taking sides in the Cold War, and committed to the pursuit of a world order built on non-aggression, non-interference, and anti-colonialism grew out of Bundung. It symbolized the coming of age of the Third World as an international political force.[47] As the leader of the NAM, India became ever more attached with its self-image as a leader of the colonized and a buffer against Western imperialism. The INC may have been an anti-colonial movement against the British, but it was certainly found lacking as a revolutionary ideal. The anti-colonialism of the party, like almost every other movement in the NAM prior to independence, became empty state rhetoric after independence. A cultish regard for the NAM as a moment of unequivocal moral standing among a band of visionary anti-colonial leaders like Nehru and Nasser also allowed for several leaders to shield their excesses in the building of their states. "Egypt established the template for military republics that styled themselves as anti-imperialist or socialist in Syria, Iraq, Algeria, North Yemen, Libya, and Sudan—all authoritarian states with repressive internal-security apparatuses that policed society, culture, and intellectual life, and crushed all opposition movements," Joel Beinin writes.[48] President Nasser also displaced upwards of 60,000 Nubians and washed away 600 villages in the creation of his Aswan Dam Project in 1964.[49]

Likewise, Arab leaders were well aware of the Indian occupation of Kashmir. "If you went to Kashmir as I did in the late 1960s, if you gave the Kashmiris a choice one would be independence, two would be Pakistan, three would be India . . . They [The Arabs] viewed the Indians as being very colonial," Rubinoff told me.[50] India's other excesses didn't go by unnoticed. In 1958, India implemented the Armed Forces Special Powers Act (AFSPA) in the northeastern Indian states of

Assam and Manipur to quell an insurgency. AFSPA provided India's armed forces "wide powers to shoot to kill, arrest on flimsy pretext, conduct warrantless searches, and demolish structures in the name of 'aiding civil power,'" Human Rights Watch wrote.[51] AFSPA was later extended to seven new states in the northeast in 1973, then in Punjab between 1983–92, and finally in Kashmir in 1990, where it is still active.

As Punyapriya Dasgupta argues, the extent to which "India's stand on Israel was dictated by considerations of international morality and how much by self-interest, was always a difficult question to answer."[52] Likewise, Sampad Patnaik writes that India had "also creatively used anti-colonialism as an assertive strategy and as a different path to great power status." Decades later, there was a certain "potency in browbeating Western sanctimony," Patnaik adds.[53] India's indifference to Israel, then, had much to do with maintaining a self-image for the sake of realpolitik.

Israeli Arms and India: A Secret History

Despite the public posturing, there had always been an intellectual and political class in India who felt kinship with the Zionist project. Nobel laureate Rabindranth Tagore, for instance, was said to have been an enthusiastic proponent of Zionism. "He wanted Zionists to come to India to teach the Kibbutz way of life; a collective, socialist life to the Indian nationalist movement," Khinvraj Jangid, director of the Jindal Centre for Israeli Studies at OP Jindal University, in Haryana, told me.[54] During the early 1950s, Israel's purported socialist project as well as its apparent "neutrality" in the early stages of the Cold War, caught the attention of some Indian political elites. Whereas Israel's participation with France and Britain in the invasion of Egypt in 1956 over Egyptian President Nasser's decision to nationalize the Suez Canal took

India closer to the Arab world, the interactions with Israel, however, did not stop. "Israel got Nepal, Burma (Myanmar) but they failed to catch the big fish, India. [But] India had a public policy and a back channel policy. There is nothing unusual about that," Rubinoff told me.[55]

In 1958, Jayaprakash Narayan, an activist and later political leader, traveled on a nine-day visit to Israel, during which he met Ben Gurion and studied Israel's cooperative and communal institutions. "Narayan sent more than 300 socialists and land reform activists to study the Israeli kibbutz movement for six months. There were exchanges. The Israeli and Indian States did not do business with each other and this was solely because of Nehru's reservations," Jangid shared with me. In a visit to Israel in October 2021, India's foreign minister Jaishanker described Narayan's visit and the interest it spawned in Israel's kibbutz movement, as "an aspect of our shared history which hasn't received the attention it deserves."[56] Nehru, too, is said to have admired the Austrian-Israeli philosopher Martin Buber as well as Ben Gurion. But the relationship could not get any more intimate. "To befriend Israel, when Israel was not caring about the Palestinian refugees, was a difficult thing for him. For Nehru, Third World solidarity was more important than a diplomatic alliance with Israel," Jangid adds.

Indian parliamentary records, too, are replete with debate over India's stance on Palestine and Israel. Opposition politicians routinely called for India's reevaluation of its foreign policy with Israel and its official insistence on supporting the Palestinian cause. In one debate in the Lok Sabha in August 1958, Congress politician Brajeshwar Prasad called on the Arab world to shift their stance on Israel:

> This little refugee nation that was born since 1948 has come to stay just as Pakistan has come to stay. It is an artificially created state like Pakistan. But we have reconciled

> with Pakistan whether we like it or not. Therefore the Arab world will have to reconcile with Israel.[57]

There was in particular much admiration for Israel's military prowess. In the autumn of 1962, a skirmish broke out in the Himalayas between China and India. Nehru wrote to a raft of world leaders, including the Israeli PM to request help, underlining the back channels that existed between the two governments. Nehru had a letter sent to Israel via the consular office in Bombay on October 27, 1962. Five days later, David Ben Gurion replied with his sympathies and an offer to help:

> All our efforts have been and are directed to the preservation of peace—in our area and throughout the world. Jerusalem, the name of our capital in Hebrew, means the city of peace.
>
> I am in total agreement with the views expressed by Your Excellency that it is incumbent upon us to do all in our power. All states big or small must be guaranteed of their sovereignty. We believe that every possible support should be lent to every measure contributing toward easing of tension on your borders so that India will once again be able to devote its undivided energies under your distinguished leadership to construction and development.[58]

Nehru replied on November 18, 1962 with the following letter of thanks:

> We are grateful for your concern for the serious situation that we face today in our border regions. I am sure you will appreciate that while India has never claimed an inch of territory belonging to another country and is traditionally and fundamentally wedded to ideals of peace and friendly settlement of disputes, she cannot but resist aggression on her own soil in the interest of safeguarding national integ-

rity and maintaining respect for standards of international behaviour.

Nehru requested the weapons be transported in ships that did not carry the Israeli flag. Ben Gurion refused. And Nehru had no choice but to accept.[59]

Upon hearing about India's purchase of Israeli weapons, Egypt's President Nasser raised objections and Nehru agreed to end arms purchases from Israel. But India had suffered an embarrassing defeat to China and felt abandoned by the rest of the world, including the Egyptians. And the military deals didn't end. The military assistance India received from Tel Aviv prompted them to continue pursuing backchannel diplomacy with the Israelis, culminating in a request for military and intelligence cooperation in 1963.[60] The Israeli government sold heavy mortars and mortar ammunition to New Delhi, though India continued to publicly deny it. Rubinoff said he asked then defense minister, Swaran Singh, in 1968 about the rumors that Israel had helped India in the 1962 and 1965 wars, "and he got up and he said this interview was now over."[61]

Communication between senior diplomats continued in the 1960s. In a letter sent on September 3, 1963, Braj Kumar Nehru, India's ambassador to Washington, assured Congressman Emanuel Celler that India had all intentions of promoting ties with Israel. "We have long recognized Israel as an independent, sovereign state and our relation with that country has always been harmonious and friendly," Braj Kumar Nehru, who was a cousin to Prime Minister Nehru, wrote.[62] Later, Israel's Chief of Military Intelligence and head of its operations reportedly traveled to Delhi to meet with India's military leaders, though the Indian government denied this trip ever happened.[63]

The country's military defeat to China in the 1962 war ushered in changes to the Indian army. "Over the next two years the country doubled its military manpower, raised a fighting air force (as opposed to a transport fleet), and reversed its position on forging relationships with foreign powers,"[64] Stephen P. Cohen and Sunil Gupta write.

> Both the United States and the Soviet Union stepped in to fill the breach in Indian defences. Moscow supplied MiG-21 fighters and also built a number of factories in India to assemble advanced weapons. The U.S. equipped eight new infantry divisions for mountain defence against the Chinese and rebuilt some defence production facilities.

In 1965, during the next India-Pakistan war, the U.S. military stopped sales to India (and Pakistan) prompting Delhi to conclude that the U.S. was an unreliable supplier. Having already received small arms from Israel in 1962, India secured more armaments from Tel Aviv in the 1965 and 1971 wars with Pakistan.

In 1965, for instance, Israel provided[65] M-58 160mm mortar ammunition to India in its war with West Pakistan. In his book *Blood Telegram*, Gary Bass[66] quotes P.N. Haksar, principal secretary to the then Prime Minister Indira Gandhi, describing the military supplies organized by the Israeli PM as a "surprising minor success" of India's efforts in 1971 to mobilize the world community ahead of its intervention in East Pakistan. According to Bass, then Israeli PM Golda Meir arranged mortars and ammunition as well as instructors with the hope that it might facilitate diplomatic ties with New Delhi.

Incidentally, Israel became one of the first countries to recognize the new state of Bangladesh following the war with West Pakistan in 1971. But attitudes in New Delhi also began to shift following the 1967 war between Israel and the Arab world. The six-day war saw the annihilation of Arab armies leaving Delhi in a state of awe. Publicly, India condemned Israel for being the aggressor and for occupying the Palestinian territories as well as the Egyptian Sinai Peninsula and Syrian Golan Heights; privately it instructed its officers to study the phenomenal destruction of the armies of Egypt and Syria.[67] In parliament, debates raged, too. M.R. Masani from the liberal Swatantra Party, described India's response to Israel as "unrealistic and wrong . . . [and] lacking in the most elementary sense of justice or reality."[68] Masani, along with other opposition parties, also called for the Indian government to adopt "an objective attitude to this dispute and to abstain from taking sides."[69]

Masani also rued the lack of diplomatic ties as it dawned on him and others, that Israel was a powerhouse in the region:

> We have been handicapped by the absence of diplomatic relations with Israel. For years, we have been asking that we should maintain relations with both sides. If we had done that, we would not have been so completely in the dark and made such a mess of our position, because we backed the wrong side on a wrong hypothesis. All these years, 87 countries have maintained diplomatic relations with both Israel and the Arab countries without forfeiting Arab friendship.[70]

In the 1970s, following tensions with Pakistan, Indian officers began traveling to Israel and securing short-term arms deals, often via third-party dealers. Yaakov Katz and Amir Bohbot wrote that India was "interested in learning new tactics, with an emphasis on the emerging use of electronic warfare, an Israeli speciality."[71] According to Kumaraswamy, the overtures to Israel demonstrated that "many Indian leaders, including Nehru, considered Israel in friendlier terms and during critical times sought understanding, if not prolonged intelligence cooperation with Israel."[72]

As ties with Israel improved in private, the Indian government's public overtures toward Israel plummeted to new depths. In 1974, the Indian government under Indira Gandhi became the first non-Arab country to recognize the Palestinian Liberation Organization (PLO) "as the sole and legitimate representative of the Palestinian people"[73] A year later, in 1975, India became one of 72 nations to vote for UN resolution 3379 that demarcated Zionism "a form of racism and racial discrimination."[74] The resolution made specific reference to a resolution adopted three months prior by the Organization of African Unity (now the African Union), which drew comparisons between the racist and colonial projects in South Africa and Israel. "The racist regime in occupied Palestine and the racist regime in Zimbabwe and South Africa have a common imperialist origin, forming a whole and having the same racist structure and being organically linked in their policy aimed at repression of the dignity and integrity of the human being," the OAU resolution 77 (XII)[75] read.

In 1980, Indira Gandhi granted the PLO full diplomatic status. *India Today*'s coverage of the development underscored what was guiding India's concessions, claiming that the move had given India

> a quantum jump in its relations with West Asia and given its political and commercial interaction in the Arab world a much sharper focus. The timing is equally significant in the context of the Afghanistan crisis. India desperately needs the support of the Arab world to avert any prospective move by Pakistan to prejudice Arab opinion with regard to India's efforts to solve the crisis.[76]

Rajiv Gandhi and Israel

It took place in the seat of the Empire: New York City. In October 1985, Shimon Peres and Rajiv Gandhi sat down for a meeting on the sidelines of the fortieth iteration of the United Nations General Assembly (UNGA). It was the first interaction between the leaders of both countries: a tremendous leap. In the days preceding the meeting and the opening session of the UNGA itself, the Israeli army had conducted an outrageous operation in Tunisia. American-made fighter jets flew almost 1,500 miles from Israel and comprehensively flattened the PLO's headquarters in Tunis, leaving behind a crater and around 60 people dead. India condemned the incident, going so far as describing Israel as "aggressive and expansionist." Condemnation notwithstanding, Rajiv still met Peres.

Later that month, on October 16, 1985, 18 Arab states called for Israel to be kicked out of the UN, citing its decades-long occupation of the Palestinians and violations of international law as proof that it did not meet the prerequisites for membership at the world body. There was precedent for this. Apartheid South Africa had been booted out of the UN in 1974. But in the case of Israel, Sweden interjected and called for a motion to have this proposal abandoned. Whereas 80 countries supported Sweden's move to end any move to have Israel's credentials revoked, 40 others voted against the motion. There were 20 other countries who abstained, India among them.[77]

That meeting in New York City between Rajiv and Peres in 1985, then, was a bellwether of the multitude of changes to come, be it India's economy, its foreign affairs or its approach to its own Hindu majority. Rajiv Gandhi, it turned out, had his own vision for India. And much of this vision was predicated on improving relations with the United States. He came without the so-called hang-ups of the past. He was considered more politically pragmatic and expressed an interest in modernizing India.[78]

Rajiv Gandhi was already one of the youngest leaders on the world stage when he became PM in 1984. He represented and carried both the hopes and dreams of young middle-class Indians, impatient to break out of an ideological mold they saw as having ensnared them for decades. These young Indians had no recollection of the independence movement, and little interest in the conventions that had defined the India that had come to being. Where the old India was perceived as being slow, stagnant, and socialist, this new India couldn't come fast enough. Writing about the mood in India in 1986, the *New York Times*' Steven R. Weisman observed that younger leaders in India were appearing to apply "less ideological but more pragmatic approaches to India's problems" and that they signaled a willingness to "turn to the West for technology and economic ideas."

Weisman noted that there was an emphasis on economic growth and the production of consumer and industrial goods as well as "a new premium on avoiding internal political confrontations." Months earlier, *India Today* also commented on the priorities of this new class: "For the first time in India, a prime minister now feels that the middle class is a political force in even arithmetical terms because it has grown so rapidly in numbers, and that it makes political sense to satisfy its aspirations even at the risk of being portrayed as anti-poor."[79]

To circumvent the so-called traditional voices in Congress, Rajiv Gandhi had closed ranks, and taken foreign policy into the ambit of his office. He also worked closely with the intelligence community and with close advisors of his own choosing.[80] One of these advisors and friends was Subramaniam Swamy, a charismatic but divisive figure in Indian politics. Swamy, a Harvard-educated economist, fervent Hindu nationalist and later member of parliament with the

Janata party, was among the early advocates of full diplomatic ties with Israel. Like many others, he became persona non grata during the Emergency Years, and escaped to the United States, organizing Indian Americans in the diaspora against Indira Gandhi. On his return, he rejoined politics and later mended fences with Indira, claiming among other things, that she had requested his help in opening a dialogue with China.[81]

The extent of Swamy's influence on Indian politics or foreign policy is difficult to quantify; however, when it comes to the normalization of ties between India and Israel, Swamy's shadow is ever looming. In 1982, he was among the first Indian MPs to publicly announce a visit to Israel. At the time, exchanges, if and when they took place, were strictly secret. But Swamy, as brazen as ever, traveled to Tel Aviv, met Yitzhak Rabin and prime minister at the time, Menachem Begin, before returning to Delhi to write an essay making a case for full diplomatic ties. His November 1982 essay in *Sunday*, a weekly magazine edited by M.J. Akbar (who later joined the BJP), inspired one particular student into becoming a fervent advocate of normalization and later, a pre-eminent scholar in the field of India-Israel relations.[82]

Swamy's influence extended further than rabble rousing. He became a broker for the Israeli state. Given the decades-long emphasis on a public show of hostility toward Israel, Swamy took it upon himself to demystify Israel in India's political imagination. In September 1991, he accused the Ministry of External Affairs of discriminating against Israelis of Indian origin who wished to visit family in India.[83] The Indian government, without asking for evidence, replied wryly: "Israeli citizens of Indian origin were entitled to the same privileges as any other foreign national."[84] Later, when India normalized ties in January 1992, legend has it that some of the very first visas for those who couldn't make the trip to the Israeli consulate in Bombay were issued from Swamy's home in the capital.[85]

It is Swamy's contention that Rajiv Gandhi helped set up the scaffolding for Hindu nationalism to thrive. "Rajiv Gandhi was the only good human being in the (Nehru-Gandhi) family and had contributed to [the] awakening of the Hindus," Swamy said in 2017.[86] Swamy's penchant for hyperbole notwithstanding, Rajiv Gandhi's influence on the rise of Hindu nationalism is striking. It was under the Rajiv Gandhi government after all, that the Babri Masjid, declared a site of dispute and closed to the public in 1949, was reopened for Hindu worshippers in 1986. It was under Gandhi that the first steps toward privatizing the economy took place.

It was also Rajiv Gandhi who advocated for the screening of the Hindu mythological television serials Ramayana and Mahabharata on the sole Indian public broadcaster Doordarshan in 1987, which helped embalm Hindutva into the public imagination. Describing the hypnotic effect of the serials on Indian society, Poonam Saxena writes that "Streets would empty out, shops would shut, telephones would be taken off the hook, appointments canceled and people who had to work on Sundays would mysteriously disappear for the duration of the shows. Cinemas were known to cancel their morning shows. It was almost like a voluntary lockdown."

Whereas the political and social foundation of Hindutva had been laid by Hindu nationalists, it was the Congress party who had helped normalize the ideology. It follows, naturally, then, that when Rajiv Gandhi took over in 1984, the idea of normalizing ties with Israel had become tangled with the very demand of progress, liberalism, and technological advancement of India.

As Hindutva began to take root as a mainstream ideology, its proponents latched on to the idea of Israel as an expression of that aspiration, again, in opposition to the "Muslim" and

"Arab" cause of Palestine. For Rajiv Gandhi, India's modernization was contingent upon a closer relationship with Israel;[87] for Hindu nationalists and supremacists, however, it was about civilizational affinity.

2
The Military-Industrial Complex

> We are being challenged by the forces of terror, the forces of terror that seeks to undermine our world, our countries, the peace and stability of our common civilization and we have agreed to cooperate in this area as well. —Benjamin Netanyahu[1]

> Our past will always be an influence, but no longer a determinant of our future. —S. Jaishankar, Indian Foreign Minister[2]

> The people of Israel have built a nation on democratic principles. They have nurtured it with hard work, grit and the spirit of innovation. You have marched on regardless of adversity and converted challenges into opportunity. India applauds your achievements. —Narendra Modi[3]

On Wednesday, January 29, 1992, more than 40 years after it had first recognized Israel, the Congress-led Indian government said it would now establish full diplomatic relations. The news might have only made it into a small corner on page 10 of the *New York Times*, but it symbolized the birth of a new era. India's advance toward Israel was in part the culmination of late twentieth century capitalism meets religious fundamentalism and the aggressive militarism that inevitably accompanied the end of the Cold War.

The dismantling of the former Soviet Union resulted in immediate geo-political reconfigurations, including the implementation of diplomatic ties between Russia and China with Israel.[4] The fall of the Berlin Wall had purportedly "liberated" India from the limitation of its post-independence convictions. Through its former Prime Ministers Indira and Rajiv Gandhi, New Delhi had already hinted at an intention to enter the global economy. The escalation of energy costs created by the Iran-Iraq War, in addition to the economic downturn and the debt crisis, had already precipitated a series of economic reforms by 1991. India's PM Narasimha Rao liberalized import and export policy and reduced government spending in the industrial sector and agreed to accede to the structural adjustments programs (SOPS) set out by international institutions like the IMF. In other words, India began its journey of integrating into the global capitalist economy.

Recognizing the shift in geo-politics and the ascent of Israel in the post-Cold War order, India understood that courting Israel could potentially grant India a front row seat with the world's new and only superpower: The United States. As narrated by author Vijay Prashad:

> The [Indian National] Congress' entry into the neoliberal regime set-up by the IMF in cahoots with global capital simultaneously came with an attempt to curry favor with the U.S. government, whose dollar and military weighed heavily on the New World Order. To be friends with Israel, in this climate, would also provide a back door to Washington, given Tel Aviv's close relationship with the U.S. after the 1967 war.[5]

The first place in which the two countries would cooperate was Kashmir.

The Story of Indian-Occupied Kashmir

In most mainstream accounts, Kashmir became a disputed territory following the invasion of Pathans from Pakistan's North West Frontier Province in October 1947. According to this narration, the Indian army was asked by the autocratic princely ruler of Kashmir at the time, Maharaja Hari Singh, to rescue the state, resulting in Kashmir's accession to India, the first war between India and Pakistan, and Kashmir being partitioned between the two states. But this narration erases significant historical context.

At the time of partition, the princely state of Jammu and Kashmir was still under the auspices of the Hindu Dogra dynasty. Maharajah Hari Singh, whose ancestors had purchased Jammu and Kashmir from the East India Company in the 1840s (a boon for helping the British defeat the Sikh Empire) ruled over a majority-Muslim populace in the state. As per the logic of partition, the British called on all princely states to accede to either India or Pakistan, bearing in mind their geography and population demographics. By virtue of the Muslim population alone (Jammu and Kashmir was 77% Muslim, while the Kashmir Valley itself was 92% Muslim),[6] the state should have joined Pakistan.

However, at the time of partition, the Maharajah requested additional time to decide, with many arguing that he would have preferred to keep the status quo and continue his repressive autocratic rule.[7] As he deliberated the fate of the state, Muslims in Jammu and Kashmir had already begun an insurrection against his rule. Singh and his Dogra army, as well as right-wing Hindu nationalist militias from India went on a rampage against the Muslim population. More than 200,000 Kashmiri Muslims were killed, and 500,000 others were displaced in the last few months of 1947. The city of Jammu was emptied out of its majority Muslim population in just a matter of weeks.

"The Jammu Massacre was an episode of ethnic cleansing orchestrated by the RSS and the Dogra royals," writes Kashmiri anthropologist Mohamad Junaid.[8] Kashmiri scholars Samreen Mushtaq and Mudasir Amin argue that the massacre of Muslims in Jammu was "part of the elimination of the indigenous population and settling in of a predominantly Hindu population . . . in a series of demographic changes that the Indian state eventually went on to carve out in the territory."[9] In response to the killing of Jammu's Muslims, Pathan Muslims from the northwest frontier province, in a move likely supported by the newly formed Pakistan state, marched to "liberate" their Muslim brethren in Jammu.

Nehru activated his intimate relationship with Lord Mountbatten, the Viceroy to India, in facilitating the takeover of Jammu and Kashmir. On October 26, 1947, the Indian government responded to an exasperated Hari Singh. But the help that came was contingent on the Maharaja Singh signing an Instrument of Accession (IoA) with the Indian government.[10] Through this agreement, Kashmir would accede to India on matters concerning communications, defense, and foreign affairs. Once hostilities would cease, the Indian leadership promised that the future of the princely state would be determined according to the will of the people.

Sheikh Abdullah, the president of the National Conference party, was given the role of prime minister of the "emergency administration" in Kashmir. Abdullah supported accession to India so long as Delhi would grant the region significant autonomy. It was agreed that elections would be held in which a "constituent assembly" would formulate a separate constitution for the state. But only pro-India parties could run, and those who wanted Kashmir to merge with Pakistan or called for independence were detained or exiled. Abullah's administration became the first of India's client regimes in Kashmir.

By then, Pakistan had officially joined the fray and the two new countries were at war over the territory. Even though India and Pakistan were now sovereign states, their armies were still under the command of British officers. Britain ordered its officers in Pakistan to resign and Pakistan was told it could not enter Kashmir. India took the dispute to the UN Security Council, expecting it would rule in its favor against what it deemed as Pakistani "aggression." But the UNSC Resolution 47 called for the removal of troops on both sides of the line of control and for a plebiscite to take place. A ceasefire came into effect in January 1949. But the plebiscite would never happen. India held on to two-thirds of the territory and Pakistan the remaining one-third.

After negotiations with its own client regime in Jammu and Kashmir, India introduced Article 370 into the Indian Constitution in 1954. The measure provided Jammu and Kashmir with semi-autonomy.[11] Article 35A that accompanied Article 370 prevented non-Kashmiris from purchasing land or becoming residents in the region. By the special status granted to Jammu and Kashmir, the state was authorized to have its own prime minister, its own legislative assembly, its own flag, constitution, and ability to make laws. But it wasn't long before these "privileges" began to erode. The promise of a plebiscite receded into the background for all besides Kashmiris; Whereas Article 370 was meant to be a temporary measure ahead of a plebiscite, Indian nationalists recast Kashmir as an integral part of India. Additionally, the projection of "India as savior" became integrated into the larger narrative of a peace-loving Indian nation led by anti-imperialists like Nehru.

"This [narrative] not only erases the decades-old struggle of the Kashmiri people for emancipation from its ruling class; it also misrepresents the actual series of events that preceded the Indian military's arrival," Junaid argues.[12] For Hindu nationalists, the measure itself was an historical error that needed "self-correction." The violent and underhanded means by which India gained control over Kashmir was lost to collective amnesia. "What needs to be underscored is that Indian control over Kashmir went against the long-held aspirations of the people of Kashmir, against the logic of partition, and against all the norms of international legal principles," Junaid writes. But why was India so intent on gaining control of Kashmir? First, Kashmir was a strategic entry point into Central Asia and China. Second, it held ideological significance to the idea of India itself. As anthropologist Mona Bhan has argued: "Kashmir was key to the constitution of the Indian nation's secular credentials and is critically important to the project of refiguring India as a Hindu nation. Without Kashmir, the very idea of India—whether in its secular incarnation or its majoritarian Hindu avatar, stands on shaky grounds." In other words, India has always relied on Kashmir for its self-definition.[13]

The World's Most Militarized Zone

Since 1990, Indian-occupied Kashmir had been enveloped in an armed uprising against Indian rule. Not only did India begin to bulk up its troops in the disputed territory—leading to what has been called the world's most militarized zone—the specter of a new war between India and Pakistan hung ominously over the region. In June 1991, no more than two weeks after Narasimha Rao was appointed Indian prime minister, six Israeli tourists and one Dutch tourist were kidnapped by militants in Srinagar, Kashmir.

The militants told journalists they had targeted the Israelis on the suspicion they were commandos sent to infiltrate the resistance movement in the valley.[14] The incident culminated in an unprecedented joint operation between Indian and Israeli diplomats to secure the release of the hostages and a media spectacle ensued in which the Indian press called on its government to normalize relations with Israel. According to the Indian police, at least 70 foreigners were evacuated during the operation. The Israeli government said that as many as 40 Israelis were in the valley at the time.[15]

As it was, the Bharatiya Janata party (BJP) party and the larger Hindu right wing were on the ascendancy in India. The ground was shifting. And the Congress-led government realized that normalizing ties with Israel came with minimal political risk. Where criticism emerged, it came from the periphery.

Meanwhile, the context in the Middle East began to alter too. As the advent of the Middle East Conference in 1991 demonstrated, the Palestinian leadership and the larger Arab world were prepared to make compromises with Israel. This provided India with cover: a sojourn with Israel wouldn't isolate New Delhi from its Arab allies. International forums like the UN, too, began to make new concessions. Israel had refused to participate in the Madrid Conference of 1991 unless the UN revoked UN Resolution 3379 that had equated Zionism to racism back in 1975. And in December 1991, the UN revoked Resolution 3379 without so much as a single concession from the Israelis. India, having been among those who voted for it in 1975 found themselves voting for its annulment. For Israel, repealing this resolution lay at the heart of international acceptance. For the rest of the world, the abrogation of Resolution 3379 underlined the former Soviet Union as a spent force and the consolidation of Israel as a surrogate of the U.S. For Indians, it was the deflection of foreign policy to the diktats of the market and the assumption of diplomatic "doublespeak." And perhaps nothing better illustrates the doublespeak than India's explanation for helping to revoke this particular resolution. India's representative at the UN explained that "no concepts or theories should be allowed to stand in the way of peace."

Decoding the hyperbole, Indian writer Punyapriya Dasgupta wrote that if New Delhi was suggesting that equating Zionism with racism was just a theory, it had to explain why it had endorsed the assertion originally. "Or is it our contention that Israel has reformed itself and indulges no longer in treating the Palestinians in ways that amount to racism?" Dasgupta asked.[16] In a stinging essay, Dasgupta added that the move to establish diplomatic ties was so peculiar that it was as if the government "must have spied redeeming features in Zionism . . . New Delhi somehow started seeing Israel as giving up the odious practices of Zionism."[17] "The slippage from the vaunted moral foundation of India's foreign policy will, in the course of time, become clearer to even those who are denying it now."

But these concerns fell to the periphery. To International Relations scholars like Kumaraswamy, critiques were interpreted as an "ideological hangover."[18] Indeed, when J.N. Dixit, the Indian foreign secretary between 1991 and 1994, wrote that he regarded the establishment "of relations with South Africa and then with Israel" as the "most significant" during his years in office, there is no sense of irony, only a steadfast belief that developments in the national interest were one and the same.[19] India's moves on the world stage were purposeful and deliberate. They represented an "evolution" of the Indian state from a purported outsider to an "insider" in the neo-liberal international order. To wit, if India wanted to be a dominant power in this new world (and did not plan on being swallowed by China or destroyed by Pakistan), it needed to become a service provider to the U.S.[20]

Whereas it had led the boycott and sanctions campaign against South Africa from the late 1940s, the "pragmatism" of the Rao government was motivated by its pursuit of adopting neoliberal economic policies.[21] India therefore joined the "global pacification industry" or the vast web of institutions, laws, and policies that operate to protect international capital.[22] Within this framework, India could simultaneously trade in weapons and surveillance technologies with Israel[23] while remaining "a friend" to the Palestinians because of its purported commitment to the question of Palestine in occasional words of support, charity, and votes at the UN.

In fact, to this day, both the Indian media and a majority of international relations scholars suggest that India only moved to implement diplomatic ties with Israel once it received the go-ahead from Arafat.[24] The story goes that two weeks before diplomatic ties were established between the two countries, PLO leader Yasser Arafat was on a visit to New Delhi during which he purportedly gave the Indian government his blessings to proceed. But the Palestinian leadership was not in any position to make demands of the Indian government and there was nothing Arafat could do to stop the inevitable.

The story of India's normalization with Israel, then, is also the story of the decline of the PLO as the credible and legitimate representatives of the Palestinian people. The PLO's recognition of Israel in 1988 in return for a two-state solution paved the way for the Palestinian cause to be buried, with the core demand—the right of return for millions of refugees—all but forsaken. The signing of the Oslo Accords in 1993, which created the Palestinian Authority government (PA) as an interim body and sanctioned Israel's control over territory, resources, and economy, only served to further entrench Israel's occupation and made the lives of Palestinians in the West Bank and Gaza Strip worse. The Oslo Accords did not accept the Palestinian right to self-determination in a sovereign state of their own. Instead, it agreed to a de-nationalized Palestinian entity that would assume a form of local governance in the occupied West Bank and Gaza Strip. Whereas the PA was supposed to prepare for Palestinian statehood, it instead became a subcontractor and a party to the Israeli occupation, coordinating and collaborating with the Israeli state, punishing and imprisoning Palestinian dissent.

An Alignment of Military Interests

India's pursuit of a closer tie-up with Israel in the 1990s came as a reconfiguration of the Israeli arms industry took place, including a move toward the privatization of the weapons industry. The privatization of security meant the management of endless conflict and therefore an insatiable want for weaponry. And as Israel, a long-time and "successful" occupier in Palestine, became the gold standard in tried and tested weapons as well as in techniques of control and surveillance, India looked on with intrigue.

Through the wars with China in 1962, with Pakistan in 1965 and 1971, India had become one of several countries with whom a secret arms trade with Israel would exist despite diplomatic restrictions. Whereas countries are more likely to sell arms to "friendly" nations, the Israeli arms trade operates as "an alternative diplomatic channel."[25] In other words, the Israeli military is able to facilitate its own deals, and administer its own customs system, with minimal supervision and oversight from civilian authorities, providing a lot more discretion and flexibility to buyers.

Israel's reputation as a bulwark of innovative weapon and defense technologies was well established by the late 1960s and 1970s. Though it had focused on "self-sufficiency" as a goal from its inception as a state, it was Israel's success during the 1967 war in which the Arab states were demolished within six days, that precipitated the expansion of its military industrial complex. Until then, France had been the main supplier of weapons to Israel.

Israel's annihilation of Egyptian and Syrian forces and with it the secular nationalist vision of Gamal Abdel Nasser significantly strengthened the American and British-backed Saudi Arabia in its unfolding cold war with Egypt. Israel's occupation of the territory assigned by the UN to the Palestinians prompted the Soviet Union to sever diplomatic ties.[26] Meanwhile, U.S. military, economic aid, and investment into Israel rose exponentially. Through the encouraged migration of American technicians and scientists, it was positioned as a major weapons manufacturer, too.[27] Israel's victory in 1967 effectively established the Jewish state as a key American watchdog state in the region.

Israel's reputation as a military and technical powerhouse continued to spread. By 1970, weapons sales made up an estimated $70m or nearly 10% of the country's gross exports.[28] However, it continued to characterize itself outwardly as a meek and defenseless nation under siege by ravenous Arabs. But internally, Israel recognized in itself the makings of a regional power, leading to a massive expansion of its domestic military-industrial complex. In order to make the arms industry feasible, Israel relied heavily on the exports of its hardware and expertise. Not only did exports lower the costs of manufacturing weapons for the Israeli army; they also created thousands of jobs and helped propel Israel toward becoming a military superpower.

Between 1966–72, the local defense industry created 20,000 new jobs, and purchases from local industries increased by 86%.[29] The arms industry became a driver of economic wealth, with the ability to wield influence and policy. Though it did not happen immediately, the late 1960s and early 1970s sowed the seeds for the privatization of Israeli security that precipitated in the creation of a revolving door for ex-military officers who moved between the army and private arms manufacturers, and who helped reinforce the Israeli economy's dependence on the military industrial complex to survive and thrive.[30] Writing about Israel's expanding arms industry, Larry Lockwood argued that the weapons trade reflected the aims of the Zionist establishment and "its long term efforts to penetrate Third World Nations" as well as foreign investors "who hope to develop Israel as a profitable technological outpost."[31]

By the early 1970s, Israel had already built up "technical programs" across parts of Africa and South America including para-military training in 13 African countries as well as in Bolivia, Ecuador, and Costa Rica. It sent military advisors to dictators like Zaire's leader Mobuto Sese Seko (now Democratic Republic of Congo) and Uganda's Idi Amin (until the relationship soured in 1972). Ehud Avriel, Israel's first ambassador to Ghana, put it succinctly: "We must break out of the encirclement by a hostile Arab World and build bridges to the emerging nations on the black continent."

Golda Meir, Israel's foreign minister (1956–66) and then as prime minister (1969–74), traveled to the African continent five times, carefully harnessing diplomatic support. And though Israel persisted with a narrative of pursuing "peace," Lockwood argued that its burgeoning arms sector suggested otherwise:

> Those governments that accepted Israeli military and police training programmes can be expected to "buy Israeli" when they shop for weapons . . . Israeli weapon manufacturers are promoting Israel's ascent as a "sub-imperialist" power—one that penetrates the markets of Third World nations while remaining heavily dependent upon American and European capital.[32]

Through the auspices of a treaty signed in 1971, the former Soviet Union became India's biggest supplier of arms by the late 1980s. But the fall of the Soviet Union and the insecurity that accompanied the new Russian Federation propelled the Indian government to rethink its approach to the arms trade. India struggled to build a successful arms manufacturing sector of its own, leaving its technology and equipment not only outdated but frequently unreliable. Israel was not only an example of a country that had built up its own military industrial-complex (through the assistance of the U.S.) but it was also willing to sell without asking too many questions, able to upgrade Russian hardware and crucially, eager to transfer technology to India itself. Though India continued working with the Russians, New Delhi saw in Israel an opportunity to leapfrog decades of stagnation.

The formal engagement on defense and security issues with the Israelis began in April 1994 in Tel Aviv. In this first interaction, between India's Air Chief Marshal S.K. Kaul and Israeli PM Yitzak Rabin, which both countries agreed to keep under wraps, the Indian delegation communicated its "immediate and long term specific requirements with the potential for mutual cooperation in defense modernization, joint research and production."[33]

On May 5, 1994, Rabin and Arafat signed what was known as the "Cairo Accord" in which Israel agreed to withdraw from Gaza and Jericho having occupied both since 1967. In India's upper house of parliament, MP John F. Fernandes, an Indian Congress party MP made reference to the deal, describing it as a "very important matter for us because it has come soon after the dismantling of apartheid in South Africa." "We have to see that this Accord is fully implemented in the future," Fernandes said. Likewise, Mariam Alexander Baby, an MP with the Communist Party of India (CPI-M) added that though he held "apprehensions about the possibility of peace being fully restored," he hoped that the process would yield "positive results."[34]

Rabin's assassination by a right-wing Israeli extremist in November 1995 and the rise of Netanyahu as prime minister in 1996 slowed formalities between the two countries somewhat, as the Congress-led government grappled with the move to the right in Israel. More political instability would come, this time in New Delhi as the BJP won the 1996 elections but fell short of achieving a majority. In 1998, the BJP prevailed once more, securing a majority and forming the National Democratic Alliance (NDA) government. The bureaucratic tightrope created by the political instability notwithstanding, it was in the 1990s that the Indian military and security establishment became fully enamored by Israeli technology. Indian officials were particularly intrigued by Tel Avi's MAFAT's (Israel's Administration for the Development of Weapons and Technological Infrastructure) willingness to work closely with India's Defence Research and Development Organization (DRDO) and provide access to its highly developed R&D.[35] By mid-1995, the Indian government agreed in principle to establish a defense attaché's office in Tel Aviv. These were later established in 1997 in both Israel and India.[36]

It was also in 1995, after three years of negotiations, that India purchased Unmanned Aerial Vehicles (UAVs) from Israel Aerospace Industries (IAI). The late 1990s saw forums like the Indo-Israeli Management Committee (I2MC). Set up by the-then Scientific Advisor to the defense Minister and secretary of the DRDO, Dr. A.P.J. Abdul Kalam,[37] the group was created to sustain dialogue between the two countries as well as facilitate work on jointly funded projects focused on weapons systems. The end goal was still to build up domestic manufacturing of weapons systems and sensors as part of India's long-stated goal of becoming self-sufficient. The Green Pine multi-functional radar, the Indian Navy's Long Range Surface-to-Air Missile (LRSAM), and the Indian Air Force's

(IAF) Medium Range Surface-to-Air Missile (MRSAM) were produced as a result of this dialogue.

There are three additional developments that precipitate the alignment of military interests: First, the election of the BJP government in 1998. The new BJP-led government, headed by Atul Bihar Vajpayee and L.K. Advani, were unfazed by the criticism that followed their new liaison with Israel. In 2000, Advani, the deputy prime minister, traveled to Israel, becoming the first Indian minister to do so. On his return to New Delhi, Advani spoke of the modern nature of international terrorism, and set up a Joint Working Group on Counter-terrorism.[38] He also lauded Israel's "integrated border management system" in reference to the systems in place along the green line that partitions Israel from the occupied Palestinian territories.

Later that year, Indian Foreign Minister Jaswant Singh also traveled to Tel Aviv, becoming the first in his portfolio to ever do so. Singh's meetings with the Israeli government in 2000 resulted in the setting up of a joint anti-terror commission. Under the guise of fighting terror, the relationship received an anti-Muslim booster shot. At the UN conference against racism in Durban, South Africa in August 2001, India refused to re-equate Zionism with racism[39] (and equally, refused to entertain any discussion that equated the Hindu caste system with racism).[40]

Second, India's nuclear tests of 1998, conducted in the Rajasthani desert between May 11–13. The U.S. responded to the testing by imposing sanctions on New Delhi. Israel was among a handful of countries who refused to condemn the tests. When the Indo-Pak War of 1999, known as the Kargil War broke out, Israel received another opportunity to demonstrate its commitment to New Delhi. According to reports from the time, the Indian army found themselves ill-prepared to handle the high-altitude mountainous region in Indian-occupied Kashmir. The government found themselves scrambling for outside assistance. Facing sanctions from the U.S. and Western Europe over its nuclear tests, Delhi naturally looked toward Israel.[41] Israel responded immediately, providing valuable satellite imagery and ammunition drones.[42] As narrated by N.A.K. Browne, India's former Air Chief Marshal:

> India's "temporary isolation" following the nuclear tests, as imposed by certain powers, only worked to Israel's advantage and this was most evident shortly thereafter during the Kargil War in 1999. Reports note that Israel supplied the Indian Army "around 40,000 rounds of 155mm and 30,000 rounds of 160mm mortar ammunition" . . . The quick response to India's request for military assistance increased Israel's credibility as a reliable arms supplier even during a crisis and helped to bolster the relationship.[43]

The war ushered in a paradigm shift in India's approach toward Israel. Even if Delhi had already started purchasing more Israeli weapons since the early 1990s, it had still seen Israel as a competitor to its domestic manufacturing. But the events of 1998/9 changed this. Israel's willingness to support India following the imposing of sanctions both before and during the Kargil War turned India and Israel into partners and co-developers.

Third, the events of September 11, 2001. Around 3,000 people lost their lives when Al-Qaeda operatives flew two planes into the World Trade Center and another into the Pentagon, culminating in the worst ever attack on American soil. The attacks gave rise to the U.S.-led "War on Terror," spanning decades and at the cost of least 900,000 lives from 80 countries worldwide.[44] New Delhi, keen to equate the freedom movement in Muslim-majority Kashmir as one of "terrorism," endorsed and expressed immediate support for this new "civilizational" war waged on the so-called Muslim world.

India would get its chance to dig its heels in further with the unprecedented attack on its Parliament on December 13, 2001. The incident, blamed immediately on Pakistani nationals led to the passage of the Prevention of Terrorism Act (POTA), providing Vajpayee's government an ability to expand its powers on matters of national security, including expanding surveillance, reducing judicial oversight and limiting public accountability in the name of fighting so-called terror.[45] POTA was referred to as India's Patriot Act, after the George W. Bush administration passed the first of many laws that gave the U.S. government sweeping powers to act in any way deemed to "protect national interests." The Patriot Act, passed 45 days after September 11, gave Bush the chance to expand surveillance on ordinary Americans, in a move that began the practice of tracking behavior, and consolidated guilt by association or by social connection.

Given India's evolving and dependable relationship with Israel, its obvious alignment in the larger War on Terror under the BJP-led government, and a diaspora hard at work in conjunction with the Zionist lobby in the DC (more on this in Chapter 4), the attack on India's Parliament provided the impetus for New Delhi to become an agent of Washington.[46] India and the U.S. had already enjoyed improved military ties in the mid-1990s prior to the nuclear tests. Both navies embarked on joint exercises in 1992, 1995, and 1996, and held programs in which Indian naval officers could visit U.S. war ships "to gain exposure to [American] technology and operations."[47] Moreover, rumors had been circulating for months that sanctions would be lifted. Just weeks before September 11, Joe Biden, who was then Chairman of the House Senate Committee, wrote to President Bush calling for sanctions to be revoked. In December, George W. Bush lifted the remaining sanctions. But even then, the sanctions were always more performative than substantive. In this way, the U.S. sought to exercise and exert dominance over both India and Pakistan, selling weapons to both nations and ultimately altering the nature of conflict between Islamabad and New Delhi. The War on Terror dragged Pakistan's attention away from Kashmir and toward Afghanistan, turning Indian-occupied Kashmir into a low-level insurgency. But India, through the U.S.-sponsored lexicon of the War on Terror continued to characterize the indigenous-led resistance movement in Kashmir as "terrorism" and therefore justified its occupation in the valley.

The events of September 11 and India's decision to immediately join the War on Terror provided, as Vijay Prashad describes it, "cover for the removal of sanctions and the increase in Indo-U.S. military contacts." But it was the burgeoning relations between India and Israel that provided the U.S. with added confidence that New Delhi was ready to be groomed as an ally of Washington.

The Years of Consolidation

In 2003, two days before the second anniversary of September 11, Ariel Sharon traveled to India, the first by an Israeli PM. The historic moment was a culmination of a fervent alignment developing between Israel, India, and the U.S.[48] With the War on Terror at this point in full swing, and all three states led by right-wing governments, the scene had been set up for a new axis to take shape.

Accompanied by three cabinet ministers and 35 executives from security, technology, and agricultural firms, Sharon met key members of Vajpayee's cabinet as well as the leader of the Indian National Congress, Sonia Gandhi. Addressing the media on a red carpet in the Mughal Gardens of Rashtrapati

Bhavan, the presidential palace in New Delhi, Sharon said he "carried greetings from Jerusalem, the capital of the Jewish people for the past 3,000 years." The ceremony was awkwardly arranged. The humidity of early September didn't help. Sharon, in a deep blue suit, appeared hurried and business-like. There were no clever quips, humorless jokes, or choreographed hugs between the leaders. Sharon addressed Vajpayee formally as "Prime Minister" without personalizing the reference with a name. Vajpayee didn't seem to mind.

Sharon's visit was a stunning intimation of the vulgarities that characterize police states. Security in Delhi was set to unprecedented levels. His entourage included four bullet-proof vehicles, brought in on a special aircraft. In New Delhi, Mumbai, and in Indian-occupied Kashmir, thousands of people took to the streets and protested his arrival, adding to the chaos and spectacle. "We, the democratic people of India, can neither accept the BJP's communally distorted vision of our country, nor the alliance with Sharon, who is the leader of one of the most racist, colonial regimes in existence today," Ranjit Abhigyan, a spokesman for the Communist Party of India (CPI-M), said.[49] By the time Sharon left, the two governments signed the "Delhi Statement on Friendship and Cooperation between India and Israel" as well as six agreements of cooperation on matters as far and as wide as the environment, education, culture, and waiving visa requirements for officials. Earlier in the week, India's Cabinet Committee on Security had endorsed the purchase of a $97m Israeli electronic warfare system for the navy.[50]

Sharon's visit to India was noteworthy for another reason: narrative and language. When both countries released a joint statement following his departure, they repeated key words that would drive the joint narrative for the next two decades: "civilization," "democracy," "shared ideals," and "terrorism."

> As ancient cultures and societies, India and Israel have left their mark on human civilization and history. As democratic countries since their inception, both nations share faith in the values of freedom and democracy. Both countries gained independence during the same period and embarked on a course of nation building to advance the well being of their respective peoples and to build modern democratic states able to face difficult challenges.[51]

Back in Washington, Sharon's visit to New Delhi was warmly received. At a time of rising global discontent with the U.S. following the invasion of Afghanistan and Iraq, India's support for the War on Terror (although it did not support the invasion of Iraq) did not go unnoticed.[52] In an article published in December 2003 in the conservative magazine *Human Events*, Joseph A. D'Agostino alluded to India as a potential U.S. ally against China and described New Delhi as wanting "to throw her lot in with us despite her former years in the Soviet orbit."[53] "India has chosen to align herself with the emerging pro-American bloc of the world's nations that includes Britain, Israel, and many of the former Soviet satellite states of Eastern Europe," D'Agostino wrote, adding that the photo-op with Sharon was proof that the pendulum had shifted.

As it happened, the BJP would lose the next election in 2004. The Indian National Congress squeezed through a victory and formed the United Progressive Alliance (UPA) government, headed by Manmohan Singh. Though there was speculation in Israel that Singh may reverse some of the gains achieved under his predecessor, the new PM nurtured the relationship especially in defense and security. Collaborations with Israel that began under the Vajpayee government were completed within months of Singh entering office. For instance, in 2003, the two countries began cooperating on a fence on the Line of Control in Kashmir. Delhi said it was to shield India from "Pakistani infiltrators." A year later, the fence was almost complete.

"The fence is similar to the barrier being built by the Israelis to control the infiltration of militant Palestinians. But the Indian fence has received far less international scrutiny than the Israeli barrier and surprisingly muted opposition from the Pakistanis," the *New York Times* wrote.[54] Similarly, research analyst Jatin Kumar argues that by 2004, Delhi had "started using Israeli equipments [sic] and tactics for border management in Kashmir."[55] "Israel also provided radars and special jamming equipment for use in Jammu and Kashmir . . . sophisticated night vision device(s) (NVD) was the first gift from Israel to India," Kumar added. Between 2000–2010, India imported around $10bn worth of arms from Israel.[56] There was also an expansion in agricultural cooperation. In 2007, for instance, the Indian agricultural conglomerate Jain Irrigation Systems purchased 50% of Israeli company NaanDan, becoming NaanDan Jain irrigations. Three years later, Prithviraj Chavan, India's technology minister, lauded the business during his visit to Israel, for achieving record exports of irrigation products to India.[57] Chavan described the partnership as a model for others to emulate. But like so many agritech companies in Israel, not only was this joint venture operating in the occupied Palestinian territories and the occupied Golan Heights, it was also active in the illegal settlements.

"India's 9/11"

On November 26, 2008, ten men linked to the Pakistan-based group Lashkar-e-Taiba, attacked several sites across the commercial capital, Mumbai, killing 195 people, including nine Israelis. "India's 9/11" or "26/11," as it became known, was significant for several reasons. The scale of the attack and the perceived failure of Indian authorities to take charge of a crisis that lasted three days, resulted in several calls for a fervently more decisive and militaristic state. Moreover, the killing of Israeli citizens meant that not only was Israel now forever tethered to an Indian tragedy,[58] its counter-terrorism and arms industry recognized a business opportunity in a country looking to enlarge its military capacity. The Indian government resolved to work closer with Israeli intelligence and began to invest heavily in mass surveillance. The following year, the Maharashtra government sent delegations to Israel to seek out "expertise in urban counter-terrorism and homeland security."[59] This also culminated in Israel periodically training commando units in the city whereas this was not a widespread exercise prior to 2008.[60]

> Part of the reason why the government of Maharashtra gravitated to Israel was because of the strategic actions of the Israeli state, which sought to capitalize on 26/11 to expand the reach of Israel's homeland security industry within India. After publicly criticizing India's handling of 26/11 as primitive and incompetent, Israeli government officials offered technical assistance and Israeli trade representatives openly declared their intention to exploit 26/11 as a commercial opportunity.[61]

Mumbai's Police Commissioner D. Sivanandan told the *Indian Express* following his return from a training exercise in Israel in which his team studied Israel's security plans for Jerusalem, that his office would "strongly recommend replication of certain Israeli solutions in India."[62] "For thousands of years, we [Indians] have been passively witnessing terror attacks. We never want to fight with anybody. That's what our main problem is and we lack the killer instinct," Sivanandan said.[63]

Indian authorities had already begun working with the Israeli company "Nice Systems" following the attacks on India's parliament in 2001. Nice Systems had already built up a reputation for handling surveillance at the Eiffel Tower, the Statue of Liberty, as well as at several high-profile airports around the world. After the attacks of 26/11 in Mumbai, the Indian government authorized the implementation of a Central Monitoring System (CMS) that would have the ability and capacity to intercept phone calls and text messages. The CMS "involved real-time monitoring of the voice calls, Internet searches, and online activity of potentially anyone with a mobile phone, landline, and Internet connection," Sangeeta Mahapatra, a visiting fellow at the German Institute for Global and Area Studies writes. Successive governments have since built layer upon layer of surveillance infrastructure, from biometric ID cards to facial recognition cameras on city streets, to spy drones at protest marches, in what Mahapatra calls "a panoply of digital-surveillance measures that have normalized the shift from targeted surveillance to mass surveillance." This was only one in a smattering of intrusive technologies introduced by New Delhi that easily placed India in the top three surveillance states in the world.[64] In 2010, Indian authorities began deploying Israeli drones to search for fighters belonging to the Naxalite movement in the forests of Chhattisgarh, Orissa and Andhra Pradesh.[65] Indian armed forces were already using Israeli-made Tavor and Galil rifles since 2009 against the insurgents made up of tribal communities fighting the Indian state. India also launched a spy satellite in 2010 jointly built by the Israel Aerospace Industries Ltd. and the Indian Space Research Organization (ISRO) to assist the Indian military surveil its border regions. This was soon followed by consultations between the Indian Home Ministry and Israel's Ministry of Public Security. Partnerships expanded in other fields, too. In 2012, India's University

Grants Commission (UGC) signed an MoU with the Israel Science Foundation (ISF) to promote collaborative research across a wide range of disciplines.

As the security industry coalesced, trade among citizens and corporations expanded. Though private citizens from Israel and India had engaged in trade over the decades, it was only in the mid-1990s that New Delhi appealed to Israeli businesses to buy Indian products. Indian exports, made up of cotton, handicrafts, and manmade yarn, amounted to $90m in 1992/3 and $130m in 1993/4. Imports from Israel, made up of fertilizers, pearls, semi-precious stones, machinery, and the like, were worth $140m in 1992/3 and $300m in 1993/4.[66] But by the new millennium, bilateral trade hovered around $1.5bn. By 2008/9 it had grown to $3.5bn and to $6.6bn by 2011/12. In 2014, trade was worth $4.52bn, driven in large part by the upsurge in arms sales.

Between 1997–2000, 15% of Israel's exports made their way to India. Over the next five years, weapon deliveries ballooned to 27%. In 2006, Israel's arms exports were worth $4.2bn of which India accounted for $1.5bn worth of imports on its own. Between 2003 and 2013, India became the single largest purchaser of Israeli arms, accounting for upwards of one-third of all arms exported out of the Jewish state. Israel had become India's second largest arms supplier after Russia. At some point in the 2000s, Prabir Purkayastha writes, Israel was supplying more arms to India than it was the Israeli army.[67] Israel's overall arms exports between 2000–2007 were close to $29.7bn, a far cry from the early 1980s when exports were closer to $1bn per annum. In 2012, exports of weapons hit $7.5bn, an increase of 129% from the previous year,[68] cementing Israel in the top ten bracket of the world's leading defense exporters, with India rapidly featuring as its most dependable buyer.

The centrality of Israeli weapons to New Delhi precipitated several high-profile corruption scandals involving the Indian government and Israeli arms manufacturers. It also appeared to assist in exonerating them from accountability, prompting Purkayastha to posit that the "same rules do not seem to apply to Israeli companies—an indication that Israel has made it into the Indian defence establishment."[69] Following 26/11, India was purchasing an implausible variety of hardware from Israel. From sensors and electro-optical systems, to surveillance and armed drones; night goggles to long-range surface to air missiles; radars that would be installed on balloons on the border with Pakistan to the upgrading of 130mm M-46 guns used by soldiers. The deals amounted to around $10bn worth of business between 2000 and 2010 alone.[70]

Israel's willingness to share its technology provided the Indian military with a unique opportunity to reverse the disappointments of its arms industry that neither lived up to expectations nor delivered the "self-sufficiency" as repeatedly promised and desired by the security establishment. Little wonder then that Richard Bitzinger described the Indo-Israeli arms trade relationship as "symbiotic."[71] N.A.K. Browne agreed: "India's quest for technology and Israel's need for economizing defence research have therefore become complimentary [sic]."[72]

By 2013, it wasn't especially clear how the relationship would proceed given the soft-pedalling of public engagements. PM Singh appeared to have avoided meeting or being seen with the Israeli government, particularly Netanyahu. But Singh's government had courted Zionist lobby groups in the U.S. in the lead up to the nuclear deal of 2005, precipitated closer economic ties with Israel even as they mercilessly pounded Gaza in 2008/9 and in 2012. The rhetoric around India's commitment to Palestine remained the same. "We are deeply concerned at the steep escalation of violence between Israel and Palestine, focused around Gaza, that threatens the peace and security of that region," the Ministry of External Affairs said in November 2012, as Israel bombed Gaza beyond repair.[73] In response to a question seeking clarity over India's relationship with Israel in parliament in December 2013, Edappakath Ahamed, India's Minister of State in the Ministry of External Affairs, replied: "India's relations with Israel stand on their own and are not at the expense of strong, time-tested and historic ties with the Arab world. Notwithstanding growing ties with Israel, there has been no change in the traditional policy of strong support to the Arab and the Palestinian cause."[74]

And Then Came Modi

Heading into elections in 2014, the BJP didn't just wangle a plan to win, they wanted to annihilate the opposition. Their slogans read, "India first" and "Time for Change, Time for Modi." The economic slowdown was emblematic of an inefficient, bloated and out of touch Indian National Congress who had led India into a "decade of decay," they proclaimed. Whereas Congress was a haven for the elite and the privileged, Modi was the common man.[75] The BJP was the real India; the people's party, as they would pronounce. Whereas Congress had kept India underdeveloped, corrupt, and poor, the BJP promised to take its "Gujarat model" across the country. Whereas Congress needlessly pandered to minorities, especially Muslims, the BJP stood for all Indians. Modi was presented as the antidote to hundreds of years of disappointment and wasted opportunity.

The BJP astutely conflated development with ethnonationalism, allowing it to both use the specter of security and foreign threats as a means to mobilize votes as a ruse to excuse its more vitriolic takes on minorities. Modi would modernize every state, transform every district, and bring affluence to every home. The demagoguery was, with the help of diaspora Indians, amplified by hundreds of vivacious rallies and spectacular 3D holograms of Modi in venues across the country. It was a masterclass in populism.

In its 2014 manifesto, the BJP said that following Indian independence in 1947, "the leaders at the helm of affairs lost the spirit and the vision, which the freedom movement had evoked. They discarded the vision and adopted the institutional framework of administration created by the Britishers which was quite alien to India's world-view."[76] "It is unfortunate that these leaders could not comprehend India's inner vitality, which was the main force responsible for India's survival despite several attacks and prolonged foreign rule and thus, failed to rekindle the spirit of India."[77] The BJP, it said,

> recognizes that no nation could chart out its domestic or foreign policies unless it has a clear understanding about itself, its history, its roots, its strengths and failings. In a highly mobile and globalized world, it is imperative for a nation to know its roots that provide sustenance to its people.

At its core, the BJP said, "India was one country, one people, one nation." Freedom of speech was encouraged so long as India came first. Foreign policy, too, would be based on the national interest and India "shall remain a natural home for persecuted Hindus and they shall be welcome to seek refuge here," the manifesto said.[78]

The BJP sold shiny dreams to a young India lagging behind in almost all developmental indicators, in which poverty was bursting at the seams and public institutions were corrupt to the core. Two decades after the economic reforms, values had shifted. Secularism—or whatever India's half-hearted attempt at it was—was no longer seen as essential and certainly not profitable; economic development was paramount and military strength provided meaning. The rising communalism of the late 1980s mixed with the nationalistic capitalism of the mid and late 1990s had created the perfect cocktail for a man of Modi's ilk to exploit. In May 2014, Modi and the BJP won the Indian national elections by a margin not seen since the days of Indira Gandhi in the early 1980s. Modi, who rose through the ranks of the Rashtriya Swayamsevak Sangh (RSS; National Patriotic Organization) as a full time worker, then as Chief Minister of Gujarat, strode into Delhi like a tempest; shaking up Indian politics forever.

As a life-long member of the RSS which had long held ambitions to turn India into a Hindu Rashtra[79] or a Hindu state, Modi took the project of reshaping India into the image of its majority to the highest level of the state. It was the RSS which had advanced Hindutva, the nationalistic agenda at the heart of this new India proposed by the BJP (more in Chapter 3). India was finally to live up to its potential and the messaging could not have been any more persuasive. Colonial subjects turned Congress peons were now impatient consumers. Modi was the safeguard who would thrust India toward its rightful destiny.

Modi Meets Bibi

In September 2014, PM Narendra Modi and Israeli PM Netayanhu met on the sidelines of the UN General Assembly. It had been five months since Modi took office and in between the Israeli invasion of Gaza ("Operation Protective Edge") had taken place. Israel flattened the Gaza Strip over a period of 50 days, killing 2,251 Palestinians, including 1,462 civilians. In Israel, 67 soldiers and six civilians were killed by Hamas rockets. Under normal circumstances, the meeting would have never happened, or at least, not under the gaze of the world's media. But not with this prime minister and certainly, not with this India. It was at this meeting that both leaders "decided to break down the remaining walls" between the two countries, as Netanyahu framed it. "We shook each other's hands and we agreed to forge an historic partnership for progress."[80] At this meeting in September 2014, Netanyahu and Modi immediately recognized in each other the single-minded determination to build states with a single culture, a single race and a single nation. Crucially, Netanyahu saw in Modi a leader who wasn't just unafraid to be associated with Israel but relished the opportunity to emulate it.

Indian academic Khinvraj Jangid says that Modi's appreciation for Israel was two-fold: "One is that it is a religious nation without any hesitation; without any guilt. And second, it is a strong military state. Physical power is very important to him."[81] During the devastating bombing campaign of Gaza earlier in the summer of 2014, India's Foreign Ministry released a statement in which it said it was "deeply concerned" over the "steep escalation of violence between Israel and Palestine" and "the loss of civilian life." But it also bemoaned "cross-border provocations resulting from rocket attacks" on Israel.[82] Days later in parliament, Modi's government managed to block an opposition party-led attempt to pass a resolution condemning Israel's disproportionate killings in Gaza. Later, it voted for a United Nations Human Rights Council (UNHRC) resolution to launch a probe into the bombardment, which calmed nerves once more. But India decided to abstain when it came to voting for the resolution (A/HRC/29/L.35) that endorsed the report in mid-2015. By that time, Modi and Netanyahu were speaking on the phone, and planning cooperation, if not regional domination. The Israeli newspaper *Haaretz* reported that Netanyahu had personally called Modi before the vote.[83] Opposition leaders from the Indian National Congress Party and Communist Party India (CPI-M) demanded to know if

Indian foreign policy had changed track. Both *The Hindu* and *Harretz*,[84] too, concluded that India's decision to abstain appeared to reflect a significant policy shift toward Israel. The Indian government, however, argued that it abstained only because it took offence to a phrase in the resolution that called for Israel to be taken to the International Criminal Court (ICC) for its crimes. It said it had found the recommendation "intrusive."[85] Commenting on India's response to the Gaza war of 2014, Sadanand Dhume, a columnist with the *Wall Street Journal* (WSJ), wrote that Delhi's response appeared ready to "suggest publicly what many officials already acknowledge privately: A burgeoning strategic partnership with Israel matters more to India than reflexive solidarity with the Palestinian cause."[86]

As BJP supporters took to the streets in support of Israel in Delhi and #IndiaWithIsrael trended on Twitter, Dhume argued, "many ordinary Indians instinctively grasp the natural confluence of interests with Israel." In his column, Dhume urged Modi to travel to Israel "to ensure that no future administration can backslide again." Whereas the election of Modi had already demonstrated that this new India was prepared to sacrifice Muslims and others for the purported chance to economically transform the country (read: corporatize it), it was only natural that Palestinians too would be discarded if it meant getting closer to Israel and the boon of global capital. By refusing to allow parliament to pass a resolution against Israeli aggression in Gaza and by abstaining from the resolution endorsing the 2015 UN report that called for accountability for Israeli crimes, India had shown that it was no longer prepared to provide Palestinians even performative support. Moreover, equivocating that both sides had an "equal responsibility" to lower tensions and prevent unnecessary loss of life, Modi's government had already amended the substantive nature of its foreign policy on the question of Palestine.

India had normalized relations with Israel in 1992 without Palestinians achieving statehood or self-determination. In 2014, New Delhi went one step further. It upgraded its public appreciation for Zionism and Israel and reduced its foreign policy to a contorted and performative "sympathy" for the Palestinian cause. It also began to illustrate a respect and intention to emulate Israeli policy at home. In 2014, the Punjab Police traveled to Israel for training on "security and anti-terror operations."[87] A year later, the Indian Police Service (IPS) began an annual program in which recent graduates would spend one week studying "best practices in counterinsurgency, managing low intensity warfare and use of technology in policing and countering terror" with the Israel National Police Academy.[88] In 2015, the Indian government began the implementation of a "smart border" along the Line of Control. These partnerships with Israel did little to deter the Indian foreign ministry from insisting that its commitment to the Palestinians remained unchanged. But the changes had arrived. And it had been a long time coming. India's decision to abstain from holding Israel accountable to the UNHCR resolution in 2015, was the surest sign that India believed in Israel's fundamental right to self-defense, and therefore, its right to exist as a settler-colonial state, unconditionally.

Brothers-in-Arms

Having completed the initial formalities, the Indian and Israeli diplomatic machines went to work. The goal: to have Modi come to Israel. In keeping with "India First," Modi decided to consolidate India's concomitant partnerships before embarking on what was likely to be a long-term partnership with Israel. Within the first two years of his tenure, Modi completed visits to UAE, Turkey, Saudi Arabia, Iran, and Qatar. The dye was cast. Simultaneous to his outreach to a collection of influential Muslim-majority countries, his surrogates began the long and hard work of building familiarity and trust with their Israeli counterparts. It began in late 2014 with Home Minister Rajnath Singh traveling to Tel Aviv for a visit, the first of its kind in 15 years. The visit was more than ceremonial. The Home Minister had specifically traveled to discuss cooperating with Israel in bulking up its own border security mechanisms as they had done under the Vajpayee government. Israel's sophisticated border technology, that included a network of "smart walls," equipped with sensors, HD video surveillance, and unmanned fortified towers with remote controlled machine guns, were the envy of militarized states everywhere. Singh is said to have been impressed after he visited an Israeli posting close to the separation fence with the Gaza Strip. Within a year, Israel was helping Delhi build a "smart fence" on India's western border with Pakistan.[89] Where fences couldn't be assembled, laser barriers were installed. These set off sirens if breached.

Then in 2015, Modi received the Israeli Naval and Air Force Chiefs and reciprocated by sending their Indian counterparts to the Air Force Chief Commanders Convention in Israel, an event that coincided with the 70th anniversary of the Israeli Air Force.[90] Later, in October 2015, Indian President Pranab Mukherjee traveled to Israel, during which he addressed the Israeli Knesset, received an honorary doctorate from the University of Jerusalem, met with Israelis of Indian origin, and laid a wreath at the tomb of the father of Zionism, Theodor Herzl. "I informed the Israeli leadership about various initiatives taken by the Government of India like 'Make in India', 'Digital India', 'Clean Ganga', 'Smart Cities', 'Start-up India', etc. and invited investment as well as participation by Israeli companies," Mukerjee said.[91]

Mukerjee also traveled to Ramallah in the occupied Palestinian territories where he met with the Palestinian Authority's

President Mahmoud Abbas, received a doctorate from Al Quds University, inaugurated a roundabout named "Maidan Al Hind," and paid tribute at the Mausoleum of Yasser Arafat. In a statement, Mukerjee said India had increased the number of ICCR scholarships to Palestinian students from 10 to 25 per year and the number of Indian Technical and Economic Cooperation (ITEC) training slots for Palestinian nationals from 50 to 100, and handed over a check of $5m as budgetary support to the Palestinian Authority. Israeli arms exports to India were worth around $1bn alone.[92]

This is how a "de-hyphenated approach" to Israel and Palestine would play out: political and economic pragmatism with Israel and charity for the compromised Palestinian leadership. In January 2016, Sushma Swaraj, then Indian foreign minister, traveled to Ramallah to meet the Palestinian leadership and later to Jerusalem, where she met Netanyahu and the broader Israeli leadership. At the invitation of Mukerjee, Israel's president, Reuven Rivlin, accompanied by a large contingent of Israeli businessmen, traveled to India for a week in November 2016. In New Delhi, Rivlin visited Gandhi's shrine, signing the guestbook with: "Love thy neighbor as thyself."[93] In Mumbai, Rivlin visited the sites of the attacks in 2008. "Mr. Prime Minister, Israel and India have changed history before, and it is time we do it again," Rivlin said. "You have called on the world to 'Make in India.' I am here to say: Israel is ready to answer this call. Israel is ready to Make in India and Make with India."[94]

Finally, in 2017, Narendra Modi arrived in Tel Aviv to a bear hug from Netanyahu. "Prime Minister, we've been waiting for you a long time [sic]," Netanyahu said. Modi's visit to Israel did not include the occupied Palestinian territories. In so doing, Modi showed that he was willing to view Israel as a single and complete entity. Palestinians were no longer part of the equation. Having visited key Arab states in advance, and having sent surrogates to deliver scholarships and loose change to the Palestinians, and having hosted and whispered sweet nothings to President Abbas in Delhi earlier in the year (that India would continue to support a two-state solution), Modi and his team ensured there couldn't be any complaints. To Israel, the gesture was precisely as Netanyahu and Israel would have wanted. Any future diplomacy between Delhi and Ramallah would amount to little more than handouts.

Netanyahu and Modi's meeting saw the India-Israel relationship move to the level of a "strategic partnership."[95] The upgrading of diplomatic ties resulted in several agreements in agriculture, technology, and water conservation. On the economy, the recently conceived India-Israeli CEO Forum met for the first time, signing twelve strategic business MoUs worth over $4.3bn. It was decided that Invest India,[96] working in conjunction with the Ministry of Commerce and Industry, would set up a special desk to promote economic partnerships, specifically Israeli investments into India. Invest India became the central agency through which all Indo-Israel ventures were administered. Meanwhile, Israel set up three economic attachés across India. It was also agreed that trade between the two countries, sitting at the time at around $4bn per annum, had the potential to reach $20bn in five years. On matters of society and culture, Modi announced the opening of an Indian cultural center in Israel. The two parties also agreed to establish a strategic partnership in water conservation and agriculture. But it was in matters of defense, counter-terrorism, and security, in which the discussions were most concentrated. Both sides agreed on pursuing joint development of weapons and crucially, the sharing and transfer of Israeli technology and a focus on the "Make in India" initiative. On counter-terrorism, both India and Israel said they had resolved to take strong measures against "terrorists, terror organizations, their networks and all those who encourage, support and finance terrorism, or provide sanctuary to terrorists and terror groups." Four months after his visit, India's air force conducted its first joint exercise[97] with the Israeli army. Likewise, in late 2017, Indian police and special Garud commandos, specialized in counter-terror operations, announced training programs with elite Israeli special forces. "The roles of the commandos of the two nations are similar. We carry out what others cannot do," wing commander K. Baharat told the *Jerusalem Post*, "We are a peace-loving country, but we need to be prepared for anything," he added.[98]

In January 2018, Netanyahu reciprocated by traveling to New Delhi, to take the journey of this new relationship full circle. In Delhi, the duo would continue with their theatrics, much to the delight of the sycophantic Israeli and Indian press. Netanyahu told Modi:

> I am a son of a historian. Our people have had thousands of years of history. India and Israel are two of the most ancient civilizations on earth. And yet, it is an amazing fact, that until you visited Israel, no leader of India, in 3,000 years of our own sovereign existence, and our history, has visited Israel.[99]

The two leaders signed nine MOU's on cybersecurity, energy production, space technology, and film production, among other industries during the visit.

The culmination of Modi's and Netanyahu's remarkable liaison provided cataclysmic advances in the political and cultural ties between the two countries. Whereas trade between the two countries had been $4.52bn in 2014, this had increased to $5.43bn by 2018. Between 2015–19, India's arm imports from Israel rose by 175%.[100] The impact and influence of Israel on matters of security and defense, the economy and lawmaking on Indian policies became conspicuous even to most lay observers. Whereas a military partnership had been a central pillar of their liaison, the implementation of a security state became the bedrock of long-term strategic partnership. "You are a revolutionary leader," Netanyahu told Modi at the end of the trip. "You're catapulting this magnificent state into the future. And you have revolutionized the relationship between Israel and India."

In response, the Palestinian leadership tried to hold on to what India had represented in the past. Ramallah showered Modi with praise when he traveled a month later, to Palestine, where he was conferred Palestine's highest civilian award, "The Grand Collar of the State of Palestine." Previous recipients include King Salman of Saudi Arabia, King Hamad of Bahrain, and President Xi Jinping of China.[101] Tayseer Jaradat, the undersecretary of Palestine's Ministry of Foreign Affairs, described Modi's visit to Palestine in February 2018 as confirming "the strong relations between the two countries, and India's firm and supportive position on Palestine." Jaradat said New Delhi's decision to vote against the US embassy move demonstrated their commitment remained intact.[102] Modi, of course, accepted the award with delight. His supporters said it was proof that India hadn't abandoned the Palestinians, while his surrogates punctuated the charade by describing the award as underlining India's new place in the world order.[103]

The Abraham Accords

On August 13, 2020, then U.S. President Donald Trump announced that the governments of the United Arab Emirates and Israel had agreed to the full normalization of relations. In what would be officially called the "The Abraham Accords: Declaration of Peace, Cooperation, and Constructive Diplomatic and Friendly Relations," the White House said it ushered in a new era of bilateral agreements between "two of the Middle East's most dynamic societies and advanced economies" that would "transform the region."[104] In so doing, the UAE became the third Arab country, after Egypt and Jordan, to sign normalization agreements with the Jewish state. In September and December, Bahrain and Morocco would follow suit. Morocco was purportedly unable to resist an American promise to back its bid for sovereignty over the occupied Western Sahara.[105] In January 2021, Sudan became the latest to normalize ties with Israel. Again, Trump offered hundreds of millions of dollars of aid, debt relief, and promised to delist Khartoum as a sponsor or terror.[106] The Abraham Accords had been implemented through a wily blend of authoritarian self-interest, trifling handouts, and old-fashioned extortion.

The Accords carried several consequences. First, they consolidated and normalized the Israeli occupation and apartheid system, signaling a departure from a long-held consensus in the Arab world that normalizing ties with Israel would only arrive after a just settlement to the conflict. "The real purpose of the Abraham Accords appeared less about saving Palestinians than allowing Gulf states to go public with, and expand, their existing ties to Israel," journalist Jonathan Cook wrote. "Regional intelligence could now be shared more easily, especially in Iran, and the Gulf would gain access to Israeli hi-tech and U.S. military technology and weapons systems."[107]

Following the official signing ceremony of the accords at the White House in September 2020, the governments of both the UAE and Israel went into PR overdrive. Not only did the two countries sign a raft of financial, technological and financial deals, both countries used every opportunity to flaunt the "freedom" granted by their "tolerant," "peace-loving" governments. *Haaretz* writer Anshel Pfeffer described the engagement with the UAE as a "consummation of a relationship both sides have been working on for a while and a realization of joint interests."[108] Israeli tourists flocked to the UAE in droves—more than 200,000 traveled to the Emirates over the next nine months. On social media, models in pajamas and draped in Israel and UAE flags, paraded for the world's cameras on the desert dunes outside Dubai. The spectacle was propelled by Israeli, Emirati and American politicians and sold with ghoulish desperation by the Western mainstream media. Here is a prime example from the Associated Press:

> The 21-year-old [Israeli model May Tager] came into the UAE on her Danish passport as traveling on an Israeli one remains complicated despite moves by the two countries to start telephone service and other outreach. The first commercial passenger flight between the two nations also took place last week, though Tager came in on a different commercial flight. Then came the breezy shoot: In the desert just on the outskirts of Dubai's skyscraper-studded downtown, wearing Delta Israel's new Princess collection of loungewear, Tager waved Israel's blue-and-white flag bearing the Star of David. Next to her was Anastasia Bandarenka, a Dubai-based model originally from Russia, who waved the Emirati flag.[109]

Second, they forged the beginnings of a new entente, featuring Israel and the UAE in opposition to Iran and political Islam, as supported by Qatar and Turkey.[110] The thirst for democracy by Arabs and North Africans, as demonstrated by the people's uprisings across much of the Arab world in 2011, posed as much of a threat to Israel as it did to Arab autocratic regimes. Israel was well aware that no democracy in the Middle East would tolerate cordial relations with a settler-colonial apartheid state in its neighborhood. The Abraham Accords, then, was also a blow to the struggles of hundreds of millions of people facing demagoguery, authoritarianism, and illiberal regimes around the world.

The erroneous branding of the Abraham Accords as "promoting coexistence and tolerance" and "coexistence and respect"—when they achieved or believed in neither—categorically pitted those who weren't willing to sign up as "extremists," "terrorists" or its derivative "terror sympathizers." The characterizations served to expand the "good" and "bad" Muslim binary produced in large part by the logic of the U.S.-led War on Terror to "good" and "bad" Muslim-majority countries based primarily on their willingness to normalize relations with Israel. Given that the U.S. government under Trump had already implemented the "Muslim ban"—which banned entry to visitors, refugees, and asylum seekers from several Muslim-majority countries like Iran, Libya, Somalia, Syria, and Yemen—on account of their proximity to "terrorism," a refusal to accept normalization with Israel carried the possibility of vicious repercussions.

The denigration and continued crippling sanctions imposed upon Iran, the vilification of political Islamic movements, and the fallacious labeling of the Abraham Accords as "peace deals" were aimed at dismantling support for Palestinian resistance and fortifying Israel and the UAE as American operatives in the region. In this script, "peace deals" was code for submission.

Mapping the Next Frontier

Israel might have been the prize, but at the outset, Modi made it clear that the United Arab Emirates was also a central pillar of his foreign policy outreach. Having consolidated economic and political ties with the UAE (and the rest of the Gulf) over several trips between 2015 and 2019, the UAE was only happy to reciprocate. In February 2019, the UAE's Shaykh Abdullah bin Zayed invited India to be a guest of honor at the Organization of Islamic Cooperation (OIC)'s Council of Foreign Ministers in Abu Dhabi. In August, the UAE endorsed the Indian government's decision to revoke the semi-autonomous status of Indian-occupied Kashmir and just under three weeks later, conferred Modi with the "Order of Zayed," the highest civilian award in the Emirates. India's Ministry of External Affairs said they understood the invitation as the "desire of the enlightened leadership of the UAE to go beyond our rapidly growing close bilateral ties and forge a true multifaceted partnership at the multilateral and international level . . . [and] as a milestone in our comprehensive strategic partnership with the UAE."[111] The UAE dubbed 2019 "the year of tolerance."

With Pakistan's growing affinity for Turkey and Qatar under former Prime Minister Imran Khan, and the cooling of ties between Islamabad and Abu Dhabi, it became convenient for Modi, Netanyahu, and Abdullah bin Zayed to slide into what observers like Mohammed Soliman called an "unlikely and unprecedented Indo-Abrahamic transregional order."[112] "Trump's major geo-political strategy was to construct a reactionary international alliance under the leadership of Washington," noted intellectual Noam Chomsky told me. The alliance was semi-formalized, but the "Abraham Accords" had given it "one level of formalization." And under this umbrella, Hungary, India, Israel, Egypt, and the Gulf Monarchies were all "natural members," Chomsky said.[113]

In October 2021, a second level of formality was added to the axis. First, the foreign ministers of Israel, the UAE, and the U.S., met in Washington. Here, the three countries set up two working groups focusing on "religious coexistence" and "water and energy." A week later, India's Foreign Minister Subrahmanyam Jaishankar traveled to Israel to meet Naftali Bennett, the tech billionaire and ultra nationalist who replaced

Netanyahu as Israeli PM in June 2021. A relationship that had blossomed under Netanyahu was about to grow barbs. During his visit, Jaishanker and Israeli Foreign Minister Yair Lapid held an historic virtual meeting with U.S. Secretary of State Anthony Blinken and UAE Foreign Minister Sheikh Al Nahyan. In a statement, the State Department said the four ministers discussed "expanding economic and political cooperation in the Middle East and Asia, including through trade, combating climate change, energy cooperation, and increasing maritime security," and appeared to confirm suspicions that the bloc would have significant geo-economic outcomes. Within this ecosystem, the UAE would provide the capital, Israel the technical expertise, and India would supply the labor, all under the watchful eye of Washington. *The Hindu* wrote that "significantly, neither the quadrilateral meeting, nor the trilateral meeting discussed the issue of Palestine."[114]

The making of a new power group left other media houses gushing over India's new place in the world as well as Trump's role in reaching this milestone. Shekhar Gupta, editor-in-chief of *The Print*, opined that the Abraham Accords were directly responsible for the unprecedented soiree between the four slugger states. He credited Trump and his son-in-law Jared Kushner for the new opportunities afforded to India. "One door he (former Indian PM Narasimha Rao) kicked open when he upgraded India's relations with Israel (in 1992) . . . the second door was kicked open by the Abraham Accords," Gupta wrote, adding: "So thank Trump for that." In Israel, the *Jerusalem Post* called the meeting "a silent revolution," "a new age in Israel's diplomatic relations," and a "quiet formation of a group of like-minded countries."[115] Over the next six months, the UAE and India signed a free trade agreement, with a similar plan said to be on the cards for India and Israel, too.[116] On 14 July 2022, the U.S.-Israel-UAE-India grouping was officially launched as the "I2U2" (India, Israel, the

United States, and UAE) or the "West Asia Quad." Within hours of its launch, it was reported that Haifa Port had been sold to the Indian company Adani Ports, operating on a joint-bid with Israeli company Gadot. Within days, the Indian flag was hoisted alongside the Israeli flag above the port.

To understand the logic and ambition of the quad, an event in New Delhi back in 2018 is instructive. During his visit to India, Israeli PM Netanyahu attended the third edition of the Indian-government-sanctioned Raisina Dialogues, run by New Delhi-based center-right think tank, Observer Research Foundation (ORF). Introducing Netanyahu, Sunjoy Joshi, Chairman of the ORF, waxed lyrical about the Israeli PM's achievements:

> Prime Minister Netanyahu leads a nation that is no stranger to volatility. Yet he has successfully managed to provide growth, prosperity and security to its people in a turbulent region. From technological innovations that have ensured food and water security in a parched environment, to creating one of the most vibrant start-up ecosystems nurtured by a world class defence and technology industry, the prowess of Israel has made light of the greatest challenges to the security and well-being of its people.[117]

The ORF itself is a cunning project; sponsored in large-part by Reliance, one of India's richest conglomerates, and built, as novelist Arundhati Roy described it, in the image of the Rockefeller Foundation, the ORF exerts an inordinate influence over Indian foreign policy.[118] The ORF presents itself as politically agnostic but routinely adopts and promotes positions that are in support of large-scale neo-liberal policies that favor big capital and the military-industrial complex. That they partner with right-wing organizations like the Heritage Foundation in the U.S. is emblematic of their neocon agenda.

Joshi's casual remarks were therefore very intentional. They were deliberately engineered to revise the Israeli narrative in India to match Modi's agenda. It rendered India's previous "hostility" with Israel as an historical error. This was therefore a program of "course correction."

At its core, however, the ORF was primarily invested in how the liaison could further stimulate unfettered capitalism. Israel was a vessel through which Indian corporations could liberate themselves. When Netanyahu finally spoke at the meeting, he predictably made a case for the centrality of the military and a free market economy in building a strong, successful and safe society. "The weak don't survive," Netanyahu told the audience. "The strong survive. You make peace with the strong. You make alliances with the strong. You are able to maintain peace by being strong . . . defence costs a great deal of money . . . [and so] the necessary requirements for innovation and ingenuity are free markets" he said. Netanyahu then characterized the pursuit of new allies as the next stage of his country's evolution. Having established both military and economic power, he said, Israel was now pursuing political power. "By political power, I mean the ability to make political alliances and relationships with many other countries."[119] Political alliances and relationships might sound banal. But if you merge economic, political, and military power under the vestige of a supreme power, the United States, this was the Empire itself.

This, then, represents the next frontier of the India-Israel alliance as part of a larger ecosystem of illiberal states that see themselves as a frontline in a continuation of the War on Terror. There are already hints that Greece, Cyprus, and Saudi Arabia may join either informally or formally.[120] In this ecosystem, these nations will look to achieve the following: expand the logic of the security state by sharing intel; jointly building military equipment; developing communication and surveillance software; flaunt nativist and jingoistic "self-reliance" as a matter of policy; and encourage the cross-pollination of investments, be it in the UAE, Indian-occupied Kashmir or the occupied Palestinian territories. The inclusion of India into this club, therefore, will expand the scale and scope of Israeli products and services, for sale in new and wider markets around the world. Netanyahu already referred to this cooperation when he said in 2017 that both countries were already working together in Africa.[121]

The plan in India on matters of security and arms production with Israel, then, was three-fold: replicate and expand; domesticate production; and finally, export to countries in Africa and the Indian Ocean region.[122] As it stands, Indian factories in conjunction with Israeli partners have already started producing: Israeli assault rifles like the Tavor, the Negev Machine Gun, and the Uzi submachine guns; Spike anti-tank guided missiles; as well as Skystriker drones.[123] Though still smaller than other countries, Indian arms exports doubled between 2018 and 2019.[124] India, then, was part of the deep entanglement of economic and political interests to keep private capital in charge and the poor, disenfranchised, and marginalized perpetually pacified.

To exemplify the extent of this quagmire, here are three examples. Firstly, in June 2017, Reliance invested 20% in an "innovation technology incubator" partially owned by OurCrowd (60%), a crowdfunding platform in Jerusalem, and Motorola Solutions (20%). A spokesperson for Reliance said they were thrilled to be involved because they were "confident of Israeli start-ups offering unique value propositions by delivering next-gen digital services."[125] A year later, Netanyahu was hosted at the Reliance-sponsored ORF event urging Indians to invest in entrepreneurs and start-ups. None of this is banal. Motorola Solutions Israel, a subsidiary of Motorola Solutions, has been providing the Wide Area Surveillance System (WASS), known as MotoEagle since 2005, used in the illegal settlements and along the separation wall, along with other communication equipment supplied to the Israeli army.[126] Reliance Defence and Engineering Ltd., said in early 2018 it would be producing Kalashnikovs with an Israeli company for the Indian army.[127]

Secondly, in the dizzying destruction unleashed upon Gaza by the Israeli military over eleven days in May 2021, at least 260 Palestinians were killed (including 129 civilians, among whom 66 were children). In Israel, twelve people, of whom two were children, were killed by rockets fired from the blockaded Gaza Strip.[128] Israel's alliance with India paid handsome dividends. In June 2021, India, along with 13 other countries, abstained from voting at the UN Human Rights Council in Geneva (UNHRC) for an investigation into the latest bombardment of Gaza.[129] Whereas it had voted for the UNHRC to launch an inquiry following the "Operation Protective Edge" in 2014 (and later refused to endorse the report which largely condemned Israel's actions), fast forward to 2021, India wouldn't even pretend to care about the details of Israeli crimes in Gaza during its eleven-day bombardment.[130] This is what the "West Asian Quad" was really about: an investment in the preservation and survival of each other's national project; a network and axis so economically, militarily, and politically interdependent, it becomes close to impossible to dismantle or rectify. Of course, the "West Asia Quad" is still "new" and ordinarily subject to changes, slowdowns, and fine tuning. India's reluctance to join the chorus of condemnation of Russia over its invasion of Ukraine in March 2022, was indicative of Delhi's determination to refrain from throwing in its entire lot with the U.S. Russia was still India's largest arm supplier and important supplier of energy, too. This relationship was not about to sever overnight. Washington, despite its reservation over India's refusal to sanction Russia, is resolute in keeping India in its pocket for its other fight with China. So much so that U.S. Congressman Ro Khanna introduced an amendment to the National Defense Authorization Act which called on lawmakers to ensure that India is not sanctioned for continuing to purchase weapons from Russia, as directed by the Countering America's Adversaries Through Sanctions Act.[131] Khanna's amendment called for the law to be waived in the case of India. He also called for the U.S. government "to assist India accelerate its transition from Russian arms." In July 2022, Congress passed the amendment.

And finally: In July 2021, a global consortium of media organizations revealed that more than 40 governments had used hacking software sold by the Israeli private intelligence firm NSO to target human rights activists, journalists and even world leaders around the globe. "The Pegasus Project" revealed that some 50,000 phone numbers in more than 45 countries were potentially targeted for surveillance by clients around the world, through software called Pegasus. The software was said to be so phenomenal, that once deployed, it would grant clients unfettered access to the phone's camera, microphone, and data. It was the hijacking of smartphones, or what Indian novelist Arundhati Roy described as the spying on our most intimate selves.[132] Up to 2,000 numbers in India had been targeted by Pegasus, with at least 300 verifiably infected. Among those on the list was Indian opposition leader, Rahul Gandhi and investigative journalist Swati Chaturvedi, the author of the award winning "I am a Troll: Inside the BJP's Secret Digital Army,"[133] which revealed how the ruling BJP party had created troll farms to target, harass, and silence critics. Given that NSO only sells Pegasus to governments, it is not a question of whether India purchased software from NSO, but rather when the relationship between Modi and NSO began, and if Delhi would be held accountable for the breach. Neither the Indian government nor NSO have ever denied working with each other. The *New York Times* reported in January 2022, that Modi most likely bought the software in 2017, as part of a larger arms deal.[134] The Indian government's refusal to allow even a parliamentary debate about Pegasus was certainly proof that military relations between India and Israel were even deeper than publicly acknowledged and that the Indian government felt it was not compelled to reveal anything it deemed to be in the national interest.

In India, outrage over the government's alleged patronage of Pegasus was mostly directed at the ruling BJP party for choosing to utilize a weapon meant to target "legitimate criminals" and "enemies of the state." The criticism cleared the Israeli state of any wrongdoing, showing that under Modi, Israel had become so rapidly integral to the revitalization of Hindu India that an assault on Israel was tantamount to an assault on the Indian nation. Alternatively, Israel had become so completely normalized in the Indian imagination that it was possible for Indian liberals to be outraged by the hacking of their phones, but still be in favor of India's close ties with the Israeli state. For example, opposition leader Rahul Gandhi described the surveillance as an act of "treason," but he stopped short of asking why Israel sold the software to the Indian government in the first place. "Pegasus is classified by the Israeli state as a weapon and that weapon is supposed to be used against terrorists" he said, as if it was any less egregious for the Indian state to weaponize the phones of anyone else in the name of national security.[135] Likewise, Indian journalist Chaturvedi, also a victim of the hacking saga, wrote in *Haaretz*: "For the sake of its relations with the democracy camp in India and around the world, Israel needs to shut down NSO and companies like it."[136] But the NSO and Pegasus aren't separate from the Israeli state. They *are* the state. Pegasus is not the only weapon Israel exports to illiberal nations, dictators and authoritarians. This *is* its business model. This is the military-industrial state. And when it comes to India, it is only getting started.

3
Hindutva and Zionism: A Story of Kinship

O Hindus! look upon Hindusthan as the land of your forefathers and as the land of your prophets, and cherish the priceless heritage of their culture and their blood, so long nothing can stand in the way of your desire to expand. The only geographical limits of Hindutva are the limits of our earth! —*V.D. Savarkar*[1]

Germany has also shown how well-nigh impossible it is for races and cultures, having differences going to the root, to be assimilated into one united whole, a good lesson for us in Hindusthan to learn and profit by. —*M.S. Golwalkar*[2]

We recognize ourselves as a nation by our faith. —*Theodor Herzl*[3]

Vinayak Damodar Savarkar (1883–1966) was little more than a low-level agitator against British rule when he was sentenced to jail in 1911. He was charged for supplying the gun used in the assassination of a British district magistrate in 1909 and sentenced to two 50-year sentences on the Andaman Islands in the Bay of Bengal.[4] Savarkar's time in jail, however, did not augment a fervent anti-British sentiment. Within months, Savarkar asked for clemency, agreeing "to serve the government in any capacity," shifting his attention to what he saw as a far greater threat facing the Indian subcontinent: Muslims.

It was, however, from 1921, following his move to a jail in the port city of Ratnagiri in Maharashtra that he began drawing a blueprint for an independent India. Over the next two years, Savarkar began articulating a program he called Hindutva, or "Hinduness," a political philosophy that asserted Hinduism as the rightful identity of any future Indian state. Hindutva, Savarkar argued, would be the framework under which the country would be governed. It is only through the adoption of Hindutva that India could "return" to its glorious past. In other words, Hindus would finally be able to reassert their pristine cultural and racial superiority and Muslims would be put in their place.

Fundamental to this program, Savarkar argued in his booklet "Essentials of Hindutva," published in 1923, was the distinguishing of Hinduism from Hindutva.[5] Being Hindu meant surrendering to the Sanskrit language and culture as heritage; demonstrating love and obedience to the motherland; and recognizing historical Hindu law and racial purity. Hinduism was also defined in contrast to that which might be considered foreign. And for Savarkar, this meant Muslims. For Hindu nationalists like Savarkar, Muslim "invasions" from Central Asia or the Arab world underscored that they were "foreign" to India. This sentiment belies the fluidity of state formation in pre-colonial India and flattens the diverse ethnic and regional political units along religious lines, a binary that has been challenged by recent South Asian historiography. To equate Muslims with British colonial rulers, then, is ahistorical.[6] By Savarkar's estimate, Hindutva, as a loose comparison, was a way of being a Hindu; an attitude, or a quality of being Hindu. In his words:

> Hindutva is not a word but a history. Not only the spiritual or religious history of our people as at times it is mistaken to be by being confounded with the other cognate term

> Hinduism, but a history in full . . . Hindutva embraces all the departments of thought and activity of the whole Being of our Hindu race.[7]

Whereas a Hindu, Savakar argued, was "primarily a citizen either in himself or through his forefathers of 'Hindusthan' and claims the land as his motherland,"[8] Hindutva had little to do with the practices or beliefs[9] of Hinduism. Instead, Hinduism was part of a larger civilizational project of "Hindutva." Savarkar's treatise on Hindutva was integral to the Hindu nationalist project.

He became one among a group of self-styled Hindu nationalist intellectuals on one end of the continuum who began carving out the idea of a country ruled by Hindus.[10] These thinkers, many of whom were educated in foreign European capitals, would build on the orientalist fascination of European philosophers and scholars who spoke dolefully of the loss of "an archaic Hindu civilization."[11] The Indian subcontinent, these British, French, and German scholars contended, had once been the cradle of all humanity and that "humanism" itself had been lifted out of Hindu values itself. They argued that Hindu society had faltered, lost its zeal and through patriotism and nationalism, would find reinvigoration. Among these, Dayananda Saraswati (1824–83), Aurobindo (1872–1950), Swami Vivekananda (1863–1902), as well as organizations like the Arya Samaj (Society of Aryans; formed in 1875) and the Hindu Mahasabha (1915), were the most prominent. As a collective, they sought to both resurrect a "forgotten" and "erased" glory of India's Hindu past as well as reformulate Hindus as a respectable, palatable, and intelligible community.[12] To accomplish this project, author Jyotirmaya Sharma says the quartet of thinkers appeared to agree on several ideas they argued would resuscitate the Hindu identity.

First, it meant transforming Hinduism into a codified religion, founded on racial and doctrinal unity. It was foreigners after all who had diluted the nation from its Hindu core and made India insular; it was now the duty to recast India anew in the vision of a glorious past. Hinduism was therefore India and India was only Hindu. "Binding them all together was a singular vision of Hindu India and its destiny," Sharma writes.[13] All questions on religion were to be henceforth directed to the Vedas[14] and the so-called golden age (400–600 CE), in what Sharma describes, as "the end of theology."[15] "There was little scope for a diversity of opinions, practices, rituals, observances, and individual choices," Sharma argues.[16] Or as author Anustap Basu explains, "it meant compacting a pantheon of a million gods in axiomatic Hindu icons like Rama or Krishna, absorbing errant, syncretic pieties, and picturing a singular Hindu telos."[17]

Second, it involved recasting Hinduism as masculine, aggressive, and militarily proficient. As Sharma writes, "Hindus had to live and die for an ideal."[18] According to this logic, the Muslim "invasions" and British colonial rule had only succeeded because Hindus had lost their way. The philosophers argued that Hindus would have to adapt, fight back, or perish. Third, to treat Hinduism as the most perfect of faiths, or as the mother of all religions. Fourth, to be forever vigilant of threats from "outsiders." The vilification of Muslims was therefore central to the revitalization of the Hindu quest for self-preservation. But this notion of self-preservation was also contingent on the creation of a majority community (for without it there would be nothing to protect). "Those who did not fall in line had to be marginalized, ignored, harassed, and if need arose, eliminated," Sharma writes. Fifth, the answers to all questions were to be found in the Vedas. The final feature was the authorization to be blunt and harsh when dealing with enemies.

Scholars argue that the codification of the Hindu identity itself was the consolidation of an upper caste identity. In other words, Hindu nationalism itself was a caste project that had instrumentalized the British Census of the late nineteenth century to include all of the different religious and cultural rituals that existed in colonial India under the banner of "Hinduism." Not only did the census compress the different castes and tribal communities into the category of "Hindu," it allowed upper caste Brahmins the opportunity to wield control over all as well as promulgate a fiction that there had once been a unified Hindu civilization. These were the origins of Hindu majoritarianism. "These Brahminical scholars and leaders who talk about Hindutva being the religion of all castes must realize that the Scheduled Castes, Other Backward Classes, and Scheduled Tribes of this country have nothing in common with the Hindus," Dalit[19] writer and activist Kancha Ilaiah argues.[20]

In his book, *Why I am not a Hindu*, Ilaiah writes that the upper castes had "reason to mix spiritualism and political power."[21]

> In fact, post-colonial Hindutva is a Brahminical modernity which works strategically in the interest of Brahmin, Baniya and neo-Kshatriya forces. Its historical aim is to subvert the political assertion of the Dalitbahujan castes which form the democratic and secular social base of India . . . The blend of spiritualism and political power is very much rooted in their casteized patriarchal authoritarianism.[22]

Likewise, Basu adds: "The modern project of a Hindu political monotheism has been to induct the privileged and the pariah into a universal, congregational plane of Hindu identity."[23] Moreover, this also meant that the so-called "Hindu-Muslim" divide was therefore a fake binary. By implication, the focus on Muslims as the eternal enemy of "the Hindus" meant

Muslims were only a distraction, scapegoats, in the pursuit of building a fictitious unified Hindu nation.[24]

Hindutva thus became the central pillar that sustained the imaginaries of the Hindu Mahasabha, the Rashtriya Swayamsevak Sangh (RSS) and the Hindu Sanghatan. The RSS, a paramilitary organization formed in 1925, became the nucleus around which a family of organizations or the Sangh Parivar would grow.[25] Even as the Indian National Congress (INC), under Mahatma Gandhi's guidance became a mass movement in the struggle to secure freedom from the British, a Hindu nationalist and supremacist movement, forged by the dogma of Savarkar and later Madhav Sadhashivrao Golwalkar (1906–73), who became integral to the expansion of the RSS, dug its heels in. Savarkar and the Hindu Mahasabhas actively collaborated with the British, prioritizing their prize of a Hindu Rashtra (Hindu state) over what Savakar described as the whims of a "pseudo-nationalist body."[26]

Be it the Congress-led civil disobedience campaign (1931–2) or the "Quit India Movement" (1942) in which Gandhi, and Jawarharlal Nehru were arrested, the Hindu nationalists were unenthused. They held a different vision for the nation. And in building a Hindu nation, there would be little place for compromise. "In our self-deception, we go on seceding more and more, in hopes of "nationalizing" the foreigners and succeed merely in increasing their all-devouring appetite," M.S. Golwalker wrote in his classic text, *We Or Our Nationhood Defined*.[27]

Flirting with European Fascists

The project of Hindu regeneration required indoctrination and discipline. Hindu nationalists and supremacists looked on as a stimulating cocktail of science, hyper-nationalism, militarization, and social revolution began spreading across the heart of Western Europe. The movement found themselves particularly enthused by Italy's Benito Mussolini who became the country's leader in 1922 and dictator by 1925.[28] Over the next decade, the nascent Hindu nationalist leadership held explicit contact with the fascist leadership in Italy and Germany, prompting academic and researcher, Marzia Casolari, to conclude that "Hindu nationalism had much more than an ideological interest and practice of fascism."[29] B.S. Moonje (1872–1948), a one-time president of the Hindu Mahasabha and a mentor to K.B. Hedgewar, the founder of the RSS, was so impressed during a visit to Italy in 1931 that he returned to India with the vision to build military schools in the image of the Balilla and Avanguardist organizations, which focused on the indoctrination of youth. Moonje met with Mussolini, too, telling the Italian leader that "India now desires to prepare herself for undertaking the responsibility for her own defence and I am working for it."[30] Describing his visit in his personal diary, Moonje wrote: "The idea of fascism vividly brings out the conception of unity amongst people . . . India and particularly Hindu India need some institution for the military regeneration of the Hindus. Our institution of the RSS under Dr. Hedgewar is of this kind, though quite independently conceived."[31] Within three years of his return from Europe, Moonje began work on Bhonsla Military School as well as the Central Hindu Military Education Society, whose goal included the "military regeneration of the Hindus and to fit Hindu youths for undertaking the entire responsibility for the defence of the motherland."[32]

To supporters of the RSS, the militarization of society was seen as a way to reassert Hindu history. Delegations of local Marathi journalists traveled on tours of Europe and returned enamored by "the socialist origin of fascism" and the transformation of Italy "from a backward country to a first class power."[33] The dismantling of democratic institutions in Italy, the decisive action toward "different" and "undesirable" citizens into "enemies" turned Hindu nationalists into disciples. They appropriated it all: from the youth military schools and populism; the khaki shorts and black berets.

The Indian National Congress and the Hindu nationalist movement ran parallel in intervening years; the former purporting secular and liberal values, in which nationhood would be defined by an all-round "Indianness," made up by the plurality of the people within it. Hindu nationalists in contrast, appealed to a Hindu Rashtra, or a Hindu State, defined by an all-round "Hinduness." Both were still, however, fundamentally upper-caste Hindu organizations; despite its discourses, the Indian National Congress was also very Hindu in nature and practice. The lines, too, were often blurred; there were members of the Indian National Congress who belonged to the Hindu Mahasabha. The upper caste hegemony distressed members of the lower castes and also influenced Muslim leaders to push for more rights and representation, and eventually a separate polity.

Nonetheless, the developments in Europe only led to a further deviation between the movements. Under Nehru, the INC was building a reputation as an internationalist, anti-colonial movement as its vigor for liberation from British rule began to intensify.[34] It did so while simultaneously refusing to support Britain's fascist foes as a new world war beckoned. Its decision to remain on "the right side of history" in World War II further augmented its reputation in the West as a movement purportedly led by principles (as opposed to revenge). In 1931, on a trip to Europe, Gandhi met Mussolini. His counterpart, Nehru, famously turned down an invitation in 1936 to meet the Italian dictator and similarly refused to meet Adolf Hitler in 1938 in protest over the Nazi annexation of Austria and occupation of the former Sudetenland (in what was then northern Czechoslovakia).[35] In contrast, Savarkar and the

Hindu nationalist movement simultaneously collaborated with the British government in India, endorsed fascist Italy, and then Hitler's expansionist project in Europe. Savarkar explicitly expressed his support for Hitler's annexation of Sudetenland in 1938 arguing that the "common desire to form a nation was essential for the formation of a nation."[36]

Responding to Nehru's snub of the German government in 1938, Savarkar, as president of the Hindu Mahasabha, in a speech titled, "India's foreign policy," delivered on August 1, 1938, said: "Who are we to dictate to Germany, Japan or Russia or Italy to choose a particular form of policy of government simply because we woo it out of academical attraction? Surely Hitler knows better than Pandit Nehru does what suits Germany best?"[37] As it so happened, the Hindu nationalist support for fascism in Europe illustrated the gravitation toward zealotry as well as a growing embodiment of ethnonationalist talking points. It was also a demonstration of "practical politics," which became the bedrock of Hindu nationalist foreign policy in the decades to come. As Savakar bluntly put it in a speech in 1938: "Any nation who helps India or is friendly toward her struggle for freedom is our friend. Any nation which opposes us or pursues a policy inimical to us is our foe."[38]

In March 1939, on the eve of World War II, the Hindu Mahasabha issued a statement endorsing the Nazi project, framing its support from an ideological affirmation for the revitalization of the culture, the symbolism and the expectation that it would provide a spark of its nascent but analogous nationalism at home:

> Germany's solemn idea of the revival of the Aryan culture, the glorification of the Swastika, her patronage of the Indo-Germanic civilization are welcomed by the religion and sensible Hindus of India with a jubilant hope . . . I think

> that Germany's crusade against the enemies of the Aryan culture will bring all the Aryan nations of the world to their senses and awaken the Indian Hindus for the restoration of their lost glory.[39]

In another speech in July 1939, in Pune, Savarkar drew explicit distinctions between Jews and Germans: "Nationality did not depend so much on a common geographic area as on unity of thought, religion, language, and culture. For this reason, the Germans and Jews could not be regarded as a nation."[40] The engagement between Hindu nationalism and European fascism had a series of implications. It established the Hindu nationalist movement as an ethnonationalist ideology with an emphasis on race, territory, and nativism as opposed to purely religion. As author Eviane Leidig has argued: "Hindutva is not centred on religion (although Hinduism does play a significant role) but rather on how religion is politicized in such a way that being Hindu generates belonging as an ethnonationalist identity."[41]Even if it was not recognized outside India as such, it recognized in itself, as part of a legion of (fascist) movements emerging across the world, especially Western Europe, as a viable alternative to "the moral bankruptcy" of liberal democracy. Crucially and most fervently for the time, it provided Hindu nationalists with a syntax and a methodology to organize, expand, and lay roots.

Hindu Nationalism and Zionism

The geo-political reconfigurations following the end of World War I had a profound impact on independence and nationalist movements across the globe. India was no different. The INC, under the leadership of Gandhi saw the events of World War I, the Balfour Declaration, the collapse of the Ottoman Empire and Caliphate, and the establishment of the British

Mandate for Palestine in 1922, as further reasons to repudiate British rule. It also fomented closer ties with Muslims in India and the assertion of an anti-imperial agenda.

In Palestine, Zionism had arrived. Palestinians were increasingly displaced, excluded from employment opportunities and denied entry into Jewish-only trade unions. As the continuous flow of Jewish refugees from Europe increased, the rate of dispossession of Palestinians only increased. The program of building a Jewish state brought together Jews (as well as dispensationalist or Christian Zionists) of various persuasions and motivations. The movement spawned political, cultural and labor Zionism (and later revisionist Zionism),[42] each with its own idea as to the character of this future state. However different these might have been, Zionism in totality agreed that this future state would need to have a Jewish majority and therefore establishing it was ultimately predicated on the act of ethnic cleansing of Palestinians. The political project went against Orthodox Jewish beliefs, but it nonetheless proceeded. However, political Zionists were so detached from the sentiments of the Jewish polity, that they were prepared to accept a homeland in Argentina and Uganda, before cultural Zionists put that matter to rest. Once the political project was endorsed, it wasn't long before the Bible was used as "proof" that Jews belonged to Palestine. And in keeping with the peculiarities of the time, the Zionists reframed their movement as one befitting a "national liberation movement."

India was the crown jewel of the British Empire, and Zionists paid attention to both the art and literature that emerged from India, as well as the mass mobilizations that threatened the British Empire.[43] However, it was Hindu nationalists who identified immediate kinship with the Zionist movement. They saw no contradiction in admiring the European fascist movement that targeted European Jews as well as the Zionist project that looked to revitalize the Jewish race by building an exclusive homeland for the Jewish people. The support of European powers for a Jewish state in the Middle East, then, turned a colonial matter into a civilizational conquest. The subtext now was that "Israel was a device for holding Islam—and later the Soviet Union—at bay," Edward Said wrote.[44] Herzl, the writer Abdul-Wahab Kayalli argued, had routinely portrayed Zionism "as a political meeting point between Christianity and Judaism in their common stance against Islam and the barbarism of the Orient."[45] Unsurprisingly, in India, Hindu nationalists saw "the Jewish question" in Europe as "the Muslim problem" in their own backyard. "India's Muslims are on the whole more inclined to identify themselves and their interests with Muslims outside India than Hindus who live next door, like Jews in Germany." Savarkar said in a speech in December 1939.[46]

For Hindu nationalists, the support for both fascism in Europe as well as Zionism won them admirers among the right wing in Europe and helped recast themselves as adjacent to the global racial elite. In Harbilas Sarda's book, *Hindu Superiority: An Attempt to Determine the Position of the Hindu Race in the Scale of Nations*, the famous Indian judge writes that his effort to glorify the Hindu past, was not meant to "run down any creed or nationality [. . .] it may be remarked that the evils of the rule of the Afghans, Turks, and others were due not to the religion they professed but by their ignorance and backwardness in civilization."[47] It is precisely this invocation of a racial, civilizational, cultural superiority and adoption of a very European tradition of pathologizing Muslims as a backward, problematic minority that lured Hindu nationalists and supremacists toward European ethno-fascism. For Hindu nationalists and supremacists, the comparison with Zionism, then, was not incidental. It merely represented an exchange in a larger, and longer conversation between Judaism and Hinduism, as "two age-old civilizations." Hindutva's affinity for the Zionist search for a homeland spoke to their interactions across the centuries.

Hindutva's construction of the Hindu proto-race (as "insider") in opposition to Muslims (as ultimate "outsider") through a focus on religion, culture, and philosophy was a marker of "civilization." In other words, Hindutva held that the people of India were all fundamentally Hindu and that Hinduism was ultimately their race-culture. It also determined who could be part of the nation. As academic Satradu Sen argues, both Zionism and Hindutva developed "an interest in deploying the language and imagery of a racialized people whose health was both a scientific and a political problem."[48] Golwalker, in particular, was caustic and influential when he articulated the place of "the other" in his book *We or Our Nationhood Defined*: "All those not belonging to the national i.e. Hindu Race, Religion, Culture and Language, naturally fall out of the pale of real 'National' life."[49]

There were other similarities in the religious ethos of both Judaism and Hinduism, which right-wing proponents latched on to, too. Both Jews and Hindus purportedly rejected conversion and were unenthused by the proselytizing habits of others (Christians and Muslims). This underscored the aforementioned anxiety of racial "contamination" or being demographically overrun by Muslims or Arabs or Palestinians. This concern is foundational to racial superiority as purported by both Zionists and Hindu nationalists. The duo also found symmetry in the vigor of the religion itself. Whereas Hinduism was about seeking eternal enlightenment, Judaism could be characterized as a journey "to search after the knowledge of God."[50] These similarities became the religious backbone for building ties between the political projects of Hindutva and Zionism, which relied on myth-making as a form of statecraft.

But the relationship didn't happen immediately. With the labor Zionist movement becoming the dominant stream in Palestine, Zionists reached out to the presiding movement in India: the INC and Gandhi. For labor Zionists, Gandhi represented a version of Hinduism that appeared to match their egalitarian vision of Zionism still in denial over the actions of the Haganah, or militia. The Hindu nationalists however chose to understand Zionism in its full totality. It is no surprise that Ze'ev Jabotinsky, the father of revisionist Zionism, or the version of Zionism that rejected labor Zionism's "negotiation" in the Holy Land, wrote his manifesto, *The Iron Wall*, in 1923, the same year that Savarkar published his treatise on Hindutva. Unlike labor Zionists, Jabotinsky was blunt about his ambitions. Hindu nationalists, too, saw the full project, understood the implications, and imbibed the values.

Jabotinsky argued that only the complete disenfranchising of Palestinians would convince them to accept the Jewish settlers:

> Culturally they [the Palestinian Arabs] are 500 years behind us, spiritually they do not have our endurance or our strength of will, but this exhausts all of the internal differences. We can talk as much as we want about our good intentions; but they understand as well as we what is not good for them.[51]

On the "Arab Question," Jabotinsky argued: "Zionist colonization must either stop, or else proceed regardless of the native population. Which means that it can proceed and develop only under the protection of a power that is independent of the native population—behind an iron wall, which the native population cannot breach."[52]

Jabotinsky and Zionist Revisionists accused labor Zionists of attempting to obscure what they all fundamentally agreed was a colonial project in Palestine. Likewise, for Hindu nationalists, the Congress party's "policy of appeasement" delayed the inevitable: the creation of a majoritarian Hindu state. Philosophically, Hindutva was fundamentally anti-Muslim. The "Hindu" identity was built almost entirely in opposition to Muslims, even placed ahead of the struggle for independence. So much so, that some of Hindutva's early ideologues extricated themselves from the larger Indian struggle for independence.[53]

In theory, Zionism shared the imperial methodology of dispossession and settlement with European colonizers, including the British, as it did with Afrikaner 'puritans' and the bigoted policy of separate development exercised under apartheid South Africa. But it also resonated in the anxieties of Muslims in colonial India, who, fearing Hindu majoritarianism and their position of "minority", began to conceptualize a separate polity of their own.

It is this fear of Hindu majoritarianism that culminated in the formation of the idea of Pakistan prompting some to suggest that Israel and Pakistan, both formed on the basis of religion, were kindred spirits, too. Other scholars argue that traces of labor Zionism, often depicted as the dominant strain of the ideology, could be found in the socialist, internationalist agenda of the Nehru government, too.[54]

These were all political movements in the making, laden with contradiction and opportunism. However, the comparisons between Zionism or Israel with both Nehru-led India and the project of Pakistan are simplistic and incomplete. For starters, the Indian struggle for freedom against the British, as flawed and contradictory as it might have been, cannot be compared to the Zionist so-called struggle for independence from the British. Through the auspices of the Balfour Declaration, it was the British who had demarcated Palestine for the Zionist settler-colonial project in Palestine in the first place.

As early as 1931, it was clear that all Zionists "concurred ideologically with the principle of Jewish sovereignty over all Palestine," Zeev Tzahor writes. If anything, labor Zionism functioned as a trojan horse for settler-colonialism. They held disagreements on strategy, on timing, on language, "there was no difference between our militarists and our vegetarians," as Jabotinsky put it.

The comparisons with Pakistan, too, are inadequate beyond the similar predicament that both Jews in Europe and Muslims on the Indian subcontinent faced in becoming a minority in the modern nation-state. Pakistan was not designed to be a settler-colonial, imperial outpost, as the Zionist state was envisioned.

The territorial lands that would ultimately make up Pakistan—as fluid as they may have been—still had geographic contiguity with the regions in which Muslims were a majority. This was the territorial demand of the founders of the Pakistan movement. They did not have extra-territorial ambitions, nor did they seek to make all of the Indian subcontinent into Pakistan. They were, primarily, concerned with questions of power sharing among Hindus and Muslims after the departure of the British. In addition, Muslims were not *settlers* in Pakistan, and nor did the Pakistan movement seek to replace existing Hindu and Sikh minority communities with Muslims, although the violence at the time of partition caused a refugee crisis across both India and Pakistan. While Pakistan was initially conceived of as a Muslim homeland, within a few months it was evident that Pakistan—unlike the Zionist state—was not invested in settling Muslims from around the world—or even North India—in the nascent nation.[55] The settler constitution of Zionism is integral to its ideology; this was not the case with Muslim nationalism on the Indian subcontinent. Furthermore, the Zionist project was much more invested in a mythical history—a trait it shares with Hindutva—than the founders of the Pakistan movement. In other words, symmetries will exist; some imagined, others more fanciful. However, when it comes to Hindu nationalism and the *complete* project of Zionism—be it cultural, political, labor, revisionist (right wing)—the two ideas share more than symmetry. They shared kinship. And their differences aside, the pursuit of consolidating dominion to create unified states with a single culture and identity, predicated on erasing the "other" is what ultimately defined their kinship.

Gandhi's Assassination and the Emergency Years

It is easy to forget that both the Indian Congress and Hindu nationalist movement had emerged during the late nineteenth and early twentieth centuries. Neither movement held a particularly long leash on history or tradition. Both developed as the context within the Indian subcontinent and around the world shifted. And though each side could distinguish itself from the other, through policy and perspective, the Congress party, with its elite educated, upper caste Hindu male leadership, often elucidated particular assertions about India's civilizational and spiritual superiority.[56] The desire of the Indian National Congress to build a secular state notwithstanding, its values and its messaging intersected with the rising Hindu nationalist sentiment of the time. Gandhi's ethic of non-violence and civil disobedience, or *satyagraha* (truth force) after all, drew inspiration from Hindu sources, like the Bhagavad Gita. His vow of *brahmacharya* (abstinence) and self-discipline was a methodology toward developing a self-righteous and moral superiority over his adversaries. Gandhi supported the protection of cows but wouldn't subscribe to legislation banning the consumption of beef (and certainly not the public lynchings) of those merely suspected of the trade in or in the consumption of beef. His prolonged dialogue with and perceived placation of Indian Muslims ultimately outweighed his asceticism as India's holy man. For this, he was assassinated on January 30, 1948 by a Hindu nationalist loosely associated with the right-wing organizations, the RSS and the Hindu Mahasabha. Gandhi's assassination, just five months after partition, precipitated the immediate arrest of scads of RSS members and the banning of the paramilitary organization for approximately a year. It pushed the organization underground, with around 20,000 of its members said to have been arrested during the raids and subsequent police investigation.[57]

But the work went on. In 1948, the RSS formed the Akhil Bharatiya Vidyarthi Parishad (ABVP) or the All India Students Council. The group focused on intimidating leftists at universities. The unbanning of the RSS in 1949 provided for the organization and Golwalkar, in particular, to embark on a new stage of its development: building a family of movements (Sangh Parivar) across all facets of the social ecosystem. In 1952, the RSS built the Vanvasi Kalyan Ashram that became in 1980 a nation-wide organization that warded off Christian missionaries by integrating "tribal" communities into Hinduism. India, under Nehru in the 1950s, attempted to inculcate a secular nationalism, in direct contrast to demands of the Hindu nationalists who saw his foreign policy as fundamentally anemic. Hindu nationalists opposed Nehru's approach to Kashmir that saw it become a semi-autonomous entity under Article 370. Hindu nationalists urged Nehru to take Kashmir forcefully. "Hindu nationalism consolidated around a new, post-independence symbolic territory of a powerful India premised on a permanently aggressive stance toward external and permanent enemies," author Chetan Bhatt writes.[58]

Under the leadership of Golwalkar, the RSS built an index of direct affiliate organizations; from labor to farmers to anti-poverty and education. They rewrote India's history and built schools designed to produce generation after generation of cadres well versed in the larger project of Hindutva. Soon enough, political parties like Bharatiya Jana Sangh (1951) and the religious group Vishwa Hindu Parishad (1964) were created to "organize and consolidate Hindu society." Jana Sangh, campaigning around re-uniting now "divided India", agitating on matters of cow protection and Kashmir, did not achieve much success in its early contest of elections.[59] That didn't matter. Golwalkar continued emphasizing the need to create ideal Hindu men who could then be transplanted across the nation. Between the 1960s and 1970s, graduates of the earliest RSS programs would find themselves in administrative, organizational, policy positions across the country. Their moment would arrive soon enough.

The Emergency as Foil for Hindu Nationalism

Following the death of her father, Jawaharlal Nehru, in 1964, Indira Gandhi was able to wrest control of the Congress party leading to her election in January 1966. PM Indira Gandhi led the country until March 1977, as well as for a second stint beginning January 1980 until her assassination in October 1984. The country Indira inherited in 1966 was one grappling with a fractured political and economic identity. India had achieved political freedom in 1947, but this hadn't come with social revolution or any semblance of redress.[60] She was thus made to face growing social strife that had emerged from a stalling economy, rising corruption and spiraling unemployment that had rolled on over the preceding two decades. In fact, the challenges were immediate. Within five months of her first year in office, a popular cartoonist named Bal Thackeray, formed a right-wing, ultranationalist, and nativist group called the "Shiv Sena" in Bombay. Thackeray spoke to the grievances of "the people" of Bombay, by blaming migrant labor and Muslims for scarcity of resources and the city's ills. His party attracted tens of thousands and soon became the gatekeepers of the city.[61]

Then, months later, a band of naked Sadhus, stormed the parliamentary complex in the country's capital demanding that the government impose a country-wide ban on cow slaughter. Seven protesters were killed when police opened fire on the crowd.[62] For days, violent demonstrations took place across New Delhi. Soon there were anti-Muslim riots in Jabalpur, Ahmedabad, and Bhiwandi; peasant rebellions in rural India which culminated in the re-emergence of communist parties (like the Communist Party of India-Marxist) in Kerala and West Bengal. The India of her father was slipping and Indira instinctively centralized power. She packed the judiciary with marionettes, dismantled procedures in institutions, surrounded herself with close allies, and ramped up state security. She controlled it all. "The difference from the previous period was that traditional master-servant deference now took on an ugly sycophantic form," author Gyan Prakash writes.[63]

In 1968, Indira set up the Research and Analysis Wing (RAW), an intelligence agency in the mold of the CIA. It reported directly to the prime minister's office. Secret ties between RAW[64] and the Israeli Mossad were set up immediately as a counter to Pakistan's burgeoning relationship with China and North Korea.[65] Though there were no diplomatic ties between India and Israel, RAW and Mossad began facilitating Israeli-India defense ties.[66] Indira naturally also looked east to Moscow. Months before the 1971 war with Pakistan, India signed a treaty with the USSR. It turned India into the biggest destination of Soviet arms by 1991.

The buoyancy over defeating Pakistan in 1971, the successful completion of its first nuclear tests in 1974 (the only one of its kind at the time to be conducted by a country outside of the United Nations Security Council) could only camouflage the deep schisms that had unfurled during Indira's tenure as PM. The rising communalism, the economic downtown precipitated by drought and the oil crisis of 1973, and the political unrest in different districts across the nation pushed her further inwards. When a judge at the Allahabad High Court ruled in June 1975 that Indira had been found guilty of electoral fraud, Indira's autocratic leanings came to the fore. She declared a State of Emergency, during which she suspended the constitution, censored the media, postponed elections, and detained more than 110,000 people without charge or trial. The Indian government ensured a media blackout and when it battled to control criticism in the Western press, it kicked out foreign journalists or asked them to sign a pledge before allowing them access. In an address to the nation broadcast over radio, Indira described the threat against India as a "deep and widespread conspiracy." She claimed that "forces of disintegration are in full play and communal passions are being aroused, threatening our unity." She also promised that the "emergency proclamation will in no way affect the rights of law-abiding citizens."[67] Predictably, it was the poor who bore the brunt of the Emergency. The PM accelerated forced sterilizations on the disenfranchised and implemented mass slum clearances. These might have encompassed "the darkest days of Indian democracy," but they were in no way an aberration in India's post-independence story.

Indira also introduced amendments to the "Maintenance of Internal Security Act" (MISA) that gave the government unprecedented power to exercise "preventative detention." When MISA had been originally introduced during the 1971 war with West Pakistan, the government told detractors it would not be used for internal dissent.[68] The episode lasted 21 months. As Gyan Prakash writes, the attempt to rubbish away the Emergency Years as a type of an accident of history seemed a deliberate ploy to subvert the deep rot within Indian democracy itself. "India's democracy, we are told, heroically recovered from Indira's brief misadventure with no lasting damage, and with no enduring unaddressed problems in its functioning."[69]

But India, like so many (post-) colonial states was a highly stratified society operating in a cesspool of deep-seated corruption that relied on power and patronage. The Emergency Years and the deeper introspection that it failed to elicit, produced a series of consequences. It revitalized the Hindu nationalist movement. Thirty years had passed since Indian independence. An entire generation, brainwashed by Hindutva, was ready to be activated. Hindu nationalist parties, their advocates and members, became central players in the agitations against Indira Gandhi. The RSS was banned once more but the Emergency reinvigorated the movement, prompting their volunteers and leaders to label the moment as "the second freedom struggle." "[The] Emergency was one of the few good events in the 60-year-old life of independent India . . . [It] galvanized the nation," RSS member Sanjeev Kelkar is quoted as having said.[70]

The heightened popularity of the Hindu right provided the Bharatiya Jana Sangh party (Indian People's Organization) with an opportunity to make its mark in mainstream electoral politics. Between 1977–9, India was run by the Janata government.[71] As L. K. Advani, who was also jailed for 19 months, and who would later become a senior member of the BJP, described the period:

> If the Emergency was the darkest period in India's post-Independence history, the righteous struggle for the restoration of democracy was undoubtedly its brightest. It so happened that I, along with tens of thousands of my countrymen, was both a victim of the Emergency and a soldier in the Army of Democracy that won the battle against it.[72]

The Emergency shattered all existing conceptions of the Indian state. Whereas Nehru, Gandhi, and the Indian National Congress had presented India as a non-violent, anti-colonial, and militarily restrained nation, Indira presented India as strong, bold, and militarily assertive.

As Khinvraj Jangid told me,

> It is Indira who believes that violence is legitimate in the name of nation and state security. This is why Hindu nationalists have a fascination with Indira Gandhi. They like her. She transformed the non-nuclear, anti-power, non-violent idea of the state into something else. She was the antidote to Nehru.[73]

When the Emergency ended, Hindu nationalists emerged emboldened, strengthened, and immensely popular. In 1980, the Bharatiya Jana Sangh merged with other parties to form the Bharatiya Janata Party (BJP). The BJP would still struggle to win elections, but the movement was no longer on the periphery. It was a disruptive force in Indian electoral politics. By the egregious actions of the Congress government during the Emergency, the Hindu Right had worked its way into the political mainstream. Indira became prime minister again in 1980. To thwart the challenge of the Hindu nationalists, the Congress party felt obliged to cede ground. It began opening up the economy (deregulation took place in the cement industry in 1982) and it moved toward emulating the identity politics of the right wing.

Indira also grew more enamored by her new secret liaison with the Israelis, to devastating effect. In June 1984, Indira sent a group of commandos to crush a Sikh rebellion in Amritsar. The ragtag group of Sikh fighters, made up of army and police officers, were holed up in the Golden Temple Complex, among the most sacred sites in Sikhism. The commandos, known as Special Group or SG commandos, had received training from an elite branch of Mossad commanders in 1983 under an agreement with RAW. The Israeli commandos were famously known for the raid in Uganda's Entebbe Airport in Uganda in 1977, following the hijacking of an Air France aircraft by Palestinian militants. Indira's Operation Blue Star, as it was known, ended in a bloodbath. "The commandos were in black fatigues and wore night-vision glasses, M-1 steel helmets, bulletproof jackets, and carried sophisticated guns including AK-47 assault rifles. The commandos were capable of jogging at a speed of 40 km per hour," Prabash K. Dutta wrote.[74]

Five months later, Indira's aggrieved Sikh bodyguards assassinated her. Congress supporters routed parts of the country in a three-day pogrom—primarily in the nation's capital—in which close to 3,000 Sikhs were killed. Witnesses recalled Sikhs being necklaced and bludgeoned on the streets of the capital. Indira's son Rajiv succeeded his mother as PM. The same SG unit was activated once more, now to protect Rajiv. Reacting to the carnage around him, Rajiv told a rally: "Once a mighty tree falls, it is only natural that the earth around it shakes." Rajiv was elected in December 1984 in a landslide.

The Emergency Years also marked a turning point in the relationship between Hindu nationalists in India and the Indian diaspora, especially those with Hindu nationalist leanings. Indians in the diaspora had been mobilized to help "restore democracy" in India. They had lobbied the American and British governments. They had taken out full page ads in the biggest and most read newspapers in the world. And they had sent resources back to India to help those purportedly standing up to PM Indira Gandhi.

"The Sangh used the Emergency to strengthen its overseas networks by engaging its members in new forms of activism to oppose the Indian government," Edward Anderson and

Patrick Clibbens write.[75] It transformed the way the Indian government and political organizations interacted with the diaspora, too.[76] The developments were among the first signs of the critical role the Indian diaspora would play in the making of a new India, impacting flows of capital, human resources and ideas. "Values that might have been important in India in the 1940s were no longer important in the 1980s. In fact, contrary values became more important," Jangid says, adding, "In 1992, it was a different India."[77]

The change in "values" played out on the streets, where rallies like the "Ram Rath Yatra," designed to instill fear into Muslims became the new Hindu motif across several states. It took place on television, as weekly serials showcasing epics like the Mahabharata and Ramayana, stirred hundreds of millions of hearts into fervent believers. It took place in cinema halls where Bollywood increasingly transported the Indian nation into Hindu diaspora homes, where patriots danced around trees in the Black Forest or under the bright lights of Times Square, but longed for the spiritual and cultural meaning of home. It took place in the Indian parliament, where some of the same actors who played gods on screen became elected officials on Hindu nationalist tickets.

In 1984, the BJP secured two seats in the Lok Sabha, the lower house. The Congress party secured 426. In 1989, the BJP adopted Hindutva as its political program, calling for the scrapping of Article 370 in the constitution that granted Kashmir special rights; it achieved 88 seats. In 1991, it was 120. In 1996, it was 161. And by 1998, it had grown to 178, enough to form a coalition government. Its rise was prodigious; its impact on the social and cultural life of India, unmistakable. The RSS, having been formed in 1925, "were in government by 1977 and were leading in many areas of public life by the stroke of the new century."[78]

4
The Indian Diaspora and the Israeli Lobby in the United States

> Since the June 1967 war, Israel has been a stage on which American Jews have played out their fantasies of toughness . . . and a pawn in their pursuit of power and privilege. If Israel has become a crazy state, and it has, it is in no small part to American Jews. —Norman Finkelstein[1]

For decades, the Zionist lobby in the U.S. has played a fundamental role in connecting the Israeli project with the imperialist project of American Empire. Since the 1960s, the beating heart of these lobbying efforts in government has been the American Israel Political Action Committee (AIPAC). Paul Findley, a Republican Congressman, found himself in the cross hairs of AIPAC in the early 1980s, eventually being voted out of office through the mobilization of the group's vast economic and community resources. Findley wrote in 1985 that AIPAC almost always got everything it wanted, "including aid increases to Israel beyond the amounts requested by the administration."

AIPAC is indubitably among the most resourced and most visible, but it is also just one part of a large Israeli lobby that advocates on behalf of Israel. The Israeli lobby includes a vast number of individuals and institutions: those who support Israel unconditionally, including annexation of the West Bank, and propose the criminalization of the Boycott Divestment and Sanctions campaign (BDS), the Palestinian civil society-led movement calling for sanctions on Israel; those who call for the US to end support for the occupation but refuse to support neither BDS nor its criminalization; and those against the Israeli occupation and the expansion of settlements but still adamant on Israel's "right to exist".

The Israeli lobby has never worked in unison, though author Don Waxman argues that what binds them is its "unwavering commitment to the survival of Israel as a Jewish state."[2] The Anti-Defamation League (ADL), for instance, formed originally in 1913, has found ways to present itself as a civil rights organization while simultaneously working with the FBI in spying and sabotaging the work of Black and Arab activists, and most routinely conflating criticism of Israel to anti-Semitism.[3] Similarly, the American Jewish Committee (AJC) formed in 1906 to defend Jewish civil and religious rights throughout the world, evolved into a custodian of Israel's image everywhere from college campuses to the halls of the U.S. Congress.[4]

Through the strength of its resources, and influence in the media and in the White House, the Israeli lobby has managed to create the impression that it—and its pro-Israel ideology—represent American Jews when it has never been given the mandate to do so. "If you're Jewish, it is assumed that you more or less uncritically support Israel because of the blood-bond. In reality it hasn't been the case," Norman Finkelstein said in 2012.[5] As a collective, the Israeli lobby has pressured U.S. lawmakers, employed smear tactics in condemning Palestinian resistance and advocacy efforts, and fiddled with university and school curriculums, all the while ostensibly claiming to keep Jews safe.

The Israeli lobby's ability to exercise influence over U.S. foreign policy has always been proportional to the interests of the U.S., but its ability to turn criticism of Israel into existential crises for Jews and to spin American backing of Israel as a moral and just undertaking, paramount to Israel's existence, has added to the mythology surrounding its scale of influence.

Not only did these organizations appear to possess the power to influence legislation on behalf of Israel, but they had the ability to influence U.S. policy toward other countries on account of those countries' ties with Israel. That these organizations were not always able to exercise power over the U.S. government was of lesser importance; the perception of influence was the point.

In 1987, India came face to face with the ADL over a tennis match. Indian authorities had refused to grant visas to the Israeli tennis team ahead of a Davis Cup tie in New Delhi in July. Two months ahead of the tie, the ADL released a scathing report titled, "India's campaign against Israel," accusing India of being among the "few countries outside the Arab world [to] have been so unrelentingly hostile to Israel."[6] It cited 17 cases of India refusing visas to Israelis since 1980, condemned its vehemently public pro-Palestinian stance and recommended U.S. sanctions.[7] The contents of the report shocked Delhi. Already reeling from a reduction of aid from the U.S. Congress,[8] Gandhi's government responded by issuing visas.

The ADL report had effectively changed Indian policy overnight. In June 1988, PM Gandhi traveled to New York City where he met with the leadership of the ADL and the AJC. The meeting had been arranged at the behest of Stephen Solarz, a U.S. lawmaker from Brooklyn, home to sizable Jewish and Indian American communities.[9] Indian PM Rajiv Gandhi reportedly told the leaders of these two Zionist lobby groups that he wanted to secure closer ties with the U.S. Academic Nicolas Blarel writes that, "in response, the Jewish organizations criticized India's prejudiced conduct toward Israel . . . they also asked India to pressure the Palestinians to renounce their call for the destruction of Israel and to follow the Egyptian example [Egypt signed a peace accord with Israel in 1979]".[10]

Though it's unclear what Gandhi promised during the meeting, within hours, news of the interaction had already made its way to Shimon Peres (the Israeli Foreign Minister), who told the Israeli media that an upgrade of relations was imminent.[11] A bewildered Indian government in New Delhi was forced to issue a clarification. Responding to a question in parliament, K.K. Tewari, the Minister of State in the Ministry of External Affairs, described Peres' invocation as "totally unrelated to the facts."[12] Within weeks, however, India reinstated Israel's consul-general in Bombay. The Israelis had been without a senior diplomat in India for six years. Again, the Indian government denied that the change had come following Gandhi's meetings with the ADL. Six months after the Israeli lobby had asked Delhi to pressure the Palestinians to recognize the state of Israel, the PLO announced its acceptance of a two-state solution and therefore recognized the state of Israel.[13]

A year later, in 1989, leading members of the ADL, as well as Congressman Solarz, traveled to New Delhi, during which they met Narasimha Rao, the foreign minister and P.K. Singh, the ministry's joint secretary, to talk about the "normalization" of ties. On their return to the U.S., Jesse N. Hordes, a member of the delegation, said that "the basic decision to change direction had already been made."[14] And it showed. It wasn't long before Delhi instructed the Maharashtra government to include the Israeli-consul general in all official events. As part of its complaint in 1987 about the Indian government's treatment of Israel, the ADL was particularly incensed by the restrictions placed on the Israeli Consulate in Bombay, going so far as to accuse New Delhi of treating its diplomatic mission with even more hostility than it did Pakistan.[15] The subsequent relaxing of travel restrictions for Israelis to India was the first step in forever altering Israel's place in India's imagination. Whereas there was still no diplomat in Israel itself, Indian embassies in London and the U.S. functioned as intermediaries for business and tour groups seeking to visit India. The Israeli lobby's impact on the Indian government had another consequence. It introduced the Indian community to the power of diaspora politics.

Setting up Hindutva in the United States

In the early 1990s, Indians comprised a tiny minority in the United States. The community that had numbered no more than 9,000 in 1960 and had grown, following the relaxation of immigrations laws in the 1960s, to around 387,000 by 1980, became close to a million by the late 1990s.[16] This community, many of whom arrived as highly educated, upper caste professionals after 1960, were raising their economic and social profile as physicians and technologists; as motel owners and engineers. They were well on their way to imbibing the ultimate American immigrant success story: hard working, law-abiding, and oblivious to their privilege as recipients of immense victories of the civil rights movement that had laid the path for their careers.[17] "The result was a form of social engineering," journalist Arun Venugopal writes.[18]

Today, there are around 4.2 million people of Indian origin in the U.S., with around 2.6 million being American citizens (1.4 million are naturalized citizens and 1.2 million were born in the United States).[19] Predominantly settled in New York and New Jersey, they are also in large numbers in Texas and California. Like other small communities in the U.S., including the Armenians and the Greeks, Indian Americans in the late 1980s and 1990s looked at Jewish Americans and saw a small, affluent community with political clout. And just as AIPAC, the ADL, and AJC had managed to present American

Jews as a monolith, wholly and utterly tethered to the idea of Israel, the Indian American groups that began to emerge in the 1990s looked to characterize themselves as representative of the larger Indian American community as well as this "new" Hindu India. As a result, a series of overlapping Hindu nationalist organizations were developed to make India synonymous with Hindutva.

The project stemmed back to the RSS. The first international branches of the RSS were launched in Kenya and Myanmar as early as 1947. The Hindu Swayamsevak Sangh (HSS), considered the overseas offshoot of the RSS, was formed in England in 1966.[20] Various reports indicate the HSS made its way to the U.S. around the same period, but it was officially founded as a non-profit in 1989. Likewise, the Vishwa Hindu Parishad of America (VHPA), a Hindu nationalist organization, was set up in New York City in 1970. At its tenth Hindu conference in New York City, the VHPA passed a resolution calling "all Hindus of the world—back home and abroad—to act in a broad and nationalistic manner rising above their personal beliefs and creeds, parochial languages, and provincial and sectarian considerations."[21] This call culminated in an expansion of organizations into the 1990s that built on what M.S. Golwalker described as the RSS's "world mission to propagate the Hindu notion of the world as a single family."[22]

In April 1991, L.K. Advani, one of the BJP's most prominent leaders, launched the Overseas Friends of the Bharatiya Janata party (OFBJP) to directly "educate American lawmakers, the American people, and the Indian American community about the true principles of the BJP."[23] The OFBJP became the protector of India's external image, even as they participated, encouraged, and funneled funds to the Temple Movement back in India. Rising communal tensions in India, the mounting death toll in heavily militarized Indian-occupied Kashmir, had drawn skepticism and concern in the West. "The BJP was getting a lot of bad press all over the world and particularly in the U.S.," Adapa Prasad, vice-president of the OFBJP in the U.S. recalls.[24] This project of stage managing the image of the Indian state was immediately put to use following the Hindu nationalist demolition of the sixteenth century Babri Masjid in December 1992, the Bombay riots and anti-Muslim pogroms that followed. The *New York Times* described the events of 1992 as "the worst outbreak of sectarian violence in India since 1984."[25]

In the face of a swelling Hindu nationalist and supremacist movement in India during the 1990s, the same Indian Americans who had once played a significant role in the agitations abroad against Indira Gandhi during the Emergency Years were now activated to consolidate the Hindu nationalist project. These Indian Americans were now deeply established in the U.S.; their organizations like the HSS, OFBJP, and VHPA were now a lot more networked, connected to a community with a lot more wealth, social status, and stability.

Take Ved Prakash Nanda, for example. A law professor at the University of Denver, Nanda authored papers and articles and testified in June 1976 before a Congressional subcommittee about human rights abuses in India during the Emergency. He later played a central role in the formation of the HSS in the United States, becoming its president in 2002.[26] Or consider Ramesh Bhutada. Originally from Maharashtra, Bhutada moved to the U.S. in 1968. Bhatuda became politically active following the arrest of his father, a member of the RSS, during the Emergency. Bhutada organized protests in Houston and formed the HSS branch in the city, later becoming the group's national vice-president.[27] Bhutada also became an energetic organizer for the OFBJP, who helped canvas for Modi's election in 2014. Five years later, Bhatuda became instrumental in the "Howdy Modi" event in Houston in 2019 that attracted some 20,000 people, including two dozen U.S. lawmakers and then President Donald Trump.

And then there is Mukund Mody, who would move from protesting against the Emergency in the 1970s to becoming an integral figure in the formation and organization of Hindutva groups in the U.S. "In the 1980s, Mody continued to work as secretary-general of FISI and to organize Hindu youth camps in America for the Vishwa Hindu Parishad (VHP). In 1990, he traveled to India to meet 'the hierarchy of the BJP' who wanted to open cells of the party in foreign countries ahead of the 1991 general elections," Edward Anderson and Patrick Clibbens write.[28] It was Mody who established the OFBJP in the U.S. in 1991. For his efforts, Mody received a special mention in Narendra Modi's memoir. In it, Mody is compared to "a sixteenth century Hindu general and Rajasthani folk hero who donated his wealth to Maharaja Pratap in order to raise an army against the Mughals."[29]

In the 1990s, Hindu nationalists in the U.S. prioritized shifting their identity from an "Indian" to "Hindu" orientation. Moreover, they looked to mobilize their activities around a "Hindu Indian state-building project."[30] In time, the emphasis on ecumenicalism and nationalism, Prema Kurien writes, became the central planks for "official American Hinduism."[31] In so doing, Indian Americans looked to Zionist organizations to maximize their impact on Capitol Hill as well as become gatekeepers of the Hindus in the U.S.[32] and defenders of anything they deemed to be offensive to Hindus.

For instance, in 1997, the VHPA formed the American Hindus Against Defamation (AHAD), modeled on the Anti-Defamation League (ADL). Just as the ADL said its aim was to "stop the defamation of the Jewish people and to secure justice and fair treatment to all," AHAD described itself as "dedicated to preserve [sic] the sanctity of Hindu symbols, icons, culture and customs."[33] There were other political initiatives. In 1993, Gopal Raju, an Indian American entrepreneur and founder of *India Abroad*, formed the Indian American Centre for Political Action (IACPA). The IACPA was created to mold a new generation of politically astute Indian Americans.[34] Raju arranged internships on Capitol Hill and hired Ralph Nunberger, a professor in international relations and a legislative liaison for AIPAC, to help him succeed. In concert with Raju's effort, U.S. Congressman Frank Pallone (New Jersey) and Bill McCollum (Florida) formed the India Caucus, an interest group that recognized India as a U.S. partner and looked to charter strengthening relations between the two countries. The other U.S. Congressman who played an integral role was Democratic lawmaker Gary Ackerman, who articulated a greater partnership between India, Israel, and the U.S. In the late 1990s, Ackerman was co-chairman of the Congressional Caucus on India and a Member of the House Foreign Affairs Committee. As the representative of New York's 5th district, known for being home to a high concentration of Jewish residents, Ackerman was therefore both influential and at the very intersection of U.S. foreign policy toward the Middle East and South Asia.

At a fundraising dinner organized by two Indian Americans in his honor in Atlanta in 1999, Ackerman described "strong India-Israel relations" as "very critical to ensuring peace and stability in a part of the world that is characterized by instability, fundamentalist religious bigotry, hatred toward the West and its values and murder and mayhem spawned by acts of cross-border terrorism."[35] He, too, described India and Israel as "ancient civilizations [that] have much in common politically and economically, and share strong democratic beliefs, traditions and values." Ackerman said, "As many of you are aware, Israel, just like India, is a special place for me [. . .] and as such, you all should consider me as your *bhai*—your brother." Within ten years, the India caucus went from eight members to a quarter of the U.S. Congress.[36] "It helped, of course, that the Indian American community had money in its pocket and its "leaders" (those with money) wanted to be players in D.C," Vijay Prashad writes.[37] For their efforts, both Ackerman and Pallone were awarded major civilian awards by the BJP government in 2002.

During its years in power between 1998–2002, the BJP routinely urged the Indian diaspora to invest back home as well as represent its interests abroad. On cue, the Indian diaspora began sending charity to Hindu nationalist projects, investing heavily in the IT, software and start-up efforts in India.[38] It simultaneously continued to underwrite efforts to lobby for a narrow pro-Hindu, pro-business agenda in DC. Whereas remittances in 1990-91 were estimated at $2.1bn or 0.7% of India's GDP, they rose to $12.3bn by 1996-7. By 2006, they had become 3.1% of the country's GDP, contributing even more than India's software exports.[39] To put these figures into perspective, India had begun to receive more remittances from the diaspora than it spent on healthcare or education.

Moreover, the strength of the dollar and the liberalization of the economy allowed Indian Americans to take a particular interest in real estate, too. So much so, it was estimated that by 2005, 20% of all properties over $250,000/Rs 10m were purchased by Indians abroad.[40] Studies showed that whereas in 1990–91, remittances from North America amounted to 24%, money sent from the Gulf was around 40%. By 2006, the scenario had flipped: Only 24% of remittances were sourced from Indian migrant workers in the Gulf, while remittances from North America had increased to 44%.[41]

The consolidation of the Indian community in America precipitated a growth in temples, Hindu associations and visits by religious figures and musicians. Naturally, the economic power wielded by the Indian American community meant that India also began catering to its needs. Even mainstream blockbuster Bollywood films began catering scripts to questions of "nostalgia," "longing," and "nationalism" faced by the diaspora. To be an authentic "Indian" was to be unequivocally devoted to the values of a certain, purportedly unobtrusive Hinduness. Raj (played by Shah Rukh Khan) in *Dilwale Dulhania Le Jayenge* (The brave hearted will take the bride, 1995) refuses to elope with Simran (played by Kajol) without the approval of her father. The film makes it clear that it is his Hindu Indian values, dipped in South Asian patriarchy that prevents him from doing so. In *Pardes* (Foreign Land, 1998), Arjun (Shah Rukh Khan), as a "good" Indian-born man is pitted against his stepbrother, Rajiv (Apurva Agnihorti), a foreign-born Indian man with every vice imaginable. Whereas Arjun is humble, cultured, and respectful, Rajiv is philandering, crass, and a borderline alcoholic. Arjun is East, Rajiv is West. No surprise that Arjun wins the girl Ganga (aptly named to represent the Ganges, the holiest river in Hinduism; Ganga is played by Mahima Chaudry). American capitalism was completely acceptable, if you retained Hindu Indian traditions, the film's subtitle "American Dreams, Indian Soul" seemed to say.

There were several other films which either packaged "longing" for homeland, like *Swades* (Our Land, 2004), about an Indian engineer at NASA, who answers a yearning to return to his village in India or like *Kabhie Khushi Kabhie Gham* also known as *K3G* (Sometimes happiness, sometimes sorrow, 2001), in which Indian families were almost always thriving upper caste industrialists living in castles abroad. In *K3G*, the main protagonist, Rahul (played by Shah Rukh Khan) falls in love with Anjali (played by Kajol), of a "lower social standing," sparking a feud in the family. The dispute is most certainly over her belonging to a lower caste, but the film doesn't say so, allowing the audiences in diaspora, where the film broke multiple records, to leave the matter unnamed in their real lives, too.

For many Indian Americans, particularly Hindus, caste was considered a burden of the past in a backwater village in rural India, or an idea invented by the British; it didn't exist in America. But in many ways, caste oppression has manifested itself in more complex ways in the U.S. Upper caste Hindus dominate the Indian American community and therefore Hinduism in America is created in their image. Their attempt to shape "India as Hindu" as well as the common tendency to treat Indians in the U.S. as a monolith has meant the silencing of Indian Muslims, Dalits, Tribals, and Christians. Their struggles as subjects of Hindutva and Brahminical oppression are erased, too.[42]

Indian Americans who fit snugly into the "upwardly mobile model minority" caricature looked to imbibe the myth of America as the land of opportunity. Whereas they were open to accepting that structural racism existed in the U.S. (given they were victims of racism, too), as highly educated Indian Americans pursuing the American dream, they differentiated themselves from Black Americans, whom in time, they saw as economic and social burdens to the system, much like the lower caste and urban poor back in India.

In other words, a segment of the Hindu American community began seeing their success as a symbol of their culture and individual hard work,[43] as opposed to a direct result of their place in a racial hierarchy or their caste that had given them the opportunity to study and the social mobility to leapfrog other communities in the U.S. As *Jews had become white folks* in the 1960s, Vijay Prashad argues that *Hindus became Jews* in the latter half of the century. They imbibed the very privilege of white and increasingly corporate America. By the late 1990s and early 2000s, these Indian Americans who had made it in the U.S. were helping shape the social, economic, and political landscape back home. They were self-styled *pioneers.*

The Guzofsky-Vyasmaan Affair

It was the summer of 2001. A website, called "Hindu Unity" and "Soldiers of Hindutva" run by Indian Americans in New York was dropped by its service provider after it received complaints that the website had been publishing names of people it deemed to be enemies of Hinduism and encouraging violence against them.[44] Rohit Vyasmaan, who helped run the website, immediately called up a man named Michael Guzofsky from Brooklyn and asked for help.[45] Guzofsky reached out to another service provider and got the site back up. Guzofksy admitted he didn't know much about Vyasmaan or the group. All he knew was that they were standing up to Muslims and he wanted to help.

Guzofsky, it turned out, wasn't just a man with a computer; he was the manager of a website belonging to the extreme Israeli group Kahane, named after Rabbi Meir David Kahane, the founder of the Jewish Defence League (JDL) in the U.S. and the Kach political party in Israel.[46] Guzofsky claimed he supported the Hindu group's first amendment right to express its views. But it didn't take much for him to reveal the real reason for championing the site. In an interview at the time with the *New York Times*, Guzofsky said the alliance was a practical one that demonstrated a common suffering at the hands of Muslims. He said the Jewish-Hindu relationship was born out of adversity. "I definitely understand their pain even if I don't know much about their faith," Guzofsky was quoted as having said.[47]

The website, "Hindu Unity," was no bastion of free speech. A project of the Bajrang Dal, an extremist movement in India, it encouraged attacks on activists or scholars who critiqued

Hindu nationalism and carried articles that called Hindus to stand up and take up arms and exterminate Muslims.[48] Whereas the Kahane group called for the expulsion of all Palestinians, the Bajrang Dal called for the purge of Muslims from India and pioneered the demolition of Babri Masjid in 1992. As political organizations, the Kahane group and Bajrang Dal were therefore almost indistinguishable.[49] "We are fighting the same war . . . Whether you call them Palestinians, Afghans or Pakistanis, the root of the problem for Hindus and Jews is Islam," said Vyasmaan, who had a photograph of Rabbi Kahane on display in his home in Queens. Months later, the attacks of September 11, 2001 in New York City and the December 13, 2001 attacks on India's parliament in New Delhi would take place.

The thirst to "protect" freedom and democracy from the civilizational threat of Muslims, became the principal cover for expanding surveillance, extra-judicial killings, torture and propel closer ties between the governments as well as right wing movements in America, Israel, and India. In 2002, Daniel Pipes, the renowned right wing academic, formed a blacklist of his own, called "Campus Watch." Whereas "Hindu Unity" had looked to vilify Muslims, secularists, and communists for critiquing Hindu nationalism, Pipes' blacklist looked to denigrate academics who expressed critical views about U.S. foreign policy or Israel.

Unsurprisingly, given the impact of the events of September 11, the space the Global War on Terror had granted neo-conservatives and right wing groups around the world, throughout the early 2000s, several Hindu nationalist organizations sprang up in a bid to reach the Indian American community and connect with a new generation. Existing organizations like the VHPA and the HSC established new chapters. These new chapters added additional activities; more literature was published that quietly played down caste oppression and erased the contribution of non-Hindus in India.

By 2005, there were 150 RSS branches in the United States as well as 40 chapters of the VHPA and 44 chapters of the Hindu Student Council. One such organization that popped up in the early 2000s was the Hindu American Foundation (HAF). Founded by Mihir Meghani, Nikhil Joshi, and Suhag and Aseem Shukla in 2003, HAF described itself as "an advocacy group providing a progressive voice for over two million Hindu Americans." HAF tried to present itself as an unaffiliated and independent defender of Hindu rights. Led by a younger generation of Hindu Americans, they peddled in the language of human and civil rights to defend Hindu supremacy in the U.S. A group of Muslim, Christian, and secular organizations which came together in 2002 under the banner of Coalition Against Genocide (CAG), wrote in 2013, that HAF was "not just like the Sangh, but is an organization born and bred within and of the Sangh."

The consolidation of these nascent gatherings came in the form of the United States India Political Action Committee (USINPAC) in 2002. Founded by three Indian American Republicans: Sanjay Puri, Jesal Amin, and Sue Ghosh Stricklett, USINPAC was built to raise India's standing in the political imagination of America's decision makers, i.e., align American power with Indian interests. Amin, like several Hindu nationalists, believed that "terrorism" in India and in Israel were connected. Vijay Prashad writes that it was Amin who was "instrumental in bringing AIPAC and AJC to help form the Hindu lobby."[50] USINPAC unashamedly adopted the organizational model of AIPAC and the American Jewish Committee (AJC) in a bid to speak the language in the halls of the U.S. Congress. Soon enough, USINPAC became the body seen to represent Indian American interests in Congress.[51] It steered clear of condemning the Patriot Act of 2001, despite the fact it was likely to impact Indian Americans, especially Muslims and Sikhs. Likewise, it tiptoed past the anti-Muslim pogroms in Gujarat in February and March 2002, that killed around 2,000 people, uprooted the lives of tens of thousands of others, and changed social dynamics in the state forever.

The War on Terror didn't merely usher in programs of surveillance and racism against the Muslim community, it facilitated the cross pollination of essentially right wing ethnonationalisms. It helped normalize anti-Muslim bigotry in different parts of the globe. Hence, the need to distinguish the Hindu identity from the "dogmatic," "irrational," "terrorist" became not merely a survivalist tactic, but an opportunity to further crystalize a civilizational-type pact between the neoconservatives and Zionists toward fulfilling the Hindu nationalist project. Meanwhile, it became routine for AIPAC representatives to travel to New Delhi or to bring Indian delegations to Israel and D.C. for dialogue. In September 2002, Indian PM Atal Behari Vajpayee met with B'nai B'rith International, the AJC, the Jewish Institute of National Security Affairs, and AIPAC where they exchanged pleasantries on "the blossoming of relations between India and Israel."[52] Writing in 2004 about Washington's new strategic partnership with India, Robert M. Hathaway noted the links being developed between the Indian American community leaders and the Republican party. He described the "connections with Indian officialdom are undoubtedly a reflection of the prevailing pro-BJP sentiment within the entrepreneurial-oriented Indian-American community.[53]

By the mid-2000s, the nascent Indian lobby had made three achievements. First, it successfully imported the morphology of Hindutva into its lobbying efforts, collapsing the vast diversity of the Indian American community (made up of Hindus, Muslims, Christians, Dalits, and other lower castes) into the needs of upper caste Hindus, thereby defining Muslims in particular as outsiders. Second, it linked its dilemma to that faced by the "Jewish" community (read: Israel) by defining its threat as the same (read: Muslims). Prashad describes it as "creating an image of the Indian as a victim of Muslim terrorism in South Asia . . . akin to the Jewish American's distress over Muslim terrorism in Israel."[54] Third, it demonstrated a "need" for support, in what was really an invitation to become business partners. "Hindutva and Indian nationalisms . . . are tied therefore to capitalism's neo-liberal avatar, and reflect the interests and dreams of the propertied, trans-national, wealthy economic and social elites of India and among elite Indian Americans," academic Raja Swamy wrote.[55]

On the other end of the spectrum, a coalition of groups, like Desis Rising up and Moving (DRUM), South Asian Americans Leading Together (SAALT), and the Indian American Muslim Council (IAMC) began mobilizing for working class rights, immigration rights and racial justice, as well as against rising Hindutva in India.[56] Christians, Dalits, Muslims, and some Hindu Americans also launched the CSFH, or Campaign to Stop Funding Hate, to halt the flow of American dollars to Hindu nationalist projects in India. Through these efforts, Narendra Modi's visa to the U.S., for instance, was revoked in 2005, but given that Modi wasn't a national figure at the time, the State Department's decision to block a tourist visa was more symbolic and had come with little risk.[57] When Modi became the head of state, the ban was revoked.

Guzofksi and Vyasmaan's exchange was not a coincidence. It was the very embodiment of a decades' worth of outreach (mostly on the part) of Hindu nationalists toward Zionists that leaned on a hatred of Muslims. "He was a great man," Vyasmaan said of Rabbi Kahane, adding: "It almost appeared as if he was speaking for the Hindus."

Modi and Hindu Americans

When Narendra Modi began running for Prime Minister in 2013, liberal interlocutors in India and abroad deliberately distorted the aims of the BJP, depicting Modi as a purveyor of "development" and "cleaner governance." In so doing, they bartered away the fate of minorities, suppressing and subverting concerns, all in the name of expanding the neo-liberal project. But it wasn't just the intellectual liberal elite, like newspaper columnists and analysts from think tanks, that lent their support to Modi. It is estimated that up to 8,000 Indians from the diaspora may have gone to India to campaign for Modi. In the U.S., fundraising events took place across multiple cities, while others carefully manicured his image or worked meticulously to deflect concerns raised by critics.

In September 2014, mere months after he became prime minister, Modi traveled to New York City to attend the UN General Assembly. His address to world leaders would be remembered most peculiarly for his request for the declaration of International Yoga Day. "By changing our lifestyle and creating consciousness, it can help us deal with climate change," Modi said.[58] Later that evening, he was greeted with the fervor of a returning war-hero meets prodigal son, by throngs of Indian Americans at Madison Square Garden in New York City. Outside the venue, a sprinkling of protesters stood with banners calling for accountability for his role in Gujarat in 2002. Inside the stadium, the *New York Times* wrote:

> They wore his face on their chests, waved it on posters, chanted his name and quoted his slogans, 19,000 fans drawn to a single star. His image stared down from the big screen at Madison Square Garden and emerged on canvas in a live speed-painting onstage. And when the man himself emerged, the capacity crowd on Sunday in New York's

> most storied arena roared as one, as if all the Knicks, all the Rangers, Billy Joel and Bruce Springsteen had suddenly materialized.[59]

In his address, Modi spoke less as a politician and more like a sage who had come to bless a gathering. He made three interventions. He emphasized the role of the Indian American community as ambassadors and credited them as key players in India's destiny. "You all have earned a lot of respect in America through your conduct, values, traditions, and ability. You have played an important role in creating a positive image of India not just in America but globally as well, since the world community lives here," Modi said.[60] He called on them to embrace the spirit of Mahatma, who had also lived abroad but ultimately returned to help the nation.

Modi specifically invited the community to invest in his "Make in India" initiative, promising to cut red tape that often hampered business back home. He asked them to believe in his project. He urged them to stand up to his detractors; to be India's ambassadors. "I have attempted to make development a people's movement . . . I want to instill the sentiments in people like 'Whatever I do, I do it for my country, let me do nothing that shames my country,'" Modi said. Finally, to show how much he cared about them, Modi announced a relaxation in travel and visa restrictions for persons and families of Indian origin. In so doing, the Indian PM made the Indian American community feel seen and heard. His acknowledgement and immediate attention to an issue that had dogged families of Indian origin in the diaspora for decades convinced many Indian Americans that Modi would be a man of action. This moment birthed a symbiotic relationship between Modi and the diaspora. He bid an entire community to be his emissary and in return he would raise its self-importance. In haste, many Indian Americans pitted their complete support for the entirety of his policies, no matter how regressive or damaging these may have been. India needed a strong man of action to "set it right." Their task as a community, then, was to make his policies palatable to an American audience.

As Muslims and Dalits and the broader left had predicted, India became increasingly authoritarian under Modi; lynchings of Muslims over mere suspicion of eating beef escalated, the killing and maiming of youth in Kashmir ballooned, and much of the media became dedicated stenographers. The election of Trump in 2016 and the shift to the right in several countries from Brazil and Hungary, the rise of the Islamic State in Iraq and Syria, and the refugee crisis in larger Europe, roused the Hindu right in the U.S. It injected Hindu supremacist projects with a certain insolence; an invincibility. In this world of alternative facts, history was elastic; only the loudest stood a chance of becoming the strongest.

Defending India

In late July 2019, Modi began sending thousands of additional troops to Indian-occupied Kashmir, spreading panic across the valley. "With each passing hour, the anxiety is deepening among Kashmiris, amid a stoic silence maintained by the state administration, which is presently under president's rule, and the Centre," *The Wire* wrote.[61] A week later, he imposed a communications blackout over the region. Landlines, cellular networks, and the Internet, were among the casualties. Kashmiri activists as well as pro-India politicians were arrested, and foreign journalists and human rights observers were barred from traveling to the region.[62]

The abrogation of Article 370 and 35A of the Indian Constitution on August 5 meant that Indian-occupied Kashmir had been fully annexed; the BJP had fulfilled a promise championed by the RSS. The shock move mobilized the small

Kashmiri diaspora across the world—in the U.S., Canada, Britain, Australia, and the Middle East. In the U.S., groups like Stand with Kashmir, a grassroots advocacy group, as well as Americans for Kashmir (A4K) a political advocacy group that raised human rights issues in Kashmir with U.S. lawmakers and policy officials—both led by young Kashmiris in the diaspora[63]—emerged, alongside previous diaspora-led organizations and initiatives. In the following weeks, a wave of protests took place across several cities, including New York, Los Angeles, Dallas, Houston, Atlanta, and San Francisco.

In September, thousands of people arrived in New York City during the UN General Assembly, attended by Modi, to show solidarity with Kashmir. The show of solidarity by multiple grassroots movements, nationalities, and faiths, including Palestinians, the Black Lives Matter movement, Indian minorities like Sikhs, Dalits, Christians, as well as Pakistanis, enraged the gatekeepers of India's image abroad. Hindu American organizations were activated to defend the move in the diaspora while the Indian government sent delegations to assuage U.S. concerns. One notable meeting took place between Harsh Shringla, India's then ambassador to India, and Steve Bannon, Trump's former aide, ideologue, and mastermind behind the right-wing shrill, *Breitbart*. Shringla tweeted out a photo of himself standing next to Bannon, along with a caption: "A pleasure to meet the legendary ideologue and 'Dharma' warrior Stephen Bannon,[64] an avid follower of the Hindu epic the Bhagavad Gita." After receiving some criticism online, he deleted the tweet with no explanation. But by then, the message was loud and clear.

On December 11, 2019, just over four months after the abrogation of Article 370, India's parliament passed the Citizenship Amendment Act (CAA). Along with the National Register of Citizens (NRC), a convoluted exercise designed to distinguish between "legal" and "illegal" citizens, the CAA promised to allow "so-called illegal migrants from Pakistan, Bangladesh and Afghanistan to apply for Indian citizenship—as long as they were not Muslim."[65] Several academics and activists pointed to a disturbing symmetry with Israel's Law of Return (more in Chapter 5).

In the U.S., the developments caught the attention of the media, U.S. lawmakers, and activists within the larger South Asian American community. If the annexation of Kashmir was the first step toward "re-establishing" Akhand Bharat (Undivided India), the CAA was the BJP-led government's most obvious stir toward the consolidation of India as a "Hindu nation" by demographic engineering. In response to the outrage in the U.S., American Sangh groups immediately launched a counterattack. Their acts of subterfuge focused on: (1) flooding congressional offices and members of Congress with phone calls, emails, and disinformation, as well as threatening to stop donations to campaigns. When U.S. Representative Pramila Jayapal introduced Resolution 745 in December 2019,[66] which called on India to "end the restrictions on communications and mass detentions in Jammu and Kashmir as swiftly as possible and preserve religious freedom for all residents," such was the pressure on the Foreign Affairs Committee that the resolution never made it to the floor;[67] (2) harassing, intimidating, and policing academics and students at universities through the onset of blacklists, online bullying, as well as the disruption of events and teach-ins; (3) expensive lawsuits and accusations of defamation;[68] and (4) tainting critics of Hindutva with the "Hinduphobia" label as well as claiming to be victims of anti-Hindu hate;[69] (5) Vilifying critics as sympathizers of "Islamic terror" or "Pakistani-sponsored terror"; (6) Creating parallel events like "Holi for Unity" to respond and confuse anti-Hindutva activists' projects like "Holi against Hindutva";[70] (7) the invocation of progressive, liberal values viz-a-viz gender or LGBTQI+

rights, or pinkwashing; (8) Using instruments of soft power, like claims of democracy, Bollywood, Yoga, the non-violence of Mahatma Gandhi as a means to both evoke a sense of civilizational superiority as well as a reason for shared interests against a common enemy (savage Muslims); (9) The mass spread of disinformation and fake news across social media and the Internet to counter news or scholarship. And though many of these tactics have existed over the past decade, or longer, academics and activists agree that the attempts to stifle critics of Hindu supremacy have become more coordinated and dangerous than ever. Unsurprisingly, these attacks followed the same methodology adopted by Zionist organizations in the U.S.

In 2015, the International Jewish Anti-Zionist Network (IJAN) released a report that detailed how several Zionist organizations were targeting critics of Israel. They called it the "Zionist Backlash Network."[71] According to IJAN, some of these tactics, included: (1) Reconfiguring criticism of Israel as anti-Semitism and being victims of anti-Jewish sentiment; (2) Pushing through legislation to censor or ban the boycott of Israel; (3) Using strategic lawsuits against public participation (SLAPP) suits to derail, intimidate activists, and waste resources; (4) Accusing Arab, Muslim, and Palestinian activists of terrorism; (5) Infiltrating Muslim civil rights organizations with spies; (6) Responding to Palestinian activism and events by creating parallel events like "Israeli Peace Week"; (7) The instrumentalization of the LGBTQI+ movement in presenting Israel as progressive and pro-queer rights as opposed to homophobic Palestinians, a tactic known as "pinkwashing."

IJAN also identified eleven wealthy individuals, many of whom were directly benefiting from the Israeli occupation, as the major funders of this vast network. Among the agents targeting Palestinians, were around 16 organizations, like the

ADL, the Simon Wiesenthal Center, Stand with U.S., and the Middle East Forum (MEF) among others, who routinely used the bogey of anti-Semitism to vilify and discredit anyone who spoke up for Palestine in the U.S. Crucially, IJAN found that the same funders, given their investment and proclivity to the U.S. wars in the Middle East, were also funders of the far right, including attacks on the labor movement as well as queer rights.

The MEF, run by Daniel Pipes, who had created "Campus Watch," and identified as a key player in the "backlash network," had received funding from eight out of the eleven donors. The MEF, in turn, funded several other Islamophobic and Zionist projects, like the Institute for the Study of Global Antisemitism and Policy (ISGAP) and Steve Emerson's Investigative Project on Terrorism (IPT). An earlier report called "Fear, Inc. 2.0: The Islamophobia Network's Efforts to Manufacture Hate in America," published by the Center for American Progress (CAP) in 2011 identified Pipes, Emerson, and Robert Spencer, founder of Jihad Watch, as leading members of a network the CAP called "Islamophobia misinformation experts." These ideologues, along with Frank Gaffney, from the Center for Security Policy, and David Yerushalmi, from the Society of Americans for National Existence, CAP argued were "primarily responsible for orchestrating the majority of anti-Islam messages polluting our national discourse."[72]

Zionist groups have since the 1960s tried to control and crush criticism of Israel in the United States. In the 1980s, the Israeli lobby turned its attention to American colleges and universities as a site of struggle for competing narratives.[73] In 1985, Paul Findley, the former Republican Congressman, wrote in detail how pro-Israeli groups—be it on Capitol Hill or at universities—engaged in "smear tactics, harassment and intimidation." He also noted their intent "to inhibit the free exchange of ideas and views."[74] He said that the Israeli lobby placed as much emphasis on academic programs as they did on "the editorial policies of student newspapers and with the appearance on campus of speakers critical of Israel."[75] Hence, the practice of writing to universities, interrupting academic lectures and book talks, accusing students, teachers, and even U.S. lawmakers of being anti-Semitic even at the slightest hint of criticism of Israel has been a product of deliberation; a tactic.

Between 2014—21, Palestine Legal, an NGO based in Chicago dedicated to protecting the constitutional rights of those who speak out for Palestinian freedom in the U.S., responded to 1707 incidents of suppression. "Having worked there since the very beginning, I can tell you the stories range from absurd to surreal to heartbreaking," Radhika Sainath, an attorney at Palestine Legal wrote.[76] In 2015, the derision for those who dared to speak up on Palestine went into overdrive. An anonymously run website called Canary Mission began posting the personal details of individuals and organizations involved in Palestine advocacy or BDS in the U.S., dubbing them as either anti-Semitic, anti-American, or supporters of terrorism. In the U.S., the allusion to "terrorism," however anonymous or whimsical, carries severe consequences. Those on the blacklist have found themselves anxious and effectively practicing self-censorship. Being listed on the site can create complications when it comes to securing visas or residency permits. It can even result in the termination of employment. It has often meant endless online harassment. As reported by *The Intercept*, there have been deportations from Israel as well as interrogations on account of the Canary Mission.[77] By 2019, there were more than a thousand people listed on the Canary Mission's website.

It is not surprising that since the abrogation of Article 370 and the CAA, Zionist and Islamophobic groups in the U.S.

have been operating in concert with each other to vilify critics of Hindutva. It is also no coincidence then that the attacks on critics have followed a similar formula. Vyasmaan and Guzofsky's interaction in 2001 had after all begun over a similar attempt to vilify critics online. Their interaction had arguably been personal. Under Modi, the relationships had become institutional. Back in 2016, the Vivekananda International Foundation (VIF) invited Daniel Pipes, founder of the right-wing Middle East Forum (MEF) to Delhi to speak to journalists, government ministers, and army officials about the threat of Muslims to secular societies. "He [Pipes] argued that Islamists who work within the system, especially in countries like the United States and India, are even more threatening than the Islamic State," a VIF report of the event read.[78] Likewise, in 2019, the Republican Hindu Coalition (RHC) and the National Indian American Public Policy Institute (NIAPPI) hosted anti-Muslim conspiracy theorist, Frank Gaffney, and Steve Bannon in an event titled: "A Call To Arms Against China's Unrestricted War On American Manufacturing." For the RHC, the event was an opportunity to bring the American right-wing establishment up to speed on "China's increased aggression and intrusion into Indian territory," as well as their "support of the terrorist harboring nation of Pakistan." Organizers claimed around 1,400 "prominent Hindu-American activists and business leaders attended the event.[79]

In 2020, several hit-pieces originating from the MEF began making their rounds on Indian news sites like *First Post, The Print* and the right-wing vessel *OpIndia*. First Martha Lee, from the MEF, took on Stand With Kashmir in *The Print*, arguing that the organization supported terrorism and carried "a dangerous agenda."[80] Likewise, months later, Clifford Smith, also from the MEF claimed in *The Print*, again, that the Boycott Divestment Sanctions (BDS) movement had expanded its net of ambitions beyond Israel to now target and undermine India. "Friends of both Israel and India must work to counter this shockingly effective political activism before it is too late," Smith wrote in a rant that argued that Ilhan Omar, the outspoken Somali-American U.S. representative in Congress, the Council for American Islamic Relations (CAIR), and Stand with Kashmir, were part of some larger pan-Islamist conspiracy against India and Israel.[81] It didn't take long before the Indian government blocked Stand With Kashmir's website and social media accounts across India (they have been blocked since at least mid-2020).

Academics working on scholarship critical of Hindutva say the efforts to intimidate aren't new. They have merely intensified. Vinayak Chaturvedi, a long-time scholar of Hindutva at the University of Irvine, California, as well as Audrey Truschke, an historian at Rutgers University, New Jersey, have meticulously documented the tactics used to intimidate them and others, on account of writing about Hindutva in the U.S.[82] Truschke says she has "lost count" of the number of death and rape threats issued against her. She now has armed security accompany her during guest lectures.[83] Likewise, student activists like Shreeya Singh, the founder of Students Against Hindutva Ideology (SAHI), told me she received hate mail for days after writing an open letter to the U.S. Congress calling on lawmakers to pass Congresswoman Pramila Jayapal's resolution on Kashmir.[84]

For Indian Muslims and Kashmiri Muslims in the U.S., the price of speaking out is even more perilous; once they become targets, they seem destined to enter an ecosystem of endless harassment and surveillance. Being heckled at university discussions is merely the tip of the iceberg. Some Kashmiri academics have found their names on pamphlets linking their work to "terror groups," or as sponsored by the *Pakistan ISI*, distributed outside lecture halls prior to or during academic panels. If they are on social media, they are bombarded by Hindutva trolls.

Given that the Indian state is a routine purveyor of enforced disappearances, fake encounter killings, politically motivated detentions without charge, and unofficial no-fly lists, the intimidation and threats of harm has yielded immediate results. Several Kashmiris in the diaspora have abandoned social media and, or, activism for the sake of family back in Indian-occupied Kashmir. Ather Zia, an associate professor in Anthropology at University Colorado, told me that her university began receiving emails from strangers in 2019 questioning her academic credentials. Zia, born in Kashmir and an academic in the U.S. for several years, said that in one email addressed to the provost of her university, she was accused of being an activist masquerading as an academic and for being anti-Semitic for comparing Kashmir with Palestine.[85] The writer also accused Zia of violating U.S. immigration law because her work "discriminates against nationals of India and Israel, adherents of Hinduism and Judaism and non-Muslim Kashmiris."[86] Zia said the university supported her but she was asked to explain to the provost why her work was being linked with terrorism. "The problem is that each time there is new leadership at the university, I have to explain it all again. In that sense, sometimes, it is very demoralizing." Zia, who was also named in the first *The Print* article, told me. [87]

There have been several other consequences for the vilification online. Zia said that during her interview for U.S. residency, immigration officials questioned her in detail about her academic work. She had to provide additional letters of support from colleagues to substantiate her case as an academic. "What if my colleagues had not been supportive? What if they harbored their own anti-Muslim sentiment and just chose not to support me?" Zia asked rhetorically. Given what has happened to Palestinian academics, like

Steven Salaita, whose tweets about Israel prompted the University of Illinois to recant a job offer, Zia is well aware of the consequences.[88] Hindu nationalists after all, rely on the willful ignorance of Indian history and politics, on anti-Muslim racism, as well as the accumulated power of its exports to escape scrutiny. "The question is whether university administrators will act to protect the academic freedom of faculty who write about India. The fear of being called 'Hinduphobic' may be too powerful for academic institutions in today's political climate," Chuturvedi wrote in a somber article in December 2021.[89]

To counter the anti-intellectual and bad faith harassment from the Hindu right, a group of academics launched the South Asia Scholar Activist Collective (SASAC) in April 2021 as a way to preserve progressive South Asian scholarship in the U.S. As their first initiative, they launched the "Hindutva Harassment Field Manual," an online resource that provides insight on how to navigate the assault on scholarship and activism while tackling the annals of disinformation put out by Hindu nationalists and supremacists. "Hinduphobia," the manual says, "rests on the false notion that Hindus have faced systematic oppression throughout history and in present times" and that "Hinduphobia" relies on flawed analogies with anti-Semitism and Islamophobia, though these are very different." The manual in itself was an intervention in recognition that scholars were under siege. Dheepa Sundaram, an assistant professor in Hindu Studies, Critical Theory, and Digital Religion at the University of Denver, told me that over the past five years, Hindu nationalists had begun employing a scholarly-like anti-racist language to argue the case of Hinduphobia, and the phrase had gained a certain currency. "We felt we were losing the battle on the term."[90]

This insidious use of "Hinduphobia" made international news in 2021 when a number of South Asian academics held the first ever conference dedicated to unpeeling the various myths perpetuated by Hindutva. Boldly titled "Dismantling Global Hindutva," the conference drew immediate condemnation from Hindu nationalists across the U.S. and especially among the right-wing media in India. The HAF accused the conference of platforming activists with "extensive histories of amplifying Hinduphobic discourse . . . [who] equate the whole of Hinduism with caste bigotry, deny the subcontinental indigeneity of Hindus and Hinduism and support or minimize violent extremist and separatists movements and deny the resulting genocides and ethnic cleansings of Hindus." HAF also expressed concerns that the event would impact Hindu students who already "report feeling under attack." It provided no proof that Hindu students in the U.S. had experienced any such hate crimes on account of discussions about Hindu nationalism at universities. The heightened media spotlight on the controversy surrounding the conference also transported a predominantly academic conversation in the U.S. into the mainstream, drawing attention from the Indian American community, journalists, and curious observers. It also showcased how Hindu nationalist and supremacist tactics in India were taking on a life of their own in the U.S., with the torrent of hate mail sent to participants and the liberal use of "Hinduphobia" showered on any criticism of Indian policies. For those who hadn't heard the phrase before, a cursory glance at the claims of the Hindu American groups left them confused.

Until 2013, the FBI's annual list of hate crimes in the U.S. did not include a specific category tracking crimes against Hindus. It was HAF who had lobbied in conjunction with the ADL for hate crimes against Hindu Americans to become a category of its own. Since then, HAF has portended to exaggerate the level of hate or crimes faced by Hindus in the U.S., as a cover for anti-caste or Muslim critiques of Hindutva. In

2019, HAF released a statement claiming that hate crimes against Hindus were on the rise.[91] Whereas the FBI had documented ten incidents in 2016 and eleven in 2017, the number of crimes against Hindus had reached 14 cases out of a total of 7,120 reported hate crimes across America in 2018.

Standing Up to Hindutva

It is not merely academics and activists who have faced the peril of Hindu nationalist groups. Take the case of Pramila Jayapal,[92] the Congresswoman from Washington's 7th Congressional district. Jayapal introduced Resolution 745 in December 2019 that focused on three things: lifting the communications blackout that has been imposed on Kashmir since August, ending detentions without charges, and respecting religious freedom. The resolution made no mention of the Indian occupation or the Kashmiri right to self-determination. But weeks later, Subrahmanyam Jaishankar, India's Foreign Minister, allegedly refused to attend a meeting on Capitol Hill on account of Jayapal's presence. The move illustrated the extent to which the Indian government expected nothing but obedience and loyalty from those of Indian origin. But it's not just government leaders or their BJP surrogates in the U.S. who have adopted a zero-sum game on Kashmir. Days after the revocation of Article 370, Tom Suozzi, Congressman of New York's 3rd district, wrote a letter to Mike Pompeo, the former Secretary of State, in which he briefly raised concerns about India's decision to unilaterally seize Kashmir. His letter was leaked on social media, prompting outrage among some Hindu Americans who proceeded to bombard his office with phone calls and mail over what they perceived as a betrayal. At the annual India Day parade on August 11 in New York, Suozzi, who attended on account of his constituency being home to a sizable South Asian community, was confronted by an Indian American named Rajender Dichpally, the director of the Gandhian Center in New York and the national general secretary of the Indian Overseas Congress (IOC). Dichpally demanded Suozzi withdraw his letter and issue an apology to the estimated 10,000 people at the rally. Suozzi refused and following the exchange with Dichpally, left the event. But two days later, Suozzi issued an apology to the Indian American community, noting that he should have consulted with the community before writing to Pompeo.

This particular incident didn't just demonstrate how influential the Indian lobby had become, it illustrated how pervasive Indian nationalism was among Hindu Americans in the U.S., despite their political affiliation in India or the U.S. Though the central divide between Congress and BJP was purportedly a question between secularism and the establishment of a Hindu Rashtra, Dichpally's intervention showcased how deeply entrenched Hindutva was within the larger Indian diaspora.

Here, the Carnegie study conducted prior to the U.S. presidential election in November 2020, is a particularly important window into the attitudes of the Indian community. First, it showed that though Hindu Americans were more likely to vote Democrat, almost seven in ten Hindu Americans approved of Modi.[93] The study also found that though the community held liberal positions on immigration, equality, religious minorities, and affirmative action, they remained mostly conservative when it came to Indian domestic policies. "His (Modi) support is greatest among Republicans, Hindus, people in the engineering profession, those not born in the United States, and those who hail from North and West India," the report noted.

Second, those Indian Americans (including Muslims and Christians) who had supported Trump were also more likely to be Modi supporters; a sizable number of Hindu Americans who preferred Biden were also fans of Modi. At times, these complexities became dark comedies. For instance, in 2020, the Biden campaign decided to appoint Amit Jani, a family associate and friend of Narendra Modi, as the Democratic party's Muslim coordinator for the election campaign later that year.[94] It was only when activists pointed out the mendacity of having an associate of Modi run Biden's outreach to Muslims, that Jani was removed. He still remained on as the party's Asian-American and Pacific Islanders (AAPI) national vote director. The parody continued as Jani sent out invitations to Pakistani Americans to join Biden rallies.[95]

In a second Carnegie Study published in 2021, authors found that Indian Americans between the ages 18–29 were more skeptical of Modi (43%) as opposed to Indian Americans over the age of 50 (25%). Those born in India, whether naturalized or not in the U.S., were a lot more supportive of Modi (53%) than those born in the U.S. (44%). The study found that engineers (66%) were more supportive of Modi than non-engineers (48%).[96] This is not an innocuous statistic. It underlined concerns that big tech in Silicon Valley, controlling algorithms and with access to personal data, were being staffed by Hindu nationalists and supremacists.[97] To place this in perspective: between 2009–20, around 70% of the 1.9m highly specialized H1-B visas issued by the State Department went to workers in the tech industry. Around 65% of these H1-B visas issued to immigrants were given to Indians.[98] Given that an estimated 150,000 Indian Americans become eligible to vote each year with around a third being made up of naturalized citizens,[99] it is therefore no exaggeration to conclude that Hindutva is being imported into the American political system. As it stands, the Carnegie Study found that just 39% of Indian Americans polled expressed concerns about developments in India, meaning the ideology overall was deep-seated within the community.

Sravya Tadepalli, who worked at HAF as an intern in 2019, said she joined the foundation on the presumption that they were a civil rights organization. Given the organization's progressive language, she was surprised to find that not only were they unopposed to Modi but were in fact purveyors of his policies. She left HAF and in 2020 joined Hindus for Human Rights, an organization that describes itself as providing "a Hindu voice of resistance to caste, Hindutva (Hindu nationalism), racism, and all forms of bigotry and oppression." But Tadepalli's experience is instructive. It demonstrated the extent to which HAF had garnered goodwill among Indian Americans, so much so that as an upper caste Hindu, unaffected by its obvious incursions, it was "difficult" for Tadepalli to recognize that they were nothing but a Trojan horse for ethnonationalism. One Indian American organizer with the South Asia Solidarity Initiative (SASI) in New York City, who asked not to be named, told me that HAF has been remarkably conscientious in building their brand.

> HAF, in particular, has spent years crafting a "progressive" branding through its support of LGBTQI+ issues, statements supporting George Floyd and addressing white Christian right wing racism. They are also part of many American anti-bullying initiatives. They have also literally created a glossary that borrows its logic from liberal and anti-racist discourse to re-cast anti-Hindutva criticisms as "hinduphobia." For example, they claim the use of "Model minority" is "Hinduphobic." It's absurd and yet carries influence. HAF has often successfully found its place in liberal American spaces. All while pushing rightwing policy interests in Congress and chilling dissent on the ground. No rightwing group I know of pulls it off as successfully as they do.[100]

Tadepalli told the podcast *Interfaithish* that growing up she sometimes heard extreme views about Muslims but always imagined it to be a marginal view.[101] "I started seeing these things really emerge in India, and really grow extremely concerning [sic], and then I saw these organizations I used to be a part of, move further to the right; that was a big wake-up call for me," Tadepalli said.[102] Tadepalli's experience illustrates the multiple levels at which Hindu nationalism, Islamophobia and caste oppression has operated among a self-described liberal Hindu American community. In this, they aren't alone. Liberal Americans of all types had perpetuated the myth of a post-racial society with the election of Barack Obama, only to find themselves in tears when Donald Trump became president. We know that they weren't crying for the chaos to come. They cried because the election of Trump exposed the country for what it always was. And just as Trump's association with Netanyahu had repulsed many young American Jews, encouraging a new generation to remove the blinkers, confront parents, boycott Birthright tours to Israel, and join new organizations like IfNotNow or flock to older anti-Zionist ones like Jewish Voice for Peace, Modi's relationship with Trump brought a certain shame to some young Hindu Americans, even if temporarily.

There are several reasons why tackling Hindutva in the U.S. has proven to be so challenging. First, there is a disconnect between the real victims of Hindutva and caste oppression and those purporting to defeat it in the U.S. Given that so-called progressive spaces tackling Hindutva are dominated by upper caste Hindus, Dalit organizers and activists argue that too much effort is being made into attempts to rehabilitate Hinduism in the U.S. as opposed to fundamentally dismantling the multiple strands of oppression that aren't born out of Hindutva alone. "The structures of caste, specifically, have been fundamentally damaging to cross-community solidarity building against Hindutva because dominant caste Indian immigrants are socialized to preserve their caste privilege at the expense of others in society," one Dalit organizer, based in New York who asked to remain anonymous, told me.[103] "Until there is a movement to center the leadership and liberation of minority groups in the ongoing redefinition of Indian diasporic identity and unlearn our internal hegemonies, I don't see how we avoid perpetuating the same structures of oppression that we seek to dismantle," the organizer added.

Second, the Indian diaspora has also become more powerful, more relevant, and more politically connected in the U.S. than ever before. Whereas one Gopal Raju had to recruit the services of an AIPAC consultant in the early 1990s to organize internships for Indian Americans on Capitol Hill, today there are Indian Americans in almost every level of government. Kamala Harris, of partial Indian heritage, is vice-president of the United States, while four Indian Americans are lawmakers in the halls of the U.S. Congress. "Capitol Hill is crammed with staff and interns of Indian-American heritage. They also appear to be over-represented in academia, the media, and other influential posts," Devesh Kapur, a professor at Johns Hopkins University, says.[104] The power of the Indian lobby has purportedly made Indian American lawmakers a lot more circumspect when it comes to critiquing India's human rights record. By way of example: When Representative Ilhan Omar introduced a resolution in late June 2022, calling for India to be characterized as a "country of Particular Concern" under the U.S. International Religious Freedom Act, none of the Indian American lawmakers in Congress supported it.

With the U.S. rapidly approaching a new cold war with China, there is little appetite in Washington to tackle Hindu nationalism. As much as the Russian invasion of Ukraine in February 2022 shifted geo-politics once more, India's continued liaison with the Russians was never likely to hamper closer Washington-New Delhi ties. But as we will see in the next chapter, for Kashmiris, Indian Muslims, Dalits, and others pushing back against Hindutva as well as the colonial violence of the Indian state—the implications are genocidal. And they have already begun.

5
Kashmir and Palestine: A Story of Two Occupations

> What is hidden within India is Hindustan. It is that which tacitly shapes the state and determines the frontiers between freedom and repression, what is allowed and what is forbidden. —Perry Anderson[1]

> There are Zionism and Israel for Jews, and Zionism and Israel for non-Jews. —Edward Said[2]

> They [India and Israel] fit together like hand in glove. —Noam Chomsky[3]

Since the 1950s, the spectacle of the "world's largest democracy" casting a ballot has trumped the workings of democracy itself. At the heart of this convoluted story of India, author Perry Anderson argues, is the "Indian Ideology," a set of nationalist ideas, primarily but not exclusively propagated by Indian liberals, that have set the contours as to how India is seen, understood and judged. It is the "Indian Ideology" that has created and sustained the belief that at its core India is non-violent, secular, exceptional, democratic, and tolerant. In this version, there is no caste prejudice or anti-Muslim bigotry. And if such incidents make their way into the public sphere, they are the works of extremists; they are not the basis of society. Where writing and scholarship on the sham of Indian secularism is abundant, they remain peripheral. In India, Anderson argues,

Gandhi's doctrines were relegated to the museum but "his saturation of politics with Hindu pathos lived on."[4]

In this way, Edward Said's argument that "the concealment by Zionism of its own history has by now become institutionalized, and not only in Israel,"[5] reverberates in the story of India, too. As Dalit writer Kancha Ilaiah argues: "While conducting the anti-colonial struggle, Brahminical leaders and ideologues did not attempt to build an anti-caste egalitarian ideology. On the contrary, they glorified brutal Hindu institutions. They built an ideology that helped Brahminical forces reestablish their full control which had, to some extent, been weakened during the political rule of the Mughals and the British."[6] The success of the BJP in India and Likud in Israel, Anderson argues,[7] could not be put down merely to the failures of their precursors in office, "but to their ability to articulate openly what had always been latent in the national movement, but neither candidly acknowledged, nor consistently repudiated."[8]

Though the Indian constitution guarantees the right to equality and the freedom of religion, in practice, dignity in India has long been predicated on one's place on the caste hierarchy or proximity to power. Whereas Muslims are ghettoized and periodically excluded from political life, Dalits are humiliated or exceptionalized. Stories of Dalits being killed for eating in front of an upper caste man[9] or drowning in human feces while clearing sewers, still occur with disturbing regularity.[10]

During the Cold War, Indian democracy was a guard against expansionist communism, despite its friendship with the former USSR. Today, it is a bulwark of neoliberalism. Journalist Andre Vltchek writes:

> In the West we have a tendency to call these violent countries [like India] "peaceful" and "tolerant" as long as they

> serve as a buffer against China, as long as they plunder their natural resources on behalf of our private companies, as long as they are willing to uphold savage capitalism.[11]

Indian economic liberalization was, after all, a dream for international corporations looking to reduce labor costs. India was not a land of humans with needs and aspirations, but rather a source of labor and a market to profit from. As a consequence, India's human rights record and the RSS and Hindutva were evidently ignored by Western observers, too. However, since 2014, the BJP-led government not only passed laws that rankled the constitution, it tampered extensively with the national narrative, as it sought to insert Hinduism into the Indian everyday as the specter of "one nation, one language, one religion" began to take form.

This Hinduization of the Indian state held several consequences, most notably, the erasure of Muslims and the saffronization of the public space.[12] As one of his first acts as PM, Modi appointed Yellapragada Sudershan Rao to lead the Indian Council of Historical Research (ICHR). Rao, a known caste-apologist, argued in an essay in 2007 that the practice of caste had been widely "misinterpreted as an exploitative social system" and described it as having worked well in ancient times.[13] Rao also deflected questionable or controversial Hindu social customs as having their roots in Muslim rule. In his position as head of the ICHR, he recategorized the Hindu epics Ramayana and Mahabharata as "historical documents." It wasn't long after, that these myths and legends entered schools and colleges as "historical facts." The presence and history of Muslims and Christians was subsequently minimized and replaced by Hindu supremacist icons in school curriculums.[14]

In BJP-run states, even India's first PM Nehru was dropped from school and university textbooks. Parallel to the assault on Indian history, came multiple attempts to regulate the lives of Muslims through the accusation of "Love Jihad," a discredited theory that argues Muslim men actively pursue Hindu women with the intention to convert them and shift the religious demographics of the country. In several BJP-led states, conversion through marriage became outlawed. The legal justifications created the civic space for civilians to take up the role of vigilantes. "We beat him in a way that no Muslim will dare to look at a Hindu woman again . . . we made a Muslim eat his own waste—thrice, in a spoon," one man told Nilanjan Mukhopadhyay, who wrote a biography of Modi. Where consensual romantic interfaith liaisons typically elicited, at most, social stigma within families, they now specifically looked to portray Muslim men as weapons of mass conversion. Indian lawyer Arundhati Katju wrote in *Foreign Affairs* that the "crusade against love jihad is not just a quixotic struggle. It marks an ominous turn in the BJP's deepening culture war."[15]

Then came the bans on beef and the slaughter of cattle in the name of creating uniformity. In late September 2015, a 52-year-old Mohammad Akhlaq was pulled out of his home in the village of Bishara in Uttar Pradesh and beaten to death over suspicions he slaughtered a cow some days earlier. Though his murder elicited widespread condemnation, BJP officials insisted on framing his murder an accident. In mid-July 2016, seven members of one Dalit family in Gujarat were flogged, tied to a car and made a public spectacle of after they were found skinning a dead cow.[16] The incident illustrated once more the extent to which vigilantism had become state sponsored. Any modicum of secularism, however fraught in India already, had now become antithetical to Hindu dignity. In 2018, the Indian government criminalized the "triple talaaq" practice in which a Muslim man was able to divorce his wife by repeating the intention to divorce (talaaq) three times.

The new law granted the state the ability to arrest without a warrant and hold men for up to three-and-half years in jail. It prompted rights activists to argue that the law was just another way for the Indian government to criminalize Muslim men, especially given that the Supreme Court had already outlawed the practice.[17]

Parallel to the attacks on Muslims and Dalits came the expansion of "anti-national" and "terrorism" labels. Several prominent Indian activists, like 84-year-old tribal rights[18] activist Father Stan Swamy, Dalit lawyer Surendra Gadling and academic Rona Wilson, were thrown in jail and charged with terrorism for purportedly playing a role in the Bhima Koregaon violence of 2018. The National Investigation Agency (NIA) described the activists as urban naxals of the Naxalite movement, working at the behest of the Maoists, trying to "spread rebellious thoughts" through the creation of an "anti-fascist front" so they could "wage war against the government."[19] It was clear that the activists were being punished for their advocacy efforts against Modi. In July 2021, the *Washington Post* reported that Arsenal Consulting, a U.S.-based digital forensic firm, had found that the personal devices of Gadling and Wilson had been taken over by hackers and that "evidence" had been planted on their devices.[20] A larger review of the forensics found that the same malware sent to the duo had also been sent to 14 other activists, underscoring the level of depravity exercised by the state. But even then, the incidents to come demonstrated that the Indian government had no intention of backing down.

In July 2021, Father Stan Swamy, already suffering from Parkinson's disease, contracted Covid-19 in jail and died. Another activist, 70-year-old Gautum Navlakha, found himself housed in a temporary prison in which 350 prisoners were stacked in six rooms sharing three toilets. The cruelty (in a time of Covid-19 pandemic no less) was by design. Father

Swamy had railed for more than three decades for the rights of tribal communities on matters of land, forest, and labor in the face of corporate takeovers. Likewise, Navlakha spoke up against India's policies in Kashmir and the tie-ups between Indian corporate oligarchs and arms manufacturers. The message was clear. There was no room for dissidents in what was fast hurtling toward a polity ruled by one dominant group.

The Rise of the Ethnocracy

In late December 2021, Hindu nationalists and supremacists gathered in the city of Haridwar in India for a three-day meeting known as a Dharam Sansad,[21] a religious parliament made up of prominent Hindu religious leaders.[22] They raised their right arm, in the form of a Nazi salute and pledged to empty the country of its Muslim population. "We all take an oath, give our word, and make a resolution that, until our last breath, we will make India a Hindu nation and keep it a Hindu-only nation," Suresh Chavhanke, a right-wing journalist, said to a crowd at the forum. "We will fight, and die, and, if required, we will kill as well. We will not hesitate a bit to make any sacrifice at any cost. To complete this resolution, our Gurudev, our teacher, our goddess Mother India, our ancestors, give us power, give us victory," he said to the chorus of those in attendance.

Swami Prabodhanand Giri, one of the leaders of the assembly, invoked the ethnic cleansing of the Rohingya minority in neighboring Myanmar in his address. "Like Myanmar, the police, politicians, the army, and every Hindu in India must pick up weapons and do this cleansing. There is no other option left," Giri said.[23] The audacious incident made its way onto video and was subsequently circulated across the internet and social media. The open and unequivocal calls for the genocide of Muslims at the Dharam Sansad immediately became a media spectacle. However, the utterances of these Monks were only the next logical step in the completion of the Hindutva project: annihilation. The calls for the "cleansing of Muslims" had the hallmarks of the RSS and their Hindu nationalist and supremacist ideals that began close to 100 years prior.[24] It was in harmony with the Hinduizing of the instruments of the Indian state as directed by the forces of Hindutva and a duplication of ultra-right-wing rallies in Israel that called for the "death of Arabs."

Since the Nakba, Israel has pursued a project of "Judaizing" Palestine. This has entailed the combined tactics of land expropriation, ethnic cleansing, geographic renaming, as well as the pursuit of apartheid policies of segregation in legal, education, social services, and living facilities.[25] Israel is, by definition, a Jewish state. It also self-describes as democratic and is considered among the family of Western nations. As the "only democracy in the Middle East," Israel is given a pass for its transgressions. Its brutality toward Palestinians are deemed "mistakes" or the result of provocations in a neighborhood of autocratic brutes. As a country, part of the ambit of "civilized nations," its deep militarism is seen as an effect, and not the cause of its troubles. But given that Israel has no Constitution and therefore no defined borders, its efforts to impose cultural, ethnic, and religious values to territory beyond the UN chartered 1948 borders shows that it has no ambition to be a democracy either.[26] "The classification of Israel as a democracy may appear to function more as a tool for legitimizing the political and legal status quo than as a scholarly exploration guided by empirical accuracy or conceptual coherence," academic Oren Yiftachel writes.[27] There are elections, a judiciary, and Palestinian citizens of Israel can vote and can run for the Knesset; Israeli journalists operate with relative freedom, too. But whereas Jews in Israel enjoy full citizenship, Palestinian citizens of Israel are at best second-class and Palestinians in the occupied territories are regarded as no more than an excess demographic. Several mainstream human rights groups, from Israeli human rights group B'tselem,[28] to Human Rights Watch and Amnesty International have categorized Israel as an apartheid state. "In the entire area between the Mediterranean Sea and the Jordan River, the Israeli regime implements laws, practices, and state violence designed to cement the supremacy of one group—Jews—over another—Palestinians. A key method in pursuing this goal is engineering space differently for each group," B'tselem wrote. [29]

Given Israel's predilection for its policies to be shaped by and contingent on a Jewish identity, its polity is best described as an ethnocracy.[30] And it's certainly not the only one. Other polities that function under the veneer of democratic norms but were nonetheless strong-armed by a dominant ethnic group that presided over different tiers of citizenship with insiders and outsiders, include Malaysia, Sri Lanka, Rwanda and now, more comprehensively, India.[31] Yiftachel's charge that Israel is a "regime premised on a main project of ethnonational expansion and control and on a parallel self-representation of the system as democratic,"[32] is a befitting description of Modi's India, too. The Hinduization of public institutions since 1947 notwithstanding, the extent to which the Modi government has attempted to complete this project is unprecedented.

> This particular government is not simply keen on having very close and deeper relations with Israel because of its strategic calculations, however misguided they may be, but they also have a very strong admiration for Israel and how it has established a Jewish state through the repression and humiliation of Palestinians.

Achin Vnaik told me, adding: "This is because this government, through its quest to establish a de jure Hindu state has learnt a number of lessons from Israel and is of course, using those lessons against what it considers to be its principal enemy: Muslims."

And this resentment is deeply rooted in a hateful mythology perpetuated and propagated by the RSS. Traces of Vladimir Jabotinsky, the father of revisionist Zionism, can be found in the work of M.S. Golwalkar, the most influential of leaders within the RSS. In 1923, Jabotinsky promised "equality" for Palestinians should they submit to the Jewish colonization. In some ways, Golwalkar took it further when he wrote in 1939 that:

> The foreign races in Hindusthan must either adopt the Hindu culture and language, must learn to respect and hold in reverence Hindu religion, must entertain no idea but those of the glorification of the Hindu race and culture . . . or may stay in the country, wholly subordinated to the Hindu Nation, claiming nothing, deserving no privileges, far less any preferential treatment—not even citizen's rights.[33]

Muslims and Christians could be citizens with limited rights, while drawing loyalty for the Hindu nation from minorities would only be achieved by the threat of violence. For Hindu supremacists then, the presence of Muslims and Christians in India was a daily reminder of their failure to resist "foreign occupation," to resist "conversion," and maintain "self-definition." Muslims were therefore "anti-nationals" by their existence alone, standing in the way of Hindu India's rejuvenation.

And central to the momentum was the creation of a legal justification for these ethnonationalist endeavors to be carried out. Hence, the Citizenship Amendment Act (CAA) was intended to differentiate citizenship within the Hindu nation. By the logic of the CAA, Hindus in India would be privileged in the same way "Jewish nationality is privileged over Israeli citizenship."[34] Therefore, Muslims would have to accept their subordination to the Hindu homeland. If they were to prove citizenship, they were still not part of the nation, unless they converted to Hinduism, or as Hindu supremacists describe it: "Ghar Wapsi" (come home). As Pinky Chaudhary, a leader of a far-right Hindu group called the Hindu Raksha Dal, told a crowd in the capital in August 2021:

> No matter who comes to power, we will not allow Muslims to rise up. We are in the process of awakening our youth. We will get mullahs out of graves and finish them from their roots . . . you will see we will create a situation where Muslims have to either convert to Hinduism or they will be sent to Pakistan.[35]

As Satradu Sen described it: there was no contradiction in being both the dominated and the domineer for the Hindu or Zionist nation.[36] "Like Zionism in the present time, it is the simultaneous consciousness of privilege and oppression, undeniable power, and irrational anxieties (being outbred, being converted, being 'defamed,' being eliminated)."[37]

The CAA legislation prompted a wave of protests in 2020, to which the Indian government responded by supporting a pogrom against Muslims in lower income neighborhoods in Delhi. Around 50 people, mostly Muslim, were killed as mobs of Hindu nationalists hunted down those who dared to complain about the beloved homeland. Like they had done in the Bhima Koregaon case, authorities used the occasion to arrest several activists, including former student activist Umar Khalid,[38] keeping him in solitary confinement for up to 20 hours a day several times over a period of eight months.[39] "Clearly, the process itself is the punishment," Khalid said from jail. Likewise, Sharjeel Imam, was another activist arrested under the UAPA and charged with various violations, including sedition for four speeches he delivered during the anti-CAA protests. Imam, a Delhi court claimed, had made statements geared to incite and provoke Indian Muslims to act against the sovereignty and the territorial integrity of India. "[His] speech also appears to challenge the territorial integrity and sovereignty of India," the court said in its order on framing charges against the activist. "It also appears to create hatred/contempt for the lawful institutions of the state and to challenge them by unlawful means." Imam had told "protesters to cut off Assam from India" in what he later explained was a call to protest by occupying roads. Authorities said he was asking for secession. Any effort to talk back against the state could result in the charge of terrorism; any effort to back the state project was understood as patriotism. Even international condemnation led nowhere. Amnesty International described the UAPA as "routinely used against people for simply expressing dissenting opinions often without evidence."[40] That was in April 2020. By the end of September, Amnesty's operations in Delhi were forced to shut down. Their offices had been raided and their accounts frozen.[41] But Amnesty wasn't the only one impacted in India; the attack was part of a larger stranglehold over civil society. Within two years of coming into power in 2014, the Indian Home Ministry had canceled the licenses of nearly 20,000 NGOs from receiving foreign funds. They were deemed to be against "the public interest."[42]

It was not surprising, then, that the Indian government would say nothing about the call for genocide by the Hindu Monks at the Dharam Sansad in Haridwar. The hate speech after all had merely built on a long drawn out architecture of hate and fear of Muslims. Instead, former Indian diplomats wrote a letter questioning the outrage it had elicited. They insinuated that sentiments espoused at the conference of top-level Hindu leaders were of a fringe nature and not representative of Modi's project.[43] Among the signatories of the letter was Lakshmi Puri, a former Indian diplomat and former deputy executive director of UN Women. For years, Puri has touted herself as a champion of girls and women's rights, winning the Eleanor Roosevelt award for human rights in 2016.[44] But as Kashmiris and Indian Muslims have repeatedly argued, Islamophobia is what tethers the liberal Indian to Hindu supremacist class in India. In the case of Puri, the analogy held true in the very same household. Lakshmi Puri is married to Hardeep Singh Puri, Modi's Minister of Petroleum and Natural Gas as well as Minister of Housing and Urban Affairs. Her defense, then, only exemplified the collective buy-in of the Indian political elite. Despite the attempts to characterize the Dharam Sansad as a marginal affair, an investigation by digital news site Article 14, found that over a period of two years, the far right in India had organized around twelve events across four states that similarly called for the genocide of Muslims, attacks on Christians, and an insurrection against the government.[45] It also found that the meetings were coordinated, that several more were planned and despite the level of hate, "the police see no conspiracy, the main organizers are free, and there are clear contradictions in the way they are treated by the justice system."

When Modi did speak on the controversies surrounding the Dharam Sansad in early 2022, his message came across loud and clear. "In the last 75 years, we only kept talking about rights, fighting for rights and wasting time. The talk of rights, to some extent, for some time, may be right in a particular circumstance, but forgetting one's duties completely has played a huge role in keeping India weak," he said.[46]

Predictably, in the months following the Haridwar meet, the rhetoric deepened, and incidents of anti-Muslim hate escalated. Swami Giri, among the main speakers at the event, was given a warm welcome in Ghaziabad in early January

2022, where he clarified his call for violence against Muslims. "Whoever has understood the Quran is a jihadi . . . Every Hindu should keep weapons at home. When you do that, you will be blessed by Ram and Krishna. You need the weapons now, to wage war against the jihadis," Giri said. In 2017, the same Giri had urged Hindu couples to produce eight children to protect their religion. "In the present times, there is threat to Hindutva and to protect it is the responsibility of every Hindu. For this, every Hindu should produce eight children so that he can contribute toward conserving, preserving and protecting Hindutva and the society."[47] It wasn't long before every facet of Muslim life became a target. Young Muslim women were banned from wearing the headscarf at several colleges in the southern state of Karnataka. When the matter was taken to court, the Karnataka High Court upheld the ban, arguing the headscarf was not obligatory for Muslim women. Legal scholars described it as constitutional overreach and cited concerns for similar moves in other states.[48] Soon after, Hindu supremacists called for a ban on halal meat stores in Karnataka, too. By mid-2022, the Indian government added an additional Israeli tactic to their arsenal: the bulldozing of Muslim homes. On the first day of Ramadan, Hindu mobs, draped in saffron scarves, marched through Muslim neighborhoods in Karauli, Rajasthan, stopping outside homes and mosques to sing songs into loudspeakers:

> We are hardcore Hindus, we will create a new history
> We will enter the homes of enemies, and will cut their heads [. . .]
> In every home the saffron flag will be seen, the rule of Ram will return.
> There is only one slogan, one name, victory to Lord Ram, victory to Lord Ram.[49]

When Muslims reacted by pelting the mobs with stones, and scuffles ensued, homes and businesses were razed to the ground. Police officers swooped in and arrested Muslims deemed to be "rioters." As they sat in jail, bulldozers arrived at the suspected rioters' homes and smashed them to the ground. The scenes would repeat themselves in Jahangirpuri in north Delhi and Khargone in the state of Madhya Pradesh. Several Indian administrations have used bulldozers in flagrant disregard of the constitution to displace the poor and the marginalized. Former Indian PM Sanjay Gandhi did it in 1982 in Jahangirpuri itself.[50] "What is new is selective political targeting now, especially by the BJP governments," Naveen Tewari and Sandeep Pandey write.[51] Then in June, authorities in Allahabad arrested Javed Muhammad, father of prominent Indian Muslim activist Afreen Fatima, alleging that he had led a protest days earlier over derogatory comments made by a BJP spokesperson about the Prophet Muhammad (Peace Be Upon Him) days earlier. As her father languished in jail, Fatima and the rest of the family were first detained, then later forced out of their home. The next morning, they watched on television as their house was razed to the ground. "What is more humiliating than seeing bulldozers laying waste to your homestead in broad daylight, as neighbors or distant strangers on television sets and smartphones spectate, either helplessly or gleefully?" Angshuman Choudhury writes.[52] The actions on Muslims are in keeping with the punitive measures exercised by the Israelis on Palestinian homes and neighborhoods for the "crime" of resisting occupation and oppression. Afreen Fatima, too, is unequivocal about the parallel. "The idea is to punish Muslims and to let them know that we (the Indian government) can say whatever we want and you can't do anything about it," Fatima told me.[53]

The goal of Hindu majoritarianism, therefore, is the subordination of the Muslim minority. "This can involve forms of internment and expulsion [in India] and in Jammu and

Kashmir, the attempt to bring about demographic changes through encouragement of Hindu migration from elsewhere," Achin Vnaik told me.[54] Vnaik added, "The nearest Indian equivalent to Israel's occupied territories is the Kashmir Valley but otherwise Muslims are spread all over the rest of India; expulsion or internment policies can only be selective and limited."

Kashmiris have long identified with the Palestinian struggle for self-determination. In back alleys of the capital Srinagar, cries of "Free Palestine" are spray painted on steel shutters next to walls with "Free Kashmir" and "Go India Go" slogans. Kashmiri youth have been killed by the Indian army in protests for Palestine, while artists and religious leaders have been detained for expressing their solidarity with Palestine. India seeks to tame Kashmiri sentiments for Palestine, knowing that it both expresses a solidarity with a global Muslim issue as well as a recognition of parallels between the two struggles. When police and army have harassed non-violent protests, Kashmiri boys and girls have resorted to stone pelting, like the "children of the stones" as Palestinian youth were referred to during the first intifada.[55]

The question of Palestine, after all, and the dispute in Kashmir emerged from the ashes of British colonialism. Whereas Palestinians were uprooted by the Nakba, hundreds of thousands of people from Jammu and Kashmir were displaced too in the weeks and months following Partition and as a result of a large-scale massacre against the Muslim population in the region of Jammu. Over the years, both the Kashmiri and Palestinian right to national self-determination have been subsequently reduced into a rubric of religious conflict: Hindu versus Muslim in Kashmir and Jew versus Muslim in Palestine. Both Palestine and Kashmir have been severely sold out by their leaders. Under the 1975 Indira-Sheikh Accord, Kashmiri leader Sheikh Abdullah, who had spent more than a decade in prison, forfeited the demand for self-determination in exchange for being the chief minister of the state. Almost 20 years later, the Oslo accords would accomplish much of the same for the Palestinians. Kashmiris were moved by the first intifada in the late 1980s in fomenting their own mass uprising against Indian rule.[56]

In the post-9/11 moment and in the context of global anti-Muslim racism, both struggles against foreign occupation were slipped under the rubric of "Islamic terrorism." Palestine and Kashmir are targets of the ethno-nationalist ideologies of Zionism and Hindutva that seek their eradication. As colonial projects, India and Israel have exercised similar modalities of control to wield power of their dominions: extrajudicial killings, arbitrary detentions, maiming, torture, economic dependencies, surveillance, home demolitions (or spaciocide),[57] restrictions on mobility, checkpoints, a network of informers, as well as the creation of a collaborator class—the Palestinian Authority in Palestine, as well as pro-India "unionist" parties in Kashmir like the National Conference and the People's Democratic party (PDP). Both countries also instrumentalize the law to protect their armed forces. Whereas the Indian government uses the Armed Forces Special Powers Act (AFPSA), to provide cover for the abuses of their soldiers, an entire cultural and legal apparatus in Israel protects Israeli soldiers from facing accountability for "unjustified use of lethal force."[58]

Several similarities notwithstanding, it is not my intention here to argue that the occupations of Palestine and Kashmir are the same. They aren't. Instead, the comparison between India and Israel is meant to illustrate the ways in which oppressive methods are shared and duplicated and crucially, justified. As Samreen Mushtaq and Mudasir Amin argue:[59]

> The colonization of Kashmir, like Palestine, is not just the influx of a settler population that would derive multiple economic and political benefits at the cost of the natives. It is to be the "crown" of a Hindutva project that wants to make itself the only legitimate sovereign of a people that refuses its control over them.

In this way, there are similarities between India's effort in Kashmir with the Chinese pursuit to assimilate Tibet and erase Uighur religious and cultural identity. In East Turkestan or Xinjiang, Beijing uses mass surveillance and the threat of incarceration to control the Uighur population. It has also flooded the region with Han Chinese to alter the demography. Former Indian army general Bipin Rawat, after all, called for "de-radicalization" camps to house Kashmiri children.[60] India's occupation of Kashmir also shares similarities with Morocco's occupation of the Western Sahara. With Israel and Morocco having established ties in December 2020 on the basis of America's recognition of Moroccan sovereignty over Western Sahara, the similarities between the Kashmiri and Sahrawi experience is only likely to grow. But where India and Israel use the liberal lexicon of democracy as well as a religious, right-wing civilizational argument to justify ethno-nationalism, China or Morocco show little interest in wrapping their programs within democratic facades.

The Israeli Model in Kashmir

In the days leading to August 5, 2019 and in the weeks and months to come, Kashmir became a site of unfathomable cruelty. Thousands of Kashmiris were detained; pro-India politicians were placed under house arrest, pro-freedom leaders as well as minors were rounded up and thrown in jail. Young boys were shipped off to Indian prisons 1,500km away in Agra and Varanasi. Foreign journalists and international human rights groups were banned from access to Kashmir. The region was placed under a complete communication blackout. Cellular phones, Internet, landline services, and even the postal services were dismantled. News traveled by word of mouth. Journalists compressed photos and video onto memory cards and smuggled them out with passengers en route to Delhi. Schools, offices, banks, and businesses were closed for months. Life came to a standstill.

On August 5, 2019, the Modi government revoked both Articles 370 and 35A, split the region into two union territories of Jammu and Kashmir, and Ladakh, and placed them under the direct control of Delhi. Kashmir had been effectively annexed. It was a stunning rebuke to the myth of Indian democracy as well as the veneer of Kashmiri autonomy. Observers warned that this move represented an intensification of India's settler-colonial project in Indian-occupied Kashmir. Under the new status of the state, India would now have the legal justification to allow non-Kashmiris to access residency rights in Kashmir as well as purchase land that had previously been restricted to Kashmiri permanent residents, or state subjects. The end goal was now within sight: Kashmir's Muslim-majority demography would be changed in favor of Indian Hindus. In time, elections would be held, and democracy would cover for the ethnocratic, colonial rule that had been imposed on the region.

Revoking Article 370 and Article 35A were long-held goals of Hindu nationalists and supremacists in India. They had resented the autonomy PM Nehru had "granted" Kashmir in 1947 and wished to see Kashmir fully integrated into India. For Hindu-supremacists, these two articles were an obstruction to the region's full integration into the Indian state and had contributed to the rise of "separatism" or "terrorism" in the region—which is how India refers to Kashmiris' decades long resistance to Indian rule. To the Hindu right, the problems in Kashmir were borne out of India's coddling of Kashmiri Muslims. The question of Kashmiri self-determination had never been on the agenda. The removal of the two Articles was therefore portrayed as ushering in a "New Kashmir" in which peace and prosperity would arrive through Indian investment and development. This had been a central plank of Narendra Modi's second election campaign, too.

Following the events of August 5, BJP politicians bragged of being able to not only buy land in Kashmir, but also "marry fair-skinned Kashmiri women."[61] In the U.S., the Hindu American Foundation (HAF) published a "Reporter's Guide" on the situation in Kashmir.[62] Central to this document were the false claims that ending Kashmir's semi-autonomy would result in equal property rights for women, more protections for the LGBTQI+ community and better opportunities for Dalits in Kashmir. Again, none of these claims were even loosely based on facts.[63] Writing in the Indian digital publication, *The Wire*, Anish Gawande, co-founder and curator of Pink List India, compared the Indian government's attempt to use the LGBTQI+ community to "pinkwashing," adding that claims of "gay liberation" in Kashmir since India annexed it was nothing but "a product of digital propaganda."[64] On "pinkwashing," an author who identifies as a queer Kashmiri Pandit wrote the following on the condition of anonymity:

> Using pinkwashing tactics, India ensures that any violent action they take against Kashmiris can be excused because they have deemed themselves the "progressive liberators" of Kashmir. Even while propagating the myth of their LGBTQ saviorism abroad and to international audiences at U.S. Congressional hearings, they continue to fan the flames of queerphobia and transphobia to court the favor of the right wing.[65]

Pinkwashing itself is a tactic almost certainly borrowed from the Israeli playbook in which a civilizing quest is used to conceal a project of ethnic cleansing. Israel denies Palestinian presence, history, and even claim to the land by taking over homes, renaming villages and towns, appropriating cuisine in the pursuit of removing the Palestinian footprint. Likewise, India, through a policy of "domestication"—or to use BJP leader Ram Madhav's words: "instilling India" into Kashmiri Muslims[66]—seeks to make Kashmiri Muslims relinquish their cultural and political identity and submit to the larger Indian Hindu project. Crucially, most Indian liberals and Hindu supremacists are in agreement that Kashmir is fundamental to India—be it secular or Hindu Rashtra.

Kashmiri scholars Samreen Mushtaq and Mudasir Amin warn against characterizing the events of August 5, 2019 as the beginning of the settler-colonial project in Kashmir, but rather as an extension of the vast matrix of control that included "spatial, demographic, and ecological manifestations" that "is both a historical practice and a present day engagement rather than a singular event of invasion."[67] While the framework of settler-colonialism may be a useful way to make the situation on ground in Kashmir comprehensible for international audiences, the authors argue that:

> the reliance on a future Indian-citizen-settler runs the risk of invisibilizing the Indian armed forces already permanently stationed in Kashmir and occupying vast tracts of land. The settler colonial framework can be a useful concept for Kashmir when its shrewd combination of assimilationist and eliminationist tactics is placed within the framework of military occupation, rather than as a distinct alternative.[68]

Collectively, this framework is set on ultimately destroying "the very idea of what it means to be a native—the elimination of history and culture such that there is a total de-familiarization with the idea of Kashmir as the homeland for the natives, going beyond disappearing, and killing the Kashmiri body."[69]

One of the most fervent manifestations of this approach came on an evening in November 2019 at the private residence of Sandeep Chakravorty, India's then consul-general to the United States. During the course of the event, Chakravorty addressed the gathering, made up of Indians and members of the Kashmiri Hindu community (known as Kashmiri Pandits). He assured the crowd that India would build settlements modeled after Israel in preparation for the return of the Hindu population to Kashmir. As Chakravorty said:

> I believe the security situation will improve, it will allow the refugees to go back, and in your lifetime, you will be able to go back . . . and you will be able to find security, because we already have a model in the world. I don't know why we don't follow it. It has happened in the Middle East. If the Israeli people can do it, we can also do it.[70]

The event was broadcast over Facebook, stirring a diplomatic controversy. Chakravorty's comments hadn't merely contradicted India's official opposition to Jewish-only settlements in the occupied territories, it demonstrated that in Kashmir, it was willing to replicate it. Kashmiri novelist Mirza Waheed wrote that the comparison with Israel "cannot have any other meaning but an endorsement of a settler-colonial project."[71] Chakravorty said his comments were taken out of context.[72] Yet, Chakravorty's call for the Israeli model replicates the demand by some right-wing Kashmir Pandit groups like Panun Kashmir, as well as the BJP itself, to create Hindu-only settlements in Kashmir, buttressed by additional security and militarized infrastructure such as walls, separate roads, and checkpoints, not unlike Jewish-only settlements in the West Bank.[73] As Azadeh Shahshahani and Zainab Ramahi argue, "The Palestinian experience may offer a window into the future for Kashmiris, with massive Israeli settlement expansion in the West Bank and dual legal systems, creating conditions that have been described as 'worse than apartheid.'"[74]

Chakravorty's comments were also especially poignant because they took place during an event in which Vivek Agnihorti, an Indian filmmaker, along with Bollywood actor Anupham Kher were trying to secure support for a project called "The Kashmir Files," a film they promised would "bring the unreported story of the most tragic and gut-wrenching genocide of Kashmir Hindus"[75] to the big screen.

But had there been a genocide of Kashmiri Pandits? When the upheavals began in the late 1980s and early 1990s, an estimated 120,000 Kashmiri Hindus left under conditions which remain contested. India refuses to allow any international investigation into the conditions that led Kashmiri Hindus to leave the valley, relying instead on right-wing narratives that Kashmiri Muslims drove them out. According to Indian government figures, 219 Kashmiri Pandits were killed between 1989–2004.[76] Meanwhile, many Kashmiri Muslims argue that while Kashmiri Pandits had left out of fear, the Indian government, under the draconian governor at the time, Jagmohan, had facilitated their departure, promising that they would return once India dealt with the armed uprising.[77] Pro-freedom leaders in Kashmir have repeatedly called for the return of Kashmiri Pandits, but have urged them to return as neighbors and not settlers. In other words, Agnihorti was promising to produce an alternate history of the Kashmir dispute in which Kashmiri Muslims were the rampaging extremists.

As Deepti Misri and Mona Bhan argue, "One of the most enduring mainstream narratives around the departures of Kashmiri Pandits in the 1990s is that they were "driven out" by their Muslim neighbors as the armed militancy took off. This is a narrative that has displaced every other analysis of these tragic departures, offering up Kashmiri Pandits as singular and exclusive victims in the violent modern history of Kashmir, even as Kashmiri Muslims have in their turn endured violent crackdowns, enforced disappearances, arbitrary detentions and a general devaluation of every form of political power, including the right to protest their oppressive conditions."[78] The Kashmir Files was finally released in early 2022. It was promoted by the BJP, made tax-free in several states. It became a box office hit.

Since August 2019, the Indian government has embarked on several devastating administrative changes in order to accelerate its settler-colonial project. One of these changes was the introduction of the category of "domicile," or permanent residency rights, which was issued by the Ministry of Home Affairs on March 31, 2020 under the title "Jammu and Kashmir Reorganization Order, 2020." This law "created a series of categories through which Indians—who had previously not been able to own land or access government jobs as they were reserved for Kashmir's "permanent residents"—would now be able to lay claim to residency rights."[79] It allows those who "have resided or studied in the state for 15 years or seven years," respectively, to qualify for domicile, entitled to residency and employment rights. In addition, children of Indian government officials, including army and paramilitary, who have served in the state for ten years are eligible to apply for government jobs."[80] All those who sought residency rights, including native Kashmiris, would now have to obtain a domicile certificate. This law makes it possible for the hundreds of thousands of Indian soldiers, as well as laborers, to retroactively or eventually, seek residency status in Kashmir. As more Indian businesses and corporations are legally able to operate in Kashmir, the number of those likely to claim permanent residency in the future will naturally increase. The "military occupation and forceful entry (will be) transformed into a natural one of belongingness over time."[81] True to form, Kashmiri resistance to this forcible demographic change—including armed resistance—will remain "terrorism," while the Hindu settler will be portrayed as the "innocent civilian."

International law prohibits occupying powers to transfer their own population into territories or change their demographic makeup as a means to avoid ethnic cleansing. The facilitation of Indian settlers into Kashmir will alter the demographic makeup of the state, thereby ending the possibility of a just solution in the region. In the interim, the Indian government will exercise delimitation—or change electoral boundaries—to grant more electoral sway to existing and future Hindu-majority districts in Kashmir. This "settler implantation and demographic gerrymandering" is intended to counter the Muslim majority.[82] In this way, decisions made by any legislative body will be deemed "democratic" and "representative" of the people of Kashmir.

The Indian government also passed another law, the "Union Territory of Jammu and Kashmir Reorganization (Adaptation of Central Laws) Third Order, 2020" pertaining to the use of land. As an occupying power, the Indian army has already swallowed vast tracts of land for its barracks and bases spread all across Kashmir. The details of these installations and the scale of these bases remain obscure, with the military using "national security" as a means of subterfuge.[83] By 2020 the Indian army held around 53,353 hectares in Kashmir with 243 hectares of additional forest land approved for use by the Indian forces between September 18, 2019 and October 21, 2019 alone. The new law, passed in October 2020, gave every Indian citizen the right to buy land in Kashmir.[84] The region was officially up for sale.

The state also repealed land reform acts from the 1950s that had placed restrictions on the amount of land that any individual could hold, meaning that Indians could now purchase unlimited amounts of land. Meanwhile the right-to-return of those state-subjects "displaced by the incomplete and unending partition of Kashmir" were immediately extinguished with the application of the Central Enemy Properties Act 1968.[85] A few months later, another law was passed that allowed the Indian army to "mark any property or area in Jammu and Kashmir as 'strategic' and take it over without any local government permissions and ignoring civilian objections."[86] For example, in January 2022, the army grabbed over 50.5 hectares of land in the tourist areas of Gulmarg and Sonmarg under this dispensation, stating that the land would be used for "operational and training requirements" of the armed forces. In this way, the Indian government had paved the way for the army and corporations to take control of the state.

The Indian state has already begun to evict indigenous communities from their homes. In late 2020, tribal communities received notice that labeled their homes as illegally occupying forest land. Their homes were demolished.[87] This bears an eerie resemblance to Israel's targeting of Bedouin communities of Naqab, where Israel gave the lands of these communities to Jewish settlers and the military. The logic of Bedoin dispossession was premised on the fact that as nomads, they had no right to the land.[88]

In Kashmir, these communities were living on lands that the Indian state wanted to use for the development of tourist infrastructure. Part of the plan is to transfer agricultural land to Indian state and private corporations.[89] Kashmir has already lost 78,700 hectares of agricultural land to non-agricultural purposes between 2015–19.[90] This decline in agricultural land—which a majority of Kashmiris still rely upon as the foundation of their economy—will disempower farmers, result in a loss of essential crops, make Kashmir less agriculturally self-sufficient, and create grounds for economic collapse in the near future. It is of course, only when Kashmiris are economically devastated that India's job in securing their land will be made even easier.

Alongside the destruction of agricultural land, the Indian government has also been charged with "ecocide" in Kashmir, which, "masked under the development rhetoric . . . destroys the environment without care, extracting resources and expanding illegal infrastructure as a way of contesting the indigenous peoples' right of belonging and using the territory for their own gain."[91] During the lockdown in late 2019, the valley saw unprecedented forest clearances.[92] In June 2020, the Jammu & Kashmir Forest Department became a government-owned corporation, allowing it to sell public forest land to private entities, including to Indian corporations. The rush to secure and extract Kashmir's resources has typically come at an immense cost to the region's vulnerable ecology, prompting local activists' fears that a lack of accountability will almost certainly exacerbate the climate crisis in South Asia. Just as Israel has secured control over Palestinian resources, India's stranglehold of Kashmir's natural resources and interference with the environment will ultimately make Kashmiris dependent on the Indian state for their livelihoods.[93] All of these shifts in land use reflect the "Srinagar Master Plan 2035," which "proposes creating formal and informal housing colonies through town planning schemes as well as in Special Investment Corridors," primarily for the use of Indian settlers and outside investors.[94] Indeed, the Indian government has signed a series of MOU's with outside investors to alter the nature of the state by building multiplexes, educational institutions, film production centers, tourist infrastructure, Hindu religious sites, and medical industries. Kashmiri investors are no competition for massive Indian and external corporations and have a fundamental disadvantage in investing in land banks that the government has apportioned toward these purposes. Back to back lockdowns have resulted in massive economic losses for Kashmir's industries, including tourism, handicrafts, horticulture, IT, and e-commerce. Furthermore, "as with other colonial powers, Indian officials are participating in international investment summits parroting Kashmir as a "Land of Opportunity," setting off a scramble for Kashmir's resources, which will cause further environmental destruction."[95] India has always kept a close eye on Kashmir's water resources and its capabilities to generate electricity, while intentionally depriving Kashmir of the electricity it produces.

As more economic and employment opportunities are opened up to Indian domiciles, Kashmiris will also be deprived of what little job security they had. In sum, "neoliberal policies come together with settler colonial ambitions under continued reference to private players, industrialization and development, with the 'steady flow of wealth outwards.'"[96] The role of the United Arab Emirates is especially important in this context, as it became the first country to explore investment opportunities in Kashmir after India annexed the region. Dubai ports giant DP World said in January 2022 they would be building an inland port while Dubai developer Emaar Properties announced it would build a mall in Srinagar, Meanwhile, the Lulu Group, an Indian Muslim owned but UAE-headquartered company, said they would set up a food processing plant.[97] It is no surprise, given the UAE's leading role in normalizing relations with Israel, that they are now being positioned as integral to the Indian settler-colonial project in Kashmir, too.

"What such investment in Kashmir will look like is easy to guess from a cursory glance at the rest of India: more trash, more cars, more pollution, more concrete, more aggressive Hindu rock music, and ever more ugly assertions of the race spirit that Golwalkar wanted Hindus to learn from Nazis.

The BJP wants to allow its Hindu majoritarian supporters to expand into Kashmir. If it looks like settler colonialism, that's because it is," Indian novelist Siddharth Deb wrote.[98]

And contrary to the claims of peace and development, these developments have come amid an atmosphere of spectacular intimidation.[99] Under the Unlawful Activities Prevention Act (UAPA), the Indian government is able to hold an individual without a trial or bail for any activity it deems to be endangering the sovereignty of India (which might mean anything from housing a militant, expressing Kashmir's right to self-determination on social media, or even expressing support for Pakistan during a cricket match against India).[100] In November 2021, prominent rights defender Khurram Parvaz from Jammu Kashmir Coalition of Civil Society (JKCCS) was taken in too.[101] And when the UAPA is not used to implicate, local intelligence officials harass and intimidate the rest. Officials are known to make unannounced visits to journalists' homes or leave cryptic messages with neighbors. For every Kashmiri journalist who has faced censure or travel restrictions, there are several who have had a visit from the intelligence services and chosen to remain silent about the harassment they face.[102] This clampdown on civil society in Kashmir is especially ominous because it has left very little space for Kashmiris to express dissent. It has also contributed to an even deeper climate of fear and lack of trust, while also making it difficult for Kashmiris to speak out on international platforms. Again, India and Israel are in lockstep with one another. In October 2021, Israel similarly designated six Palestinian civil society groups "terrorist organizations."[103]

The Indian government has also passed a stringent "New Media Policy" which allows "government officers to decide on what is 'fake news' and take action against journalists and media organizations."[104] Local journalists have already argued that the pressure is so immense on them to toe the line, they are now the purveyors of endless government PR.[105] Mosques, religious organizations, and charitable institutions have also been placed under greater scrutiny. Ordinary Kashmiris are also being targeted for their words on social media. They are threatened with termination of employment if they utter "anti-national" ideas.[106] Kashmir, for all intents and purposes, is now under a colonial administration. Whereas the Indian state had exerted control over Kashmir through a military occupation and a puppet legislature in the past, Kashmiris have now become bystanders in their own home, Mohamed Junaid says.[107]

Today, political or civic space in Kashmir has been emptied out. Whereas the pro-freedom leadership is either under arrest or house arrest, the pro-India political leaders, or representatives of the various client regimes India had installed in Kashmir, have become parodies, quite like the Palestinian Authority. In the devastating words of Kashmiri journalist Muzamil Jaleel, "On August 5, 2019, India launched the final assault on the homeland of Kashmiris. The plan is, and always has been, to rob Kashmiris of their land, flood it with settlers, and eventually render the natives into a disempowered minority that's not fully human, but human object, a thing."[108]

Resistance and Beyond

All indicators suggest that a project of ethnic cleansing is well underway in India. Minorities are being squeezed under a rubric of an all-consuming Hindu majoritarian project backed by giant oligarchs and corporations that threaten to tear apart a fragile country that has never been a nation. In the ethnocracy, no one is safe. Not journalists. Not Muslims. Not Christians. Not activists. Not even Hindus are safe if they do not conform to the fascist agenda. The assault on dignity has empowered none besides giant corporations and has turned citizens into a morass of disenfranchised subjects. The state is now firmly in the hands of a fiction called the nation.

In Kashmir, the Indian government's abrogation of the special constitutional clauses that provided certain protections over land and employment was an articulation of the expansionist project, or Akhand Bharat. The consequences have been catastrophic for Kashmiris. But Western democratic states have neither the political inclination nor the moral authority to hold Modi accountable. Delhi knows this. Meanwhile, Muslim majority countries, especially those in the Gulf, have in India an infinite resource of cheap human labor needed to build their luxury cities, a customer of energy, and now a geo-political ally. The fragile protections granted by the facade of the global capital economy has gifted Indian foreign policy a certain arrogance. India's unemployment rate is soaring. The economy has shown growth but only because of the soaring number of new billionaires. The government, meanwhile, has yet to come clean over the shocking number of Covid-19 deaths. None of these developments have gone unnoticed. The world is well aware of the immense cruelties unfolding across the country. But where governments can't or won't act, Indian soft power is beginning to take a beating among ordinary people in many parts of the world.

Whereas the story of India's descent into a proto-fascist state has many parts, its burgeoning relationship with the Israeli state and attempt to duplicate its methods is perhaps among the least discussed. The pace at which this relationship has accelerated over the past decade has appeared to catch some by surprise. But India's fraught experiment with democracy is part of the story here, too. In the interim, as "confusion" reigns, both the Indian and Israeli states have focused on exaggerating people to people contacts through Bollywood, yoga, and tech.

In recent years, there has been an increased awareness among grassroots activists, organizations, academics, and journalists about the close relations between India and Israel and what it portends. In January 2020, BDS India, the Indian news sites *News Click* and the *People's Dispatch* released a report detailing the extent of the India-Israel military relationship. The report, titled: "Israel-India Military Relations: Ideological Paradigms of Security" argued that Israel's military ideology, methodology, and technology was sustained by the billion-dollar arms trade and collaboration with India. It described the import of these Israeli methods as "ominous" and "a threat to democracy and human rights wherever it is implemented." Affixed to the report, a warning: "The significant role of Israel in this steadily growing military-industrial complex in India should be cause of serious concern for our civil society."[109] And this is not without precedent.

Israeli weapons, developed and field tested on Palestinians, have periodically found their way to some of the most autocratic and dangerous countries in the world. These include the genocides in Bosnia, Rwanda, and Myanmar. The Israeli arms industry therefore is not merely an introduction to technology, it is an invitation to Israeli governance and surveillance. Increasingly, anti-war activists, socialists, and those fighting for native and indigenous rights across the globe, be it in Hawaii or Ferguson, are recognizing the extent to which the Israeli occupation of Palestinians has served as a model for others to, if not emulate, then replicate in ways that help surmount the will of not just their own respective colonial or occupied territories, but also, increasingly, their citizens. It is here where the consequences of this relationship between India and Israel becomes clear: they are the blueprint and serve as a model for authoritarian regimes around the world.

Consider Elbit Systems, Israel's biggest arms manufacturer. It describes itself as "an international electronics defense company," which is to say it's in the business of producing products to repress at the behest of its clients. It builds several deadly weapons used by the Israeli military, including the Hermes 900, used since 2014 to survey and conduct airstrikes in the Gaza Strip. Elbit provides much of the technology for the apartheid barrier and the illegal checkpoints in Palestine. Most importantly for this discussion, Elbit's aspiration for market dominance is to shut down the competition by buying them out. "Elbit buys companies in quick succession, and each new market that opens to the firm through a new acquisition means it is involved in another conflict," Shir Hever writes.[110] In other words, the expansion of war and conflict is its primary business. It is unsurprising that Elbit has its products in more than a dozen countries, including Colombia, Rwanda, Cameroon, Azerbaijan, and India.

Yet, even as governments around the world come together to kill, repress, and surveil, grassroots people's movements have attempted to build solidarity across multiple struggles. In August 2020, activists with the group Palestine Action, rallied outside three London offices belonging to the Israeli-company Elbit Systems. The rallies were one in a series of direct actions at the arms manufacturer over several months. The activists held banners, drenched the office walls with red paint and called on the landlord of the premises to kick the company out over its role in the continued oppression of Palestinians and indigenous people in other parts of the world. Elbit Systems has four factories in the United Kingdom that produce parts for the drones used by Israel. The activists also spray painted several slogans on the sites, including: "Tested on Palestinians, Used in Kashmir."[111] A tiny gesture it may have been, but for those under occupation, it carried a message that will forever reverberate.

Postscript and Acknowledgements

In the early months of 2011, I traveled to Indian-occupied Kashmir for *Al Jazeera English* to report on the scourge of enforced disappearances, the experiences of Kashmiri Hindus (known as Pandits), and the aftermath of the uprising that had taken place six months prior.

Tens of thousands of Kashmiris had taken to the streets in the summer of 2010, chanting *azadi* (freedom) from Indian rule prompted by the killing of three Kashmiri villagers by the Indian army.* Indian troops crushed the rallies, killing at least 120 Kashmiris, mostly young men. The protests had received scant international attention.

In earnest, we called the series *Kashmir: The Forgotten Conflict*. As our series unfolded online, the Indian government exercised a variety of intimidatory tactics to deter us from continuing with our work. They accused us of bias, summoned members of our senior management to Delhi to explain the reasons for the spotlight on Kashmir, and unofficially blocked visas for Doha-based staff (even those who wanted to travel to India as tourists). We later found out that it was one particular article that had ruffled feathers. It was called: "Kashmir: South Asia's Palestine." It's difficult to forget an episode like that.

In 2012, I moved to cover the African continent, focusing my attention on southern and central Africa instead. But the story followed me. On a reporting trip to the eastern Democratic

* Muzamil Jaleel (2010) "Fake encounter at LoC: 3 arrested, probe ordered," *Indian Express*, May 29 https://indianexpress.com/article/news-archive/web/fake-encounter-at-loc-3-arrested-probe-ordered/ (last accessed April 2022).

Republic of Congo, for instance, I met UN peacekeepers from the Jammu and Kashmir infantry. Their commanding officer proudly told me that they used their experience hunting militants in the mountains of Kashmir in keeping local Congolese rebels at bay. One man's occupier was another man's 'peacekeeper', I remember thinking.

As a reporter tasked with covering the African continent, foreign interference and influence is a recurring theme. The U.S., France, China, and Russia were obvious culprits. But a scratch beyond the surface and Turkey, the UAE, India, and Israel were establishing major footprints, too. Israel's efforts were particularly nefarious for they were specifically looking to wrench African countries away from their historic support for the Palestinians. During his term in office, Benjamin Netanyahu had launched a "charm offensive" in Africa, re-establishing diplomatic ties and expanding its bouquet of services, from agriculture to water conservation, humanitarian aid to private security, to countries across the continent. Israel's willingness to discreetly provide technology, military assistance, and riot and crowd control expertise to regimes on the continent made Israel an enemy of the people. But via its Mashav program, Israeli flags could be seen flying in the most remote towns and villages, be it in the Central African Republic or Ghana.

Parallel to these developments, the story in India was shifting dramatically. The rise of Narendra Modi in India exposed fault lines in the newsroom. Like so many in the western media, colleagues talked up Modi's economic plans for Delhi and underplayed the consequences for minorities and Kashmiris. Those who pushed back were deemed troublemakers or labeled activists. Even as the context in India rapidly changed, several colleagues and editors held firm to the "idea of India." Under Modi and Netanyahu, the relationship moved into a strategic partnership. In 2017, Netanyahu said during a historic visit to Delhi that his office was working in conjunction with Modi's government in making in-roads on the African continent.*

In July 2018, I traveled back to Kashmir as a freelancer to work on a documentary about Kashmiris who had been blinded by lead-plated pellets fired by Indian forces during protests. Since around 2010, Indian forces had been using pellets to maim youth who dared to express dissent against Indian rule in the valley. In 2016, around 1,100 Kashmiris were partially or fully blinded by pellets in what became known as the world's first mass blinding.** The vast surveillance architecture, the targeting of journalists, and the destruction of homes showed that Israeli tactics were very much present in the valley.

By the time Kashmir was annexed in August 2019, and a senior Indian diplomat in New York called for building Israeli-like settlements in Kashmir, followed by the passing of the Citizenship Amendment Act (CAA) that reverberated with Israel's Right of Return Law, a new certainty had arrived: India wanted to become a version of Israel.

It was clear that a project of this nature was long overdue.

This book may be about India and Israel, but at its core, this is a story about narrative and ideas we carry about India and Israel and their connection to each other. There remains a hesitancy to cover India properly. And this book seeks to counter that hesitation.

I am therefore extremely grateful to Pluto Press for giving me the opportunity to not only write on the new alliance

* Ministry of Foreign Affairs (2017) "Statement by PM Netanyahu at his meeting with Indian PM Modi," MFA, https://mfa.gov.il/MFA/PressRoom/2017/Pages/Statement-by-PM-Netanyahu-at-his-meeting-with-Indian-PM-Modi-5-July-2017.aspx (last accessed October 2021).

** AJE Staff (2021) "UN chief asks India to end use of pellet guns on Kashmir children," *Al Jazeera English*, June 30, https://aljazeera.com/news/2021/6/30/un-chief-pellet-guns-kashmir-children#:~:text=Indian%20security%20forces%20and%20police,%E2%80%9Cworld's%20first%20mass%20blinding%E2%80%9D. (last accessed August 2022).

between India and Israel but to challenge the distorted ideas we have all held about India's foreign policy prior to the arrival of Narendra Modi. I am especially thankful to my editor Neda Tehrani for believing in this project and for treating a complicated manuscript with such immense kindness and care. I would also like to acknowledge the entire Pluto team for their efforts: from design to marketing and copy-editing. Thank you: Melanie Patrick, Emily Orford, Robert Webb, Carrie Giunta, James Kelly, Alex Diamond-Rivlin, Patrick Hughes, and Dave Stanford.

I am also very thankful to my editors at *Al Jazeera English* who supported my work on Kashmir. These include my editor Carla Bower and my former managers Mohamed Nanabhay and Imad Musa.

I started work on this book just over a year into a new role with *Middle East Eye* and I am thankful to management for not only encouraging me to engage on the topic rigorously but giving me time to write the book for Pluto. Special thanks to David Hearst, Omayma Abdellatif, and Simon Hooper. I am especially grateful to my editor Faisal Edroos and colleague Umar Farooq for their friendship and relentless enthusiasm for the project.

Though there has been a wave of articles on the similarities between India and Israel over the past two years, we are only really at the beginning stages of academic scholarship on the topic. I am therefore thankful to the many scholars, activists, and academics who took time to talk with me to try and make sense of a rapidly shifting terrain. These include: Kavita Krishnan, Apoorvanand, Noam Chomsky, Ather Zia, Achin Vnaik, Khinvraj Jangid, Yara Hawari, Nerdeen Kiswani, Dheepa Sundaram, Afreen Fatima, Arthur Rubinoff, Arie Dubnov, Abdulla Moaswes, Dheepa Sundaram, Shreeya Singh, Nikhil Mandalaparthy, Rabbi Alise Wise, Suchitra

Vijayan, Priyamvada Gopal, and the activists at SASI. The book most certainly benefited from their insights.

The book was commissioned in the heart of 2020, amid the Covid-19 pandemic. Besides the immense insecurities that came with the time, travel was difficult and access to archival and library resources severely restricted. I am very grateful to The Department of African and African American Studies at Harvard University for providing me with access to university resources. A very special thank you to Cornel West, Tommy Shelby, and Giovanna Micconi, for helping arrange this. The librarians at Harvard also lived up to their billing, helping me access several articles and book chapters remotely. Similarly, I received assistance from Janine Pickardt at the United Nations Digital Library.

After the first drafts were completed, there were several friends who sacrificed their weekends to offer a close reading of the manuscript, offering honest and critical feedback. Thank you to Theresa Mathews, Saif Khalid, and Linah Alsaafin. I am honored that Linah accepted my invitation to write the foreword. As she argued in her terrific essay, the book takes my encounter with the question of Palestine full circle.

No project can exist without the support of family and friends, who played some role or another, sometimes not even to their knowledge: These include: Sorin Furcoi, Maria Costea, Ikbal Moosa, Naeem Mayet, Muhammed Patel, Zaahir Essa, Divesha Essa, Laika Essa, Aamina Moosa, Yusuf Osman, Ashwin Desai, Mohammed Haddad, Sameera Essa, Fatma Naib, Safiyyah Patel, Raja Abdulhaq, Fathima Paruk, Safiyah Patel, Shereena Qazi, Fatima Cassim, Laila Alarian, Zena Altahhan, Zainab Iqbal, Megan O'Toole, Sarita Sagar, Jo Rushby, Girish Singh, Dhilan Kalyan, Ahmed Tootla, Muhammad Zakaria Suleman, Alia Chughtai, Soud Hyder, Sehrish Suleman, Atiya Husain, Mohammad Alsaafin, Sophia Qureshi, Marina Sofi, Riyaad Minty, Rabail Sofi, Farzana Gardee, Gulshan Khan, Layan

Fuleihan, Sarwat Malik, Raheel Hassan, Osha Mahmoud, Mohamed Setar, Tahmid Quazi, Rashaad Amra, Mohamed Raiman, Khadeeja Manjra, Ayesha Jacub, Farid Sayed, Asad Hashim, Zeenat Adam, Nashwa Nasreldin, Imam Rashied Omar, Wajahat, Mariya Petkova, Yasser Ally, Yusuf Kajee, Shajei Haider, Nate Mathews, Suvaid Yaseen, Ali Alarian, Horia el Hadad, Birce Bora, Malika Bilal, Mohamad Junaid, Leena Alarian, Mohammed Ziyaad Hassen, Nathi Ngubane, Hafsa Adil, Faras Ghani, Saleem Patel, and Hafez Fuzail Soofie. I'm indebted to several friends in the US, in India, and in Kashmir whom I cannot name for their own safety.

Much love to my family in South Africa, in particular my parents Rooksana and Ebrahim, my sister, Shenaaz, to whom I owe everything; the Ayob and Essa clan in Durban and Johannesburg; much love to my family in the United States, Dr Rubina Shah and Yousuf Kanjwal, Shifa Kanjwal, Faroukh Mehkri, Omar Kanjwal, Samra Ahmed, and Asma Khaliq. For the love and endless care, the Kanjwal and Shah family in Kashmir.

Finally, this book wouldn't exist without the insistence and support of my wife, Hafsa Kanjwal, to whom this book is dedicated.

This book was written during a time of immense grief for loved ones back home in South Africa. The Covid-19 pandemic stole away our beloved uncle Mohamed Saleem Ayob and my starry-eyed cousin Azhar Bux, who was married for barely a month before he fell ill. We also lost uncle Ebrahim Patel following his long fight with cancer and my beautiful aunt Halima Essa in the ensuing chaos. Never have I ever felt so far away from home. This book is in their memory, too.

New York
July 2022

Notes

Chapter 1

1. Punyapriya Dasgupta (1988) *Cheated by The World: The Palestinian Experience*, Orient Longman, New Delhi, p. 283.
2. P.R. Kumaraswamy (2010) *India's Israel Policy*, Columbia University Press, New York, p. 48.
3. Jawaharlal Nehru (1937) Eighteen months in India, Kitabistan, Allahabad, p. 139.
4. Ibid., p. 143.
5. Kumaraswamy, *India's Israel Policy*, p. 44.
6. Arthur G. Rubinoff (1995) "Normalization of India-Israel Relations: Stillborn for Forty Years," *Asian Survey*, Vol. 35, No. 5, May, p. 488.
7. Kumaraswamy, *India's Israel Policy*, p. 56.
8. Ibid., p. 31.
9. Dasgupta, *Cheated by The World*, p. 283.
10. Kumaraswamy, *India's Israel Policy*, p. 38.
11. Ibid., p. 39.
12. In partition historiography, debates exist whether or not the Muslim League actually wanted a separate nation-state, or if they were using the two-nation theory to make claims for greater autonomy within a broader, more federal India in which Muslims would be able to self-govern Muslim-majority regions, and not be subject to Hindu majoritarian rule.
13. The All India Congress Committee (AICC) is considered the central decision-making body within the Indian National Congress.
14. Moin A. Zaidi (2018 [1985]) "Immutable Policy of Friendship and Cooperation, New Delhi: Indian Institute of Applied Political Research," in Kumaraswamy, *Squaring The Circle: Mahatma Gandhi and the Jewish National Home*, KW Publishers, New Delhi, p. 126.
15. Ibid., p. 127.

16. Ibid., p. 129.
17. Nehru, *Eighteen months in India*, p. 142.
18. Ibid., pp. 143–4.
19. Leonard A. Gordon (1975) "Indian Nationalist Ideas about Palestine and Israel," *Jewish Social Studies*, Vol. 37, No. 3/4, Summer–Autumn, p. 226.
20. Perry Anderson (2013) *The Indian Ideology*, Verso Books, London and New York.
21. Interview with Arthur G. Rubinoff on March 25, 2021.
22. Rubinoff, "Normalization of India-Israel Relations, p. 489.
23. Rashid Khalidi (2020) *The Hundred Years' War on Palestine: A History of Settler Colonialism and Resistance, 1917–2017*, Metropolitan Books, New York, p. 25.
24. Emanuel Celler (1947) "Celler deplores Nehru's Espousal of Arab State in Palestine," *Israel Archives*, April 28, https://archives.gov.il/archives/Archive/0b07170680031e2e/File/0b0717068oc6cf62 (last accessed December 2021).
25. Gordon, *Indian Nationalist Ideas about Palestine and Israel*, pp. 221–34.
26. UNSCOP (1947) "United Nations: Special Committee on Palestine (UNSCOP)," September 3, https://jewishvirtuallibrary.org/united-nations-special-committee-on-palestine-unscop#chapt7 (last accessed: March 2022).
27. Kumaraswamy, *India's Israel policy*, p. 100.
28. Ibid., p. 101.
29. Ibid.
30. P.S. Gourgey (1947) "Letter to Eliahu Epstein," *Israel Archives*, October 2, https://archives.gov.il/archives/Archive/0b0717068 0031e2e/File/0b0717068oc6cf62 (last accessed December 2021).
31. Khalidi, The Hundred Years' War on Palestine, p. 56.
32. Sunil Parushotham (2019) "Violence and in the making of Indian Democracy," in Alf Gunvald Nilsen, Kenneth Bo Nielsen, and Anand Vaidya (eds.), *Indian Democracy*, Pluto Press, London, p. 42.
33. Socialcops (2015) "We Bet You Don't Know Why the Indian Census Was Created," August 24, https://blog.socialcops.com/intelligence/we-bet-you-dont-know-why-indian-census-was-created/ (last accessed May 2022).

34. R.B. Bhagat (2001) "Census and the Construction of Communalism," *EPW Commentary*, November 24, http://sacw.net/2002/CensusandCommunalism.html (last accessed: June 2022).
35. Ibid.
36. Suchitra Vijayan (2021) "Midnight's Borders: A People's History of Modern India," Melville House, New York.
37. Anderson, *The Indian Ideology*, p. 77.
38. National Archives of India (1950) File No 46 (15)—AWT/48, Vol. 5, https://indianculture.gov.in/flipbook/120646 (last accessed: January 2022).
39. Ibid.
40. Ibid.
41. Interview with Arthur G. Rubinoff on March 25, 2021.
42. Rubinoff, Normalization of India-Israel Relations, p. 492.
43. Kumaraswamy, *India's Israel policy*, p. 14.
44. Rubinoff, Normalization of India-Israel Relations, p. 491.
45. Dasgupta, *Cheated by The World*, p. 287.
46. Ibid.
47. Joel Beinin (2020) "Egypt's Gamal Abdel Nasser Was a Towering Figure Who Left an Ambiguous Legacy," *Jacobin*, September 28, https://jacobinmag.com/2020/09/egypt-gamal-abdel-nasser-legacy (last accessed: January 2022).
48. Ibid.
49. Wiliam C. Mann (1988) "Displaced by Aswan Dam 23 Years Ago: Egypt's Nubians Dream of Home," *LA Times*, January 3, https://latimes.com/archives/la-xpm-1988-01-03-mn-32292-story.html (last accessed: March 2022).
50. Interview with Arthur G. Rubinoff on March 25, 2021.
51. HRW (2008) "Getting Away with Murder: 50 Years of the Armed Forces (Special Powers) Act," *Human Rights Watch*, August, https://hrw.org/legacy/backgrounder/2008/india0808/ (last accessed: July 2022).
52. Punyapriya Dasgupta (1992) "Betrayal of India's Israel Policy," *Economic and Political Weekly*, Vol. 27, No. 15/16, April 11–18, pp. 767, 769, 771–2.
53. Sampad Patnaik (2015) "Anti-colonialism is an old strategic tool of India—Shashi Tharoor merely repackaged it," *Scroll*, July 31, https://scroll.in/article/744066/anti-colonialism-is-an-old-

strategic-tool-of-india-shashi-tharoor-merely-repackaged-it (last accessed: March 2022).

54. Interview with Khinvraj Jangid on August 25, 2021.
55. Interview with Arthur G. Rubinoff on March 25, 2021.
56. PTI (2021) "Jaishankar unveils plaque at 'Bhoodan Grove' in Israel," *Times of India*, October 18, https://timesofindia.indiatimes.com/india/jaishankar-unveils-plaque-at-bhoodan-grove-in-israel/articleshow/87103606.cms (last accessed: January 2022).
57. Raghunath Keshav Khadilkar (1958) *Lok Sabha Debates (Fifth Session)*, Second Series Vol. XVIII No. 7, New Delhi: Lok Sabha Secretariat, p. 1744, https://eparlib.nic.in/bitstream/123456789/1560/1/lsd_02_05_19-08-1958.pdf#search=1958%20israel.
58. Kallol Bhattacherjee (2017) "With Nehru writing to its PM, Israel gave arms to India in 1962," *The Hindu*, May 27, https://thehindu.com/news/national/with-nehru-writing-to-its-pm-israel-gave-arms-to-india-in-1962/article18591835.ece (last accessed January 2022).
59. Ibid.
60. Nicolas Blarel (2015) *The Evolution of India's Israel Policy: Continuity, Change and Compromise Since 1922*, Oxford University Press, New Delhi, p. 157.
61. Interview with Arthur G. Rubinoff on March 25, 2021.
62. Bhattacherjee, "With Nehru writing to its PM."
63. Blarel, *The Evolution of India's Israel Policy*, p. 157.
64. Stephen P. Cohen and Sunil Dasgupta (2010) *Arming without Aiming: India's Military Modernization*, Brookings Institution Press, Washington D.C., pp. 7–8.
65. Harsh V. Pant and Ambuj Sahu (2019) "Israel's arms sales to India: Bedrock of a strategic relationship," *ORF Issue Brief*, No. 311, September, Observer Research Foundation.
66. PTI (2013) "Israel secretly provided arms to India in 1971: Book," *Times of India*, November 1, https://timesofindia.indiatimes.com/india/israel-secretly-provided-arms-to-india-in-1971-book/articleshow/25068719.cms (last accessed August 2021).
67. Nicolas Blarel and Jayita Sarkar (2019) "Substate Organizations as Foreign Policy Agents: New Evidence and Theory from India,

Israel, and France," *Foreign Policy Analysis*, Vol. 15, No. 3, July, pp. 413–31.

68. Lok Sabha Secretariat (1967) *Lok Sabha debates*, Vol. VI, No. 40, July 15, p. 12136, https://eparlib.nic.in/bitstream/123456789/2389/1/lsd_04_02_15-07-1967.pdf#search=israel%201967 (last accessed January 2022).
69. Ibid., p. 12135.
70. Ibid., p. 12138.
71. Yaakov Katz and Amir Bohbot (2017), *The weapon Wizards: How Israel became a high-tech military superpower*, St. Martin's Press, New York, p. 231.
72. P.R. Kumarasamy, (2010) *India's Israel Policy*, Columbia University Press, New York, p. 241.
73. MEA (2018) *India Palestine Relations*, Ministry of External Affairs, August, https://mea.gov.in/Portal/ForeignRelation/Updated_Note_on_India-Palestine_Relations_for_MEA_Website.pdf (last accessed January 2022).
74. UN (1991) "Racism and racial discrimination/Revocation of resolution 3379 ('Zionism as racism')," https://un.org/unispal/document/auto-insert-180327/ (last accessed June 2022).
75. African Union (1976) "Resolutions of the Twenty-Sixth Ordinary Session of the Council of Minister," AU, https://au.int/sites/default/files/decisions/9591-council_en_23_february_1_march_1976_council_ministers_twenty_sixth_ordinary_session.pdf (last accessed March 2022).
76. Christopher Raj (1980) "India grants full diplomatic status to PLO," *India Today*, April 30, https://indiatoday.in/magazine/international/story/19800430-india-grants-full-diplomatic-status-to-plo-821663-2014-02-04 (last accessed January 2022).
77. United Nations Digital Library (1985) "Provisional verbatim record of the 37th meeting, held at Headquarters, New York, on Wednesday, October 16, 1985: General Assembly, 40th session," https://digitallibrary.un.org/record/100057?ln=en(last accessed November 2021).
78. Warren Unna (1985) "Indian Update," *New York Times*, October 6, https://nytimes.com/1985/10/06/books/indian-update.html (last accessed November 2021).

79. T.N. Ninan (1985) "India's middle class represents the emergence of a major political and economic force," *India Today*, December 31, https://indiatoday.in/magazine/cover-story/story/19851231-indias-middle-class-represents-the-emergence-of-a-major-political-and-economic-force-802280-2014-01-29 (last accessed February 2022).
80. Nicolas Blarel (2015) *The evolution of India's Israel policy: continuity, change and compromise since 1922*, Oxford University Press, New Delhi p. 223.
81. P.R. Guris (2017) "Dr Subramanian Swamy remembers Indira Gandhi," YouTube, March 5, https://youtube.com/watch?v=oLQ38f1165c&ab_channel=PGurus (last accessed January 2022).
82. P.R. Kumaraswamy (2018) "My Israel Journey," *Middle East Institute*, New Delhi, February 2, http://mei.org.in/dateline-76 (last accessed November 2021).
83. Rajya Sabha Debates (1988) "Endorsement of Indian Passport for Israel," Parliament of India: Official debates of Rajya Sabha Session 147, July 28, https://rsdebate.nic.in/bitstream/123456789/281624/1/PQ_147_28071988_U285_p107_p107.pdf (last accessed October 2021).
84. Rajya Sabha debates (1991) "NRI Status to People Of Indian Origin In Israel," Parliament of India: Official debates of Rajya Sabha, Session 160, September 11, https://rsdebate.nic.in/bitstream/123456789/249493/1/PQ_160_11091991_S226_p35_p36.pdf (last accessed October 2021).
85. Shailaja Neelakanthan (2017) "First Israel visas in India were issued from this MP's residence," *Times of India*, July 4, https://timesofindia.indiatimes.com/india/first-israel-visas-from-india-were-issued-from-this-mps-residence/articleshow/59438603.cms (last accessed November 2021); Interview with Subramaniam Swamy, November 16, 2021.
86. PTI (2017) "Rajiv Gandhi only good human being in family: Subramanian Swamy," *Economic Times*, March 26, https://economictimes.indiatimes.com/news/politics-and-nation/rajiv-gandhi-only-good-human-being-in-family-subramanian-swamy/articleshow/57841096.cms?utm_

source=contentofinterest&utm_medium=text&utm_campaign=cppst (last accessed November 2021).
87. Interview with Khinvraj Jangid on August 25, 2021.

Chapter 2

1. Benjamin Netanyahu (2017) "Statement by PM Netanyahu at his meeting with Indian PM Modi," Ministry of Foreign Affairs, July 5, https://mfa.gov.il/MFA/PressRoom/2017/Pages/Statement-by-PM-Netanyahu-at-his-meeting-with-Indian-PM-Modi-5-July-2017.aspx (last accessed October 2021).
2. S. Jaishankar (2021) *The India Way*, HarperCollins India, New York, p. 20.
3. Indrani Bagchi (2017) "We've waited 70 yrs for you, Israeli PM tells Modi as he lands in Tel Aviv," *Times of India*, July 5, https://timesofindia.indiatimes.com/india/weve-waited-for-70-years-for-you-israel-welcomes-pm-modi-on-historic-visit/articleshow/59445531.cms (last accessed October 2021).
4. China announced diplomatic relations with Israel on January 24, 1992, just five days before India's announcement which made it to page three of the *New York Times*.
5. Vijay Prashad (2003) *Namaste Sharon: Hindutva and Sharonism*, Leftword Books, Delhi.
6. Perry Anderson (2013) *The Indian Ideology*, Verso Books, London and New York, p. 79.
7. Ibid.
8. Ratik Asokan (2020) "A culture of resistance, in The Baffler," September 30, https://thebaffler.com/latest/a-culture-of-resistance-asokan (last accessed October 2021).
9. Samreen Mushtaq and Mudasir Amin (2020) "India's settler colonialism in Kashmir is not starting now, eliminating the natives is a process long underway," Polis Project, June 27, https://thepolisproject.com/read/indias-settler-colonialism-in-kashmir-is-not-starting-now-eliminating-the-natives-is-a-process-long-underway/ (last accessed January 2021).
10. A copy of the IoA is available on *The Wire*: Venkatesh Nayak (2019) "The Backstory of Article 370: A True Copy of J&K's Instrument of Accession," *The Wire*, August 5, https://thewire.

in/history/public-first-time-jammu-kashmirs-instrument-accession-india (last accessed January 2022).

11. Kelly Buchanan (2019) "FALQs: Article 370 and the Removal of Jammu and Kashmir's Special Status," Library of Congress, October 3, https://blogs.loc.gov/law/2019/10/falqs-article-370-and-the-removal-of-jammu-and-kashmirs-special-status/ (last accessed June 2022).
12. Ratik Asokan (2020) A culture of resistance, *The Baffler*, September 30, https://thebaffler.com/latest/a-culture-of-resistance-asokan (last accessed January 2021).
13. Mona Bhan (2022) "Development: India's Foundational Myth," in Thomas Blom Hansen and Srirupa Roy (eds.), *Saffron Republic: Hindu Nationalism and State Power in India*, Cambridge, UK: Cambridge University Press.
14. Steve Coll (1991) "Israeli tourist battles with Kashmir captors," *Washington Post*, June 28, https://washingtonpost.com/archive/politics/1991/06/28/israeli-tourist-battles-with-kashmiri-captors/059fb732-528a-49d8-acc6-dfebba3bc449/ (last accessed August 2021).
15. Bernard Weinraub (1991) "Kashmir Rebels Kill Israeli Tourist, Marking New Phase in Conflict," *New York Times*, June 28, https://nytimes.com/1991/06/28/world/kashmir-rebels-kill-israeli-tourist-marking-new-phase-in-conflict.html (last accessed August 2022).
16. Punyapriya Dasgupta (1992) "Betrayal of India's Israel Policy," *Economic and political weekly*, Vol. 27 No. 15/16, April 11, p. 771.
17. Ibid.
18. P.R. Kumarasamy, (2010) *India's Israel Policy*, Columbia University Press, New York.
19. J.N. Dixit (1996), *My South Block Years: Memoirs of a Foreign Secretary*, UBS Publishers' Distributors Ltd, New Delhi; N.A.K. Browne (2017) "A Perspective on India–Israel Defence and Security Ties," *Strategic Analysis*, Vol. 41, No. 4, pp. 325–35.
20. Prabir Purkayastha (2014) "The military fulcrum of strategic relations" in Gita Hariharan (ed.), *From India to Palestine*, Leftword Books, New Delhi.

21. Interview with Khinvraj Jangid, Director of the Jindal Centre for Israel Studies at OP Jindal Global University in New Delhi, August 25, 2021.
22. "Global Pacification Industry" refers to the methods of governments around the world in controlling and repressing ordinary people who demonstrate dissent. As described in Jeff Halper (2015) *War Against the People: Israel, the Palestinians and Global Pacification*, Pluto Press, London.
23. Richard Bitzinger (2013) "Israeli Arms Transfer to India: Ad Hoc Defence Cooperation or the Beginnings of a Strategic Relationship?" S Rajanathan School of International Studies, April, https://rsis.edu.sg/rsis-publication/idss/219-israeli-arms-transfers-to-indi/#.YWmpVEbMLP8 (last accessed October 2021).
24. UPI Archives (1992) "India to establish ties with Israel," *UPI*, January 29, https://upi.com/Archives/1992/01/29/India-to-establish-ties-with-Israel/4957696661200/ (last accessed August 2021).
25. Shir Hever (2018) *The Privatisation of Israeli Security*, Pluto Press, London.
26. Mumtaz Ahmad Shah and Dr. Tarbraz (2020) "India's Israel policy: From Nehru to Modi," *Journal of Critical Reviews*, Vol. 7, No. 9.
27. Larry Lockwood (1972) "Israel's Expanding Arms Industry," *Journal for Palestine Studies*, Vol. 1, No. 4, July, p. 83.
28. Ibid., pp. 73–91.
29. Farah Naaz (2000) "Israel's Arms Industry," *Strategic Analysis*, Vol. XXIII, No. 12, March, https://ciaotest.cc.columbia.edu/olj/sa/sa_oonaf01.html (last accessed June 2022).
30. Shir Hever's (2018) *The Privatisation of Israeli Security*, Pluto Press, London, is an instructive guide on how high public spending on the military led to calls for the privatization of the Israeli security industry that benefited Israeli elites and helped cement the occupation of the Palestinian territories.
31. Lockwood, "Israel's Expanding Arms Industry," p. 89.
32. Ibid., p. 91.
33. Browne, "A Perspective on India–Israel Defence and Security Ties," p. 327.

34. Rajya Sabha (1994), "Palestine-Israel Peace Accord," Parliament of India: Official debates of Rajya Sabha, Session 170, May 5, pp. 307–10, https://rsdebate.nic.in/handle/123456789/193285?viewItem=search (last accessed October 2021).
35. Browne, "A Perspective on India–Israel Defence and Security Ties," p. 328.
36. Browne opened the defense attaché's office in Tel Aviv on April 7, 1997.
37. Browne writes without a shred of irony: "Dr Kalam remained a highly respected figure with the Israeli defense research community. 'I have come to pray for peace in the Holy Land,' he once remarked after visiting the famous Al Aqsa mosque in the heart of Jerusalem." p. 328.
38. Kanchi Gupta (2014) "India-Israel relations: From UPA to Modi," Observer Research Foundation, November 12, https://orfonline.org/research/india-israel-relations-from-upa-to-modi/ (last accessed October 2021).
39. Itzhak Gerberg (2008) "The changing nature of Israeli-India relations: 1948–2005," PhD Thesis, University of South Africa, March, https://uir.unisa.ac.za/bitstream/handle/10500/2936/dissertation_gerberg_%20i.pdf;sequence=1 (last accessed October 2021).
40. CNN (2001) "India shuns calls to talk caste with U.N.," CNN, August 17, https://cnn.com/2001/WORLD/asiapcf/south/08/17/india.caste/ (last accessed October 2021).
41. Nicolas Blarel and Jayita Sarkar (2019) "Substate Organizations as Foreign Policy Agents: New Evidence and Theory from India, Israel, and France," *Foreign Policy Analysis*, July, Vol. 15, No. 3, July, pp. 413–31.
42. Mumtaz Ahmad Shah and Dr. Tarbraz (2020) "India's Israel policy: From Nehru to Modi," *Journal of Critical Reviews*, Vol. 7, No. 9.
43. Browne, "A Perspective on India–Israel Defence and Security Ties," p. 327.
44. Jill Kimball (2021) "Costs of the 20-year war on terror: $8 trillion and 900,000 deaths," News From Brown, September 1, https://brown.edu/news/2021-09-01/costsofwar (last accessed October 2021).

45. Even here, the legacy of Indira Gandhi and the Congress looms large. POTA was passed by the BJP, but it arguably had its roots in another piece of legislation called TADA, passed following the assassination of Indira Gandhi in 1984. Terrorist and Disruptive Activities (Prevention) Act OR TADA that gave the state sweeping powers. It has been reported that by 1994, close to 80,000 people had been arrested under TADA. Just 1% of these detainees were ever convicted of any crime. For more on POTA, read: Jayanth K. Krishnan (2004) "India's Patriot Act: POTA and the Impact on Civil Liberties in the ties in the World's Largest Democracy in Minnesota Journal of Law and Inequality," Vol. 22, No. 2, December.
46. Arundhati Roy (2008) "The monster in the mirror," *Guardian*, December 12, https://theguardian.com/world/2008/dec/12/mumbai-arundhati-roy (last accessed October 2021).
47. Prashad, "Namaste Sharon."
48. Ibid.
49. Associated Press (2003) "Indians protest at Sharon visit," *Guardian*, September 9, https://theguardian.com/world/2003/sep/10/india.israel (last accessed October 2021).
50. Amy Waldman (2003) "The Bond Between India and Israel Grows," *New York Times*, September 11, https://nytimes.com/2003/09/07/world/the-bond-between-india-and-israel-grows.html (last accessed October 2021).
51. MEA (2003) "Delhi Statement on Friendship and Cooperation between India and Israel," Ministry of External Affairs (MEA), September 10, https://mea.gov.in/bilateral-documents.htm?dtl/7730/Delhi+Statement+on+Friendship+and+Cooperation+between+India+and+Israel (last accessed June 2022).
52. India supported the U.S.-led War on Terror, but its parliament passed a resolution in April 2003 against the war in Iraq. This did not stop support for Bush. A 2005 Pew Global Attitudes Survey found that India was the only country out of 16 countries (besides the U.S.) where a majority of those surveyed expressed confidence in Bush. For more info, see https://pewresearch.org/global/2006/02/28/india-pro-america-pro-bush (last accessed May 2021).

53. Joseph A. D'Agostino (2003) "Conservative Spotlight: USINPAC," *Human Events*, December, https://humanevents.com/2003/12/11/conservative-spotlight-usinpac (last accessed May 2021).
54. Amy Waldman (2004) "India and Pakistan: Good Fences Make Good Neighbors," July 4, https://nytimes.com/2004/07/04/world/india-and-pakistan-good-fences-make-good-neighbors.html (last accessed July 2022).
55. Jatin Kumar (2019) "India-Israel cooperation in border Management," Manohar Parrikar Institute for Defence Studies and Analyses, October 19, https://idsa.in/idsanews/india-israel-cooperation-in-border-management-jatin (last accessed July 2022).
56. Bitzinger, "Israeli Arms Transfer to India."
57. Amiram Cohen (2010) "NaanDan Ups India Exports 30x Since Jain Came on Board," *Haaretz*, May 24, https://haaretz.com/1.5046032 (last accessed October 2021).
58. Jonathan Spyer (2021) "The 2008 terror attacks in Mumbai helped shape Israel-India relations," *Jerusalem Post*, November 25, https://jpost.com/international/the-2008-terror-attacks-in-mumbai-helped-shape-israel-india-relations-687000 (last accessed June 2022).
59. Rhys Machold (2016) "Learning from Israel? '26/11' and the anti-politics of urban security governance," *Security Dialogue*, August 1, https://jstor.org/stable/26294164 (last accessed June 2022).
60. Ibid.
61. Ibid.
62. Ritu Sarin (2009) "From Israel, lessons on fighting terror," *Indian Express*, July 21, https://indianexpress.com/article/news-archive/web/from-israel-lessons-on-fighting-terror/ (last accessed June 2022).
63. PTI (2009) "India lacks killer instinct," *Times of India*, July 23, https://timesofindia.indiatimes.com/city/mumbai/india-lacks-killer-instinct/articleshow/4809345.cms (last accessed June 2022).
64. Niharika Sharma (2019) "India's among the world's top three surveillance states," October 16, https://qz.com/india/1728927/

indias-among-the-worlds-top-three-surveillance-states/ (last accessed October 2021).

65. TNN (2010) "Govt to deploy drones for recce along Red corridor," *Economic Times*, April 9, https://economictimes.indiatimes.com/news/politics-and-nation/govt-to-deploy-drones-for-recce-along-red-corridor/articleshow/5776820.cms?from=mdr (last accessed July 2022).
66. Rajya Sabha debates (1994) "Indo-Israeli-ties," Parliament of India: Official debates of Rajya Sabha, Session 171, August 8, https://rsdebate.nic.in/bitstream/123456789/204068/2/IQ_171_08081994_U1819_p132_p133.pdf (last accessed October 2021).
67. Purkayastha, "The military fulcrum of strategic relations," p. 63.
68. Gili Cohen (2013) "Israel's Military Exports Totaled Some $7.5 Billion in 2012," *Haaretz*, July 23, https://haaretz.com/.premium-military-exports-to-asia-leaping-1.5298570 (last accessed October 2021).
69. Purkayastha, "The military fulcrum of strategic relations," p. 65.
70. Bitzinger, "Israeli Arms Transfer to India."
71. Ibid., p. 3.
72. Browne, "A Perspective on India–Israel Defence and Security Ties," p. 328.
73. MEA (2012), "Official Spokesperson's response to a media question on violence in Gaza," Ministry of External Affairs, November 18, https://mea.gov.in/outoging-visit-detail.htm?20823/Official+Spokespersons+response+to+a+media+question+on+violence+in+Gaza (last accessed October 2021).
74. Rajya Sabha (2013), "India's relation with Israel," Parliament of India: Official debates of Rajya Sabha, No. 230, December 9, https://rsdebate.nic.in/bitstream/123456789/627819/2/PQ_230_09122013_U56_p402_p402.pdf (last accessed October 2021).
75. Christophe Jaffrelot (2015) "The Modi-centric BJP 2014 election campaign: new techniques and old tactics," Contemporary South Asia, Vol. 23, No. 2, Special Issue on Indian Elections 2014: Explaining the landslide.

76. BJP (2014) Election Manifesto, BJP, http://library.bjp.org/jspui/bitstream/123456789/252/1/bjp_lection_manifesto_english_2014.pdf p. 1 (last accessed March 2022).
77. Ibid.
78. Ibid.
79. Prem Shankar Jha (2019) "Hindutva Has Nowhere to Go Except Down the Road to Tyranny," *The Wire*, July 4, https://thewire.in/politics/hindutva-muslims-rss-hindu-rashtra (last accessed March 2022).
80. Government of Israel (2014) "Statements by PM Netanyahu and Indian PM Narendra Modi," July 4, https://gov.il/en/departments/news/eventindiaisrael040717 (last accessed March 2022).
81. Interview with Khinvraj Jangid, Director of Jindal Centre for Israel Studies at OP Jindal Global University in New Delhi, August 25, 2001.
82. MEA (2014) "Official Spokesperson's response to a media question on escalation of violence in Gaza and Israel," Ministry of External Affairs, July 10, https://mea.gov.in/outoging-visit-detail.htm?23602/Official+Spokespersons+response+to+a+media+question+on+escalation+of+violence+in+Gaza+and+Israel (last accessed June 2022).
83. Khalid, Saif (2015) "The beginning of an Israel-India 'romance'?" *Al Jazeera English*, July 10, https://aljazeera.com/features/2015/7/10/the-beginning-of-an-israel-india (last accessed October 2021).
84. Barak Ravid (2015) "UN Human Rights Council Adopts Resolution Condemning Israel Over Gaza War Report," *Haaretz*, July 3, https://haaretz.com/.premium-unhrc-condemns-israel-over-gaza-war-inquiry-1.5375179 (last accessed October 2021).
85. Suhashni Haider (2014) "India abstains from UNHRC vote against Israel," *The Hindu*, July 3, https://thehindu.com/news/India-abstains-from-UNHRC-vote-against-Israel/article60340928.ece (last accessed March 2022).
86. Sadanand Dhume (2014) "Revealed: The India-Israel Axis," *Wall Street Journal*, July 23, https://wsj.com/articles/revealed-the-india-israel-axis-1406133666 (last accessed October 2021).

87. Harpeet Bajwa (2014) "Israel to train Punjab cops in anti-terror operations," *Indian Express*, https://indianexpress.com/article/india/india-others/Israel-to-train-punjab-cops-in-antiterror-operations/ (last accessed June 2022).
88. PTI (2018) "IPS officers visit Israel to learn best policing practices," *Economic Times*, July 13, https://economictimes.indiatimes.com/news/defence/ips-officers-visit-israel-to-learn-best-policing-practices/articleshow/48541981.cms (last accessed October 2021).
89. Jatin Kumar (2019) "India-Israel cooperation in border Management," *Manohar Parrikar Institute for Defence Studies and Analyses*, October 19, https://idsa.in/idsanews/india-israel-cooperation-in-border-management-jatin (last accessed July 2022).
90. Israeli Air Force (2015) "Commander Convention. Day 2," IAF, https://iaf.org.il/4473-50213-en/IAF.aspx (last accessed October 2021).
91. Pranab Mukherjee (2015) "Media statement by the president of India upon the conclusion of his state visit to Jordan, Palestine and Israel en route from Tel Aviv to New Delhi," Representative Office of India in Ramallah, October 16, https://roiramallah.gov.in/press.php?id=54 (last accessed March 2022).
92. The number of ITEC training slots was subsequently increased to 150 in 2017.
93. Raphael Ahren (2016) "Israel and India hail growing defence ties as Rivlin visits," *Times of Israel*, November 15, https://timesofisrael.com/israel-and-india-hail-growing-defense-ties-as-rivlin-visits/ (last accessed October 2021).
94. Ibid.
95. MEA (2017) India-Israel Joint Statement during the visit of Prime Minister to Israel, Ministry of External Affairs, July 5, https://mea.gov.in/bilateral-documents.htm?dtl/28593/IndiaIsrael_Joint_Statement_during_the_visit_of_Prime_Minister_to_Israel_July_5_2017 (last accessed October 2021).
96. Press Trust of India (2017) "Pacts worth $4.3 billion inked at India-Israel CEO forum: Ficci," *Hindustan Times*, July 6, https://hindustantimes.com/india-news/pacts-worth-4-3-billion-inked-at-india-israel-ceo-forum-ficci/story-EGNs6NGfqQBqdwJoEhhvKI.html (last accessed October 2021).

97. *Haaretz* (2017) India Air Force in Israel for First-ever Joint Military Exercise, *Haaretz*, November 2, https://haaretz.com/israel-news/india-air-force-in-israel-for-first-ever-joint-military-exercise-1.5462139 (last accessed October 2021).
98. Anna Ahronheim (2017) "Indian special forces in Israel to train with the IDF's most elite units," *Jerusalem Post*, November 19, https://jpost.com/Israel-News/India-Israel/Indian-special-forces-in-Israel-to-train-with-the-IDFs-most-elite-units-513820 (last accessed October 2021).
99. Narendra Modi (2018) "Here's what Israeli PM Netanyahu said about India and PM Modi," YouTube, https://youtube.com/watch?v=n1SxGdpbsWA&ab_channel=NarendraModi (last accessed October 2021).
100. Azad Essa (2022) "India and Israel: The arms trade in charts and numbers," *Middle East Eye*, June 3, https://middleeasteye.net/news/india-israel-arms-trade-numbers (last accessed June 2022).
101. PTI (2018) "Grand Collar of the State of Palestine' by President Mahmoud Abbas, recognizing his key contribution to promote relations between India and Palestine," *The Hindu*, https://thehindu.com/news/national/modi-conferred-grand-collar-of-the-state-of-palestine/article22714293.ece (last accessed October 2021).
102. Aseel Al-Akhras (2018) "India and Palestine . . . strong and solid historical relations," *Wafa*, February 10, http://wafa.ps/ar_page.aspx?id=7Cy7Fga81091068755 4a7Cy7Fg (last accessed October 2021).
103. PTI (2018) "Amit Shah congratulates Narendra Modi for being conferred 'Grand Collar of the State of Palestine,'" *FirstPost*, February 11, https://firstpost.com/india/amit-shah-congratulates-narendra-modi-for-being-conferred-grand-collar-of-the-state-of-palestine-4345643.html (last accessed October 2021).
104. Seán Federico-O'Murchú (2020) "Read the full statement by the U.S., Israel and UAE on normalizing Israel-UAE relations," CNN, August 13, https://edition.cnn.com/2020/08/13/middleeast/mideast-trump-full-statement-uae-israel-intl/index.html (last accessed October 2021).

105. Michelle Kelemen (2020) "Morocco Agrees To Join Trump Administration's Abraham Accords," NPR, December 10, https://npr.org/2020/12/10/945136662/morocco-agrees-to-join-trump-administrations-abraham-accords (last accessed October 2021).
106. Middle East Eye (2021) "Sudan signs agreement normalizing ties with Israel," *Middle East Eye*, January 6, https://middleeasteye.net/news/sudan-us-israel-sign-abraham-accords (last accessed October 2021).
107. Jonathan Cook (2020) "How Gulf states became business partners in Israel's occupation," *Middle East Eye*, December 14, https://middleeasteye.net/opinion/how-gulf-states-became-business-partners-israels-occupation (last accessed June 2022).
108. Anshel Pfeffer (2020) "Don't Compare MBZ and Bibi to Sadat and Begin—the UAE-Israel Deal Is Much Bigger Than Peace," *Haaretz*, August 18, https://haaretz.com/middle-east-news/.premium-bibi-and-mbz-aren-t-begin-and-sadat-uae-deal-is-much-bigger-than-peace-1.9079484 (last accessed October 2021).
109. Fay Abuelgasim (2020) "Model diplomacy: Israeli waves flag in UAE pajama photoshoot," Associated Press, September 8, https://apnews.com/article/united-arab-emirates-dubai-entertainment-israel-diplomacy-95a119884c2f6f8d88c658off3cb3e16 (last accessed October 2021).
110. Mohammed Soliman (2021) "An Indo-Abrahamic alliance on the rise: How India, Israel, and the UAE are creating a new transregional order," *Middle East Institute*, July 28, https://mei.edu/publications/indo-abrahamic-alliance-rise-how-india-israel-and-uae-are-creating-new-transregional (last accessed October 2021).
111. Dipanjan Roy Chaudhury (2019) India invited as Guest of Honour for 1st time ever by OIC; Delhi's big pitch in Islamic World, *Economic Times*, February 23, https://economictimes.indiatimes.com/news/politics-and-nation/india-invited-as-guest-of-honour-for-1st-time-ever-by-oic-delhis-big-pitch-in-islamic-world/articleshow/68125198.cms (last accessed October 2021).
112. Mohammed Soliman (2021) "An Indo-Abrahamic alliance on the rise: How India, Israel, and the UAE are creating a new transregional order," *Middle East Institute*, July 28, https://mei.

edu/publications/indo-abrahamic-alliance-rise-how-india-israel-and-uae-are-creating-new-transregional (last accessed October 2021).

113. Interview with Noam Chomsky, June 26, 2021.
114. Suhashni Haider (2021) "India, Israel, UAE, U.S. decide to launch quadrilateral economic forum," *The Hindu*, October 19, https://thehindu.com/news/national/jaishankar-takes-part-in-new-quadrilateral-with-israel-uae-and-us/article37064989.ece (last accessed October 2021).
115. Seth J. Frantzman, (2021) "The Israel-UAE-India-US partnership is a quiet revolution," *Jerusalem Post*, October 19, https://jpost.com/international/the-israel-uae-india-us-partnership-is-a-quiet-revolution-analysis-682452 (last accessed October 2021).
116. Husain Haqqani and Aparna Pande (2022) "Without summits, a West Asia 'Quad' makes progress," *The Hill*, May 28, https://thehill.com/opinion/international/3504446-without-summits-a-west-asia-quad-makes-progress (last accessed June 2022).
117. ORF (2018) Speech by Sunjoy Joshi, on ORF, January, https://orfonline.org/wp-content/uploads/2018/01/Speech_by_Sunjoy_joshi.pdf (last accessed March 2022).
118. Arundhati Roy (2014) *Capitalism: A ghost story*, Haymarket Books, p. 71.
119. ORF (2018) "Inaugural Address by Benjamin Netanyahu, Prime Minister of Israel," Raisina Dialogues, January 16, https://youtube.com/watch?v=AQ41bY5UnEo&ab_channel=ORF (last accessed October 2021).
120. Seth J. Frantzman (2020) "From Greece To India, via Israel: A New Middle East Alliance Is Expanding," *Newsweek*, November 27, https://newsweek.com/greece-india-via-israel-new-middle-east-alliance-expanding-opinion-1550780 (last accessed June 2022).
121. MFA (2017) "Statement by PM Netanyahu at his meeting with Indian PM Modi," Ministry of Foreign Affairs, July 5, https://embassies.gov.il/MFA/PressRoom/2017/Pages/Statement-by-PM-Netanyahu-at-his-meeting-with-Indian-PM-Modi-5-July-2017.aspx (last accessed June 2021).

122. In 2021, India released a list of 152 military items it was willing to export. Some of the big items included: Cruise missiles, torpedoes and light combat helicopters.
123. Azad Essa (2022) "India and Israel: The arms trade in charts and numbers," *Middle East Eye*, June 3, https://middleeasteye.net/news/india-israel-arms-trade-numbers (last accessed June 2022).
124. Nayanima Basu and Snehesh Alex Philip (2021) "Buy weapons from us, India says as it pushes exports to compete with China in neighbourhood," *The Print*, March 16, https://theprint.in/defence/buy-weapons-from-us-india-says-as-it-pushes-exports-to-compete-with-china-in-neighbourhood/622216/ (last accessed October 2021).
125. OurCrowd (2017) "OurCrowd, Motorola Solutions and Reliance Industries Launch Incubator to give Jerusalem Startups a Global Competitive Edge," May 30, https://blog.ourcrowd.com/incubator/ (last accessed October 2021).
126. WhoProfits (2017) "Motorola Solutions," https://whoprofits.org/company/motorola-solutions/ (last accessed October 2021).
127. Rahul Wadke (2018) Reliance Defence, Israeli company to make Kalashnikov weapons, *The Hindu*, January 15, https://thehindubusinessline.com/companies/reliance-defence-israeli-company-to-make-kalashnikov-weapons/article9345795.ece (last accessed October 2021).
128. HRW (2021), "Gaza: Apparent War Crimes During May Fighting," in Human Rights Watch, July 27, https://hrw.org/news/2021/07/27/gaza-apparent-war-crimes-during-may-fighting (last accessed October 2021).
129. Shubajhit Roy (2021) "Palestine to India: Silence at UN body stifles fight for rights," *Indian Express*, June 3, https://indianexpress.com/article/india/palestine-to-india-silence-at-un-body-stifles-fight-for-rights-7341617/ (last accessed October 2021).
130. Ibid.
131. Ro Khanna, "Release: Khanna, Sherman, Schweikert Urge Stronge US-India Defense Partnership," July 8, Congressman Ro Khanna, https://khanna.house.gov/media/press-releases/release-khanna-sherman-schweikert-urge-stronger-us-india-defense-partnership (last accessed July 2022).

132. Arundhati Roy (2021) "This is no ordinary spying. Our most intimate selves are now exposed," *Guardian*, July 26, https://theguardian.com/commentisfree/2021/jul/27/spying-pegasus-project-states-arundhati-roy (last accessed September 2021).
133. Swati Chaturvedi (2016) *I am a Troll: Inside the BJP's Secret Digital Army*, Juggernaut, New Delhi.
134. Ronen Bergman and Mark Mazzetti (2022) "The Battle for the World's Most Powerful Cyberweapon," *New York Times*, January 28, https://nytimes.com/2022/01/28/magazine/nso-group-israel-spyware.html (last accessed July 2022).
135. Tribune News Service (2021) "Use of Pegasus spyware on Indians a treason, says Rahul Gandhi; demands Shah's resignation," *Tribune India*, July 23, https://tribuneindia.com/news/nation/use-of-pegasus-spyware-on-indians-a-treason-says-rahul-gandhi-demands-shahs-resignation-287151 (last accessed October 2021).
136. Swati Chaturvedi (2020) "I Was Targeted by NSO Spyware. Here's How Israel Is Helping Modi Undermine India's Democracy, *Haaretz*, July 25, https://haaretz.com/israel-news/.premium-i-was-targeted-by-nso-israel-is-helping-modi-undermine-india-s-democracy-1.10028100 (last accessed October 2021).

Chapter 3

1. V.D. Savarkar (1923) "Essentials of Hindutva," Savakar, http://savarkar.org/en/index.html (last accessed October 2021).
2. M.S. Golwalkar (1939) *We or our nationhood defined*, 2006 edition, Pharos Publishing, Delhi, pp. 87–8.
3. Theodor Herzl (1960) *The Complete Diaries of Theodor Herzl, Book One: May–June 1895*, Theodor Herzl Foundation, Inc., New York, p. 56.
4. Ajaz Ashraf (2016) "History revisited: Was Veer Savarkar really all that brave?" *Scroll*, May 27, https://scroll.in/article/808709/the-hollow-myth-of-veer-savarkar (last accessed October 2021).
5. In 1928, the booklet was republished as "What is a Hindu?"
6. David Gilmartin and Bruce B. Lawrence (eds.) (2000) *Beyond Turk and Hindu: Rethinking Religious Identities in Islamicate South Asia*, University Press of Florida, Gainesville, FL.

7. Savarkar, "Essentials of Hindutva."
8. Ibid.
9. Vaibhav Purandare (2019) "Hindutva is not the same as Hinduism said Savarkar," *Telegraph India*, August 22, https://telegraphindia.com/india/hindutva-is-not-the-same-as-hinduism-said-savarkar/cid/1699550 (last accessed November 2021).
10. Jyotirmaya Sharma (2011) *Hindutva: Exploring the idea of Hindu nationalism*, Penguin Books, New Delhi, p. 11.
11. Chetan Bhatt (2001) *Hindu Nationalism: origins, ideologies and modern myths*, Routledge, New York, p. 10.
12. Sharma, *Hindutva: Exploring the Idea of Hindu Nationalism*, pp. 11–13.
13. Ibid., p. 11.
14. The Vedas are considered among the oldest of Hindu scriptures. Savakar, however, believed that one could be Hindu without believing the religious authority of Vedas.
15. Sharma, *Hindutva: Exploring the Idea of Hindu Nationalism*, p. 14.
16. Ibid., p. 11.
17. Anustap Basu (2020) *Hindutva as Political Monotheism*, Duke University Press, North Carolina.
18. Sharma, *Hindutva: Exploring the Idea of Hindu Nationalism*, p. 12.
19. Kancha Ilaiah (2002) *Why I am not a Hindu*, Samya, Calcutta, p. viii. According to Ilaiah, "Dalit" is a Marathi word that means "suppressed and exploited people." Ilaiah writes that "the term 'Dalit' became really popular only after the emergence of the 'Dalit Panthers' movement in Maharashtra in the 1970s. 'Dalit' as it is usually understood encompasses only the so-called untouchable castes."
20. Ilaiah, *Why I am not a Hindu*, p. 101.
21. Ibid., p. 43.
22. Ibid.
23. Basu, *Hindutva as Political Monotheism*, p. 2.
24. Divya Dwivedi, Shaj Mohan, and J. Reghu (2020) "The Hindu Hoax: How upper castes invented a Hindu majority," *Caravan*, December 31, https://caravanmagazine.in/religion/how-upper-castes-invented-hindu-majority (last accessed June 2022).
25. Sharma, *Hindutva: Exploring the Idea of Hindu Nationalism*, p. 7.

26. Sharik Laliwala (2019) "During the Quit India Movement, the Hindu Mahasabha Played the British Game," *The Wire*, August 8, https://thewire.in/history/quit-india-movement-hindu-mahasabha-british (last accessed November 2021).
27. Golwalkar (1939) *We or our nationhood defined*, p. 55.
28. Marzia Casolari's painstaking work on the links between Hindu nationalists and European fascists is an incredible feat. See Marzia Casolari (2000) "Hindutva's Foreign Tie-up in the 1930s: Archival evidence," *Economic and Political Weekly*, January 22, p. 218.
29. Ibid.
30. B.S. Moonje's diary quoted in Casolari, "Hindutva's Foreign Tie-up in the 1930s: Archival evidence," p. 220.
31. Ibid.
32. NMML, Moonje paper, subject files, n24, 1932–6, "The Central Military Education Society," undated, estimated 1935, in Marzia Casolari (2000) "Hindutva's Foreign Tie-up in the 1930s: Archival evidence," *Economic and Political Weekly*, January 22, p. 221.
33. Casolari, "Hindutva's Foreign Tie-up in the 1930s," p. 219.
34. Bimal Prasad (1962) *The origins of Indian foreign policy: The Indian National Congress and World Affairs, 1885–1947*, second edition, Bookland, Calcutta, pp 84–5.
35. J. Nehru (1946) *The Discovery of India*, Oxford University Press, New Delhi, p. 18.
36. MSA, Home Special Department, 60D (g) Pt II, 1937, "Extract from the weekly confidential report of the District Magistrate, October 21, 1938, in Casolari, "Hindutva's Foreign Tie-up in the 1930s," p. 223.
37. Savakar 'India's foreign policy', August 1, 1938, Hindu Mahasabha, quoted in Casolari, "Hindutva's Foreign Tie-up in the 1930s," p. 223.
38. Ibid.
39. Spokesperson of the Hindu Mahasabha, March 25, 1939, quoted by M. Hauner, in Casolari, "Hindutva's Foreign Tie-up in the 1930s," p. 224.
40. Speech by Savarkar on July 29, 1939 in Pune, quoted in Casolari, "Hindutva's Foreign Tie-up in the 1930s," p. 223.
41. Eviane Leidig (2020) "Hindutva as a variant of right-wing extremism," *Patterns of Prejudice*, Vol. 54, No. 3, May, pp. 215–37.

42. Political Zionism focused on a state, at times, any state, anywhere; Cultural Zionism focused on revitalizing the future state as a center of Jewish culture and protection of Judaism; Labor Zionism focused on building an equitable, purportedly left, social democracy; revisionist Zionism or right-wing Zionism, opposed social democracy and was enamored by the fascist movements of Europe.
43. Arie M. Dubnov (2016) "Notes on the Zionist passage to India, or: The analogical imagination and its boundaries," *Journal of Israeli History*, Vol. 35, No. 2, pp. 177–214.
44. Edward Said (1979) *The Question of Palestine*, Times Books, New York, p. 29.
45. Abdul-Wahab Kayalli (1977) "Zionism and Imperialism: The Historical Origins," *Journal of Palestine Studies*, Vol. 6, No. 3, Spring, p. 111.
46. Speech by Savarkar in 1939, Hindu Mahasabha, quoted in Casolari, "Hindutva's Foreign Tie-up in the 1930s," p. 224.
47. Harbilas Sarda (1906) *Hindu superiority: an attempt to determine the position of the Hindu race in the scale of nations*, Rajputana Printing Work, Ajmer, p. xxxi.
48. Satadru Sen (2015) "Fascism without Fascists? A comparative look at Hindutva and Zionism," *Journal of South Asian Studies*, Vol. 38, No. 4, p. 702.
49. M.S. Golwalkar (2006 [1939]) *We or our nationhood defined*, Pharos Publishing, Delhi, p. 99.
50. Moses Hess (2019 [1862]) *Rome and Jerusalem: A Study in Jewish Nationalism*, Anodos Books, p. 45.
51. Ze'ev Jabotinsky (1923) "The Iron Wall," November 4, http://en.jabotinsky.org/media/9747/the-iron-wall.pdf (last accessed November 2021).
52. Ibid.
53. Truschke, Audrey (2020) "Hindutva's dangerous rewriting of history," *South Asia Multidisciplinary academic journal*, Vol. 24/25, https://journals.openedition.org/samaj/6636 (last accessed November 2021).
54. Khinvraj Jangid (2021) "Imagining Nations, Creating States: Nehru, Ben-Gurion and an Analogical Study of India and Israel in Post-colonial Asia," *Israel Studies*, Vol. 26, No. 1.

55. Vazira Fazila-Yacoobali Zamindar (2010) *The Long Partition and the Making of Modern South Asia*, Columbia University Press, New York.
56. Prasad, *The origins of Indian foreign policy*, p. 10.
57. Bhatt, *Hindu Nationalism*, p. 145.
58. Ibid., p. 159.
59. Ibid., p. 163.
60. Gyan Prakash (2019) *Emergency Chronicles: Indira Gandhi and Democracy's Turning Point*, Princeton University Press, Princeton, NJ.
61. Prakash, *Emergency Chronicles*, p. 82.
62. Shoaib Daniyal (2016) "Looking back: The first Parliament attack took place in 1966—and was carried out by gau rakshaks," *Scroll*, August 28, https://scroll.in/article/814368/did-you-know-the-first-parliament-attack-took-place-in-1966-and-was-carried-out-by-gau-rakshaks (last accessed November 2021).
63. Prakash, *Emergency Chronicles*, p. 147.
64. P.R. Kumarasamy (2010) *India's Israel Policy*, Columbia University Press, New York, p. 241.
65. Achin Vanaik (2021) "Palestine Question and Changing Indian Perspectives," May 26, Facebook, https://facebook.com/IndiaRadicalSocialist/videos/2934821333428351 (last accessed October 2021).
66. Kumarasamy, *India's Israel Policy*, p. 241.
67. Indira Gandhi (1975) "Speech and Proclamation," *New York Times*, June 27, https://nytimes.com/1975/06/27/archives/speech-and-proclamation.html (last accessed November 2021).
68. Gyan Prakash (2019) *Emergency Chronicles: Indira Gandhi and Democracy's Turning Point*, Princeton University Press, Princeton, NJ, p. 175.
69. Ibid., p. 375.
70. Sanjeev Kelkar (2011) *Lost Years of the RSS*, Sage Publications, New Delhi, p. 133, cited in Edward Anderson and Patrick Clibbens (2018) "'Smugglers of Truth': The Indian diaspora, Hindu nationalism, and the Emergency (1975–77)," *Modern Asian Studies*, Vol. 52, No. 5 p. 1735.
71. Anderson and Clibbens, "'Smugglers of Truth,'" p. 1731.

72. Ibid.
73. Interview with Khinvraj Jangid, director of the Jindal Centre for Israel Studies, at OP Jindal Global University in New Delhi, August 25, 2021.
74. Prabash K Dutta (2018) "Israel's invisible hand behind Operation Blue Star of 1984," *India Today*, June 6, https://indiatoday.in/india/story/operation-blue-star-special-group-commandos-mossad-training-israel-1251738-2018-06-06 (last accessed June 2022).
75. Anderson and Clibbens, "'Smugglers of Truth,'" p. 1733.
76. Ibid., p. 1734.
77. Interview with Khinvraj Jangid, Director of Jindal Centre for Israel Studies, at OP Jindal Global University in New Delhi, August 25, 2021.
78. Ram Madhav (2021) "The Sangh and Modernity," *Open Magazine*, June 18, https://openthemagazine.com/essays/the-sangh-and-modernity/ (last accessed November 2021).

Chapter 4

1. Norman Finkelstein (2012) "Jewish American Relationship with Israel at the Crossroads," The New School YouTube channel, October 8, https://youtube.com/watch?v=6uxAJhF_3Iw&ab_channel=TheNewSchool (last accessed December 2021).
2. Don Waxman (2010) "The Israel Lobbies: A Survey of the Pro-Israel Community in the United States," *Israel Studies Forum* Vol. 25, No. 1, Summer, p. 9.
3. Drop the ADL (2020) "The ADL is not an ally," https://droptheadl.org/the-adl-is-not-an-ally/ (last accessed April 2022).
4. Paul Findley (1985) *They dare to speak out: People and Institutions Confront Israel's Lobby*, Lawrence Hill and Company, Westport, CT.
5. Finkelstein, "Jewish American Relationship with Israel at the Crossroads."
6. JTA (1987) "ADL Report Traces India's Ostracism of Israel over Several Decades," JTA, May 8, https://jta.org/archive/adl-report-traces-indias-ostracism-of-israel-over-several-decades (last accessed November 2021).

7. Nicolas Blarel (2015) *The Evolution of India's Israel Policy: Continuity, Change and Compromise since 1922*, Oxford, UK, p. 226.
8. Shekhar Gupta (1987) "US House committee to slash by $15 mn the proposed $50 mn development aid to India," *India Today*, April 30, https://indiatoday.in/magazine/international/story/19870430-us-house-committee-to-slash-by-15-mn-the-proposed-50-mn-development-aid-to-india-798789-1987-04-30 (last accessed November 2021).
9. P.R. Kumarasamy (2010) *India's Israel Policy*, Columbia University Press, New York, p. 227.
10. Robert Lifton (2012) *An entrepreneur's Journey: Stories From a Life in Business and Personal Diplomacy*, AuthorHouse, Bloomington, p. 256, cited in Blarel, *The Evolution of India's Israel Policy*, p. 227.
11. Kumarasamy, *India's Israel Policy*, p. 228.
12. Rajya Sabha debates (1991) "Upgrading ties with Israel," Parliament of India: Official debates of Rajya Sabha, Session 147, August 11, 1988, https://rsdebate.nic.in/bitstream/123456789/279828/1/PQ_147_11081988_U2011_p39_p41.pdf (last accessed October 2021).
13. "Steve Lohr (1988) "Arafat says PLO accepted Israel," *New York Times*, December 8, https://nytimes.com/1988/12/08/world/arafat-says-plo-accepted-israel.html (last accessed June 2022).
14. Kumarasamy, *India's Israel Policy*, p. 228.
15. JTA (1987) "ADL Report Traces India's Ostracism of Israel over Several Decades," JTA, May 8, https://jta.org/archive/adl-report-traces-indias-ostracism-of-israel-over-several-decades (last accessed November 2021).
16. Shreya Sarkar (2021) "Indian Americans Are Progressing, But With Power Comes Responsibility," *The Quint*, September 12, https://thequint.com/us-nri-news/indian-americans-in-us-and-what-does-the-expansion-of-their-footprint-means-us-census-2020#read-more (last accessed November 2021).
17. Vijay Prashad (2012) *Uncle Swamy: South Asians in America Today*, The New Press, New York.
18. Arun Venugopal (2021) "The Truth Behind Indian American Exceptionalism," *The Atlantic*, Jan/Feb, https://theatlantic.com/magazine/archive/2021/01/the-making-of-a-model-minority/617258/ (last accessed April 2022).

19. Sumitra Badrinathan, Devesh Kapur and Milan Vaishnav (2020) "How Will Indian Americans Vote? Results From the 2020 Indian American Attitudes," Survey, in Carnegie Endowment for International Peace, October 14, https://carnegieendowment.org/files/IAAS_full_final.pdf (last accessed December 2021).
20. According to the HSS (UK) website, the HSS branch in the United Kingdom was started by Indians from East Africa, https://hssuk.org/about/ (last accessed September 2021).
21. Williams (1988) cited in Prema Kurian (2007) *A place at the multicultural table: The Development of an American Hinduism*, Rutgers University Press, New Brunswick, NJ, p. 52.
22. Walter K. Andersen and Shridhar D. Damle (2018) "How the RSS operates in foreign countries in general and the USA in particular," *Scroll*, Aug 9, https://scroll.in/article/889509/how-the-rss-operates-in-foreign-countries-in-general-and-the-usa-in-particular (last accessed September 2021), excerpted from Walter K. Andersen and Shridhar D. Damle (2018) *The RSS: A View to the Inside*, Penguin Random House India, Haryana, India.
23. L.K. Advani cited in Neha Thirani Bagri (2016) "How the BJP turned a small band of non-resident Indians into a global PR machine" September 28, https://qz.com/india/790858/?utm_term=mucp (last accessed September 2021).
24. Bagri, "How the BJP turned a small band of non-resident Indians into a global PR machine."
25. Edward A. Gargan (1992) "At least 200 killed in India as Muslim-Hindu riots rage," *New York Times*, December 8, https://nytimes.com/1992/12/08/world/at-least-200-killed-in-india-as-muslim-hindu-riots-rage.html html (last accessed June 2022).
26. Edward Anderson and Patrick Clibbens (2018) "'Smugglers of Truth': The Indian diaspora, Hindu nationalism, and the Emergency (1975–77)," *Modern Asian Studies*, Vol. 52, No. 5, p. 1757.
27. Pieter Friedrich (2020) "Money Trail: Diaspora Diplomacy's Financial Whitewashing of Hindutva," September 27, *The Polis Project*, https://thepolisproject.com/money-trail-diaspora-diplomacys-financial-whitewashing-of-hindutva/#.YUOiMtNKiBt (last accessed September 2021).
28. Anderson and Clibbens, "'Smugglers of Truth,'" p. 1758.
29. Ibid.

30. Arun Chaudhuri (2012) "American Hindu Activism and the Politics of Anxiety," PhD dissertation, Graduate Program in Anthropology York University Toronto, Ontario September 2012, p. 64, https://collectionscanada.gc.ca/obj/thesescanada/vol2/003/NR92758.pdf?is_thesis=1&oclc_number=913611576 (last accessed November 2021).
31. Kurien, *A place at the multicultural table*, p. 52.
32. Ibid.
33. VHP-A (1997) American Hindus Against Defamation (AHAD), https://ahad.hindunet.org/ (last accessed December 2021).
34. Prashad, *Uncle Swamy: South Asians in America Today*, p. 55.
35. Arthur J, Pais (1999) "*Bhai* Ackerman hails growing Israel-India ties on Rediff," September 20, https://rediff.com/news/1999/sep/20us.htm (last accessed September 2021).
36. Carl Jaison (2019) "India's cheerleaders in the US Congress – A preview," Observer Research Foundation, July 29, https://orfonline.org/expert-speak/indias-cheerleaders-in-the-u-s-congress-a-preview-53545/ (last accessed August 2022).
37. Prashad, *Uncle Swamy: South Asians in America Today*, p. 51.
38. Chaudhuri "American Hindu Activism and the Politics of Anxiety."
39. Muzaffar Chisti (2007) "The rise of remittances to India: A closer look," *Migration Policy*, February 1, https://migrationpolicy.org/article/rise-remittances-india-closer-look (last accessed December 2021).
40. Ibid.
41. Ibid.
42. Interview with a Dalit organizer, May 16, 2022.
43. Kurian, *A place at the multicultural table*.
44. Ingrid Therwath (2012) "Cyber-hindutva: Hindu nationalism, the diaspora and the Web," *Social Science Information*, Vol. 51, No. 4, p. 551–77.
45. Dean E. Murphy (2001) "Two Unlikely Allies Come Together in Fight Against Muslims," *New York Times*, June 2, https://nytimes.com/2001/06/02/nyregion/two-unlikely-allies-come-together-in-fight-against-muslims.html (last accessed May 2021).

46. "Meir Kahane (1931–1990)," *Jewish Virtual Library*, https://jewishvirtuallibrary.org/rabbi-meir-kahane (last accessed May 2021).
47. Therwath, "Cyber-hindutva: Hindu nationalism, the diaspora and the Web."
48. Murphy, "Two Unlikely Allies Come Together in Fight Against Muslims."
49. The website "Hindu Unity" was registered until 2015. It no longer exists.
50. Prashad, *Uncle Swamy: South Asians in America Today*, p. 91.
51. Allison Marz Freedman (2009) "USINPAC and the U.S.-India Nuclear Deal: Lasting Influence or One-Shot Victory?" March 1, *CUREJ: College Undergraduate Research Electronic Journal*, University of Pennsylvania, p. 43.
52. Ganesh S. Lakshman (2002) "American Jews moot India-US-Israel coalition against terror," *Hindustan Times*, September 14, cited in Amit Gupta (2004) "The Indian Diaspora's Political Efforts in the United States," ORF, September, https://orfonline.org/wp-content/uploads/2004/09/OccasionalPaper_n14.pdf (last accessed May 2021).
53. Robert M. Hathaway (2004) "Washington's new strategic partnership," *Indian Seminar*, https://india-seminar.com/2004/538/538%20robert%20m.%20hathaway.htm (last accessed May 2021).
54. Prashad, *Uncle Swamy: South Asians in America Today*, p. 67.
55. Raja Swamy (2004) "Zionism and Hindutva in the U.S.," *Ghadar*, p. 2 http://ghadar.insaf.net/June2004/pdf/zionism.pdf (last accessed November 2021).
56. Sangay Mishra (2016) *Desis Divided: The Political Lives of South Asian Americans*, University of Minnesota Press, Minneapolis, MN.
57. James Mann (2014) "Why Narendra Modi Was Banned From the U.S.," *Wall Street Journal*, May 2, https://wsj.com/articles/why-narendra-modi-was-banned-from-the-u-s-1399062010 (last accessed December 2021).
58. Narendra Modi (2014) "Full text of PM Modi's speech at UNGA," *Business Standard*, September 28, https://business-standard.com/article/current-affairs/full-text-of-pm-modi-s-speech-at-unga-114092800002_1.html (last accessed December 2021).

59. Vivian Yee (2014) "At Madison Square Garden, Chants, Cheers and Roars for Modi," September 28, *New York Times*, https://nytimes.com/2014/09/29/nyregion/at-madison-square-garden-chants-cheers-and-roars-for-modi.html (last accessed December 2021).
60. Narendra Modi (2014) "Text of Prime Minister Shri Narendra Modi's address to the Indian community at Madison Square Garden, New York," Prime Minister's Office, September 28, https://pib.gov.in/newsite/PrintRelease.aspx?relid=136737 (last accessed December 2021).
61. Mudasir Ahmed (2019) "Deployment of Additional Troops: Kashmiris Suspect 'Sinister' Motives," *The Wire*, July 27, https://thewire.in/government/kashmir-additional-troops-rumours-valley (last accessed June 2022).
62. Anirbam Baumik (2019) "India explains not allowing foreign journalists in J&K," *Deccan Herald*, November 15, https://deccanherald.com/national/india-explains-not-allowing-foreign-journalists-in-jk-776602.html (last accessed June 2022).
63. I attended Stand with Kashmir events and helped volunteers connect with journalists.
64. Dharma Warrior translates roughly into "Justice warrior."
65. Shoaib Danyaal (2020) "CAA was passed three months ago. Why has the Modi government still not implemented it?" *Scroll*, https://scroll.in/article/955754/caa-was-passed-three-months-ago-why-has-the-modi-government-still-not-implemented-it (last accessed December 2021).
66. Congress (2019) "H.Res.745—Urging the Republic of India to end the restrictions on communications and mass detentions in Jammu and Kashmir as swiftly as possible and preserve religious freedom for all residents," Congress.gov https://congress.gov/bill/116th-congress/house-resolution/745/cosponsors?searchResultViewType=expanded&KWICView=false (last accessed June 2022).
67. Rashmee Kumar and Akela Lacy (2020) "India lobbies to stifle criticism, control messaging in US Congress amid rising anti-Muslim violence," in *Intercept*, March 16, https://theintercept.com/2020/03/16/india-lobbying-us-congress/ (last accessed June 2022).

68. Niha Masih (2021) "Under fire from Hindu nationalist groups, U.S.-based scholars of South Asia worry about academic freedom," *Washington Post*, October 3, https://washingtonpost.com/world/2021/10/03/india-us-universities-hindutva/ (last accessed June 2022).
69. Feminist Critical Hindu Studies Collective (2021) "Hinduphobia is a smokescreen for Hindu nationalists," *Religion News Service*, September 10, https://religionnews.com/2021/09/10/hinduphobia-is-a-smokescreen-for-hindu-nationalists-dismantling-global-hindutva-conference/ (last accessed June 2022).
70. Mat McDermott (2020) "HAF supports US students rallying around 'Holi For Unity,'" Hindu American Foundation, March 5, https://hinduamerican.org/press/hindu-american-foundation-holi-for-unity (last accessed June 2022).
71. International Jewish Anti-Zionist Network (2015) "The Business of Backlash: The Attack on the Palestinian Movement and Other Movements for Social Justice," IJAN, March, http://ijan.org/resources/business-of-backlash/ (last accessed June 2022).
72. Center for American Progress (2011) "Fear, Inc. The Roots of the Islamophobia Network in America," Centre for American Progress, https://palestineportal.org/wp-content/uploads/2016/10/CAP_FearInc_RootsOfIslamophobiaNetworkInAmerica.pdf (last accessed June 2022).
73. Findley, *They dare to speak out*, p. 181.
74. Ibid., p. 180.
75. Ibid.
76. Radhika Sainath (2021) "When It Comes to Palestine, Free Speech Rights Are Under Attack," *Jacobin*, May 23, https://jacobinmag.com/2021/05/palestinian-israeli-conflict-occupation-free-speech-palestine-exception (last accessed November 2021).
77. Alex Kane (2018) "It's killing a student movement: Canary Mission's Blacklist of Pro-Palestine Activists is taking a toll," *Intercept*, November 22, https://theintercept.com/2018/11/22/israel-boycott-canary-mission-blacklist/ (last accessed November 2021).
78. VIF (2016) Interaction with Daniel Pipes, VIF, https://vifindia.org/event/report/2016/february/27/interaction-with-

daniel-pipes-president-of-the-middle-east-forum (last accessed December 2021).

79. RHC (2019) "On Present Danger: China," *Republican Hindu Coalition*, August 20, https://rhc-usa.org/2019/08/political-all-stars-and-top-business-leaders-join-to-celebrate-prime-minister-modis-landslide-victory-and-expose-chinas-unrestricted-warfare-against-us-manfactrers/ (last accessed June 2022).
80. Martha Lee (2020) "Stand With Kashmir not an innocent hashtag, it supports violent Islamists and terrorists," *The Print*, May 26, https://theprint.in/opinion/stand-with-kashmir-not-innocent-supports-violent-islamists-terrorists/429425/?amp&__twitter_impression=true (last accessed December 2021).
81. Clifford Smith (2020) "BDS and the Islamic lobby in US has found a new target after Israel—democratic India," *The Print*, December 17, https://theprint.in/opinion/bds-and-the-islamic-lobby-in-us-has-found-a-new-target-after-israel-democratic-india/532861/ (last accessed December 2021).
82. Vinayak Chuturvedi (2020) "Annoy the Alt-Right in the U.S. today, and you could get 'swatted,'" *The Hindu*, November 7, https://thehindu.com/society/annoy-the-alt-right-in-the-us-today-and-you-could-get-swatted/article33038406.ece (last accessed December 2021).
83. Audrey Truckhe (2021) "Hindu Supremacists Threaten Academic Freedom in the United States," *Academe Blog* https://academeblog.org/2021/09/18/hindu-supremacists-threaten-academic-freedom-in-the-united-states/ (last accessed December 2021).
84. Interview with Shreeya Singh on December 7, 2021.
85. Interview with Ather Zia, Assistant Professor of Anthropology at University of Colorado, November 24, 2021.
86. Ibid.
87. Ibid.
88. Sunaina Mitra (2018) *Boycott! The Academy and Justice for Palestine*, University of California Press, Oakland, p. 123.
89. Vinayak Chaturvedi (2021) "The Hindu Right and Attacks on Academic Freedom in the U.S.," *The Nation*, December 1, https://thenation.com/article/culture/hindu-right-academic-freedom/ (last accessed December 2021).

90. Interview with Dheepa Sundaram, December 8, 2021.
91. HAF (2019) "Newly released US government statistics show 14 cases of hate crimes targeting Hindu Americans in 2018," Hindu American Foundation, November 14, https://hinduamerican.org/press/anti-hindu-rate-crimes-united-states-rise-fbi-report (last accessed June 2022).
92. Pramila Jayapal (2019) "India's foreign minister refused to meet me. I won't stop speaking out on human rights," *Washington Post*, December 23, https://washingtonpost.com/opinions/2019/12/23/indias-foreign-minister-refused-meet-me-i-wont-stop-speaking-out-human-rights/ (last accessed June 2022).
93. Sumitra Badrinathan, Devesh Kapur, and Milan Vaishnav (2020) "How Will Indian Americans Vote? Results From the 2020 Indian American Attitudes," Carnegie Endowment for International Peace, October 14, https://carnegieendowment.org/files/IAAS_full_final.pdf (last accessed December 2021).
94. Azad Essa (2020) "Biden campaign accused of 'cosmetic' changes as pro-Modi aide remains," *Middle East Eye*, March 9, https://middleeasteye.net/news/biden-appoints-hillary-clintons-muslim-advisor-canvas-muslim-vote (last accessed October 2021).
95. Azad Essa (2020) Pakistani Americans, a Biden rally and the Modi supporter who organized it," *Middle East Eye*, August 18, https://middleeasteye.net/news/joe-biden-campaign-rally-pakistan-americans (last accessed April 2022).
96. Sumitra Badrinathan, Devesh Kapur, and Milan Vaishnav (2021) "How Do Indian Americans View India? Results From the 2020 Indian American Attitudes Survey," Carnegie Endowment for International Peace, February 9, https://carnegieendowment.org/2021/02/09/how-do-indian-americans-view-india-results-from-2020-indian-american-attitudes-survey-pub-83800 (last accessed July 2022).
97. Soumya Shankar (2019) "India's Liberal Expats Are Modi's Biggest Fans," *Foreign Policy*, May 7, https://foreignpolicy.com/2019/05/07/indias-liberal-expats-are-modis-biggest-fans/ (last accessed July 2022).

98. Badrinathan, Kapur, and Vaishnav, "How Will Indian Americans Vote?"
99. Ibid.
100. Interview with Indian American organizer with South Asia Solidarity Initiative (SASI) in New York City, December 5, 2021.
101. The context in which Tadepalli narrated her experience is also instructive to the extent to which the Jewish and Indian communities are interacting on questions of nationalism, religion and politics. Tadepalli was invited to speak about her experience during a podcast called "Interfaith-ish," in which she joined Sarah Brammer-Shlay, a co-founder of IfNotNow, the Jewish youth group calling for an end to U.S. support for the Israeli occupation. Both narrated their stories they grew up with around Israel and India.
102. Sravya Tadepalli (2021) "Conflicting narratives," Interfaith-ish Podcast, November, https://soundcloud.com/interfaithish/episode92 (last accessed December 2021).
103. Interview with Dalit organizer on May 16, 2022.
104. Prakash Nanda (2021) "How Are Jewish Americans Helping The Indian Diaspora In Raising Their Clout In The US Government?" *Eurasian Times*, January 21, https://eurasiantimes.com/jewish-americans-help-the-indian-diaspora-in-raising-its-clout-in-the-usa/ (last accessed December 2021).

Chapter 5

1. Anderson explains Hindustan is originally a Persian word that signified the land beyond the Indus, was "transformed into a sectarian slogan as Hindustan by the Sangh" (the group of organizations that make up the Hindu right wing), in Perry Anderson (2013) *The Indian Ideology*, Verso Books, London and New York, p. 145.
2. Edward Said (1979) *The Question of Palestine*, Vintage Book, New York, p. 107.
3. Interview with Noam Chomsky, June 26, 2021.
4. Anderson, *The Indian Ideology*, p. 147.
5. Said, *The Question of Palestine*, p. 58.
6. Kancha Ilaiah (2002) *Why I am not a Hindu*, Samya, Calcutta, p. 114.

7. In his book The Indian Ideology, Perry Anderson compares the rise of Likud in Israel, the BJP in India, as well as the Fianna Fail in Ireland. For a more detailed analysis: Perry Anderson (2013) *The Indian Ideology*, Verso Books, London and New York, pp. 146–8.
8. Anderson, *The Indian Ideology*, p. 147.
9. Vineet Khare (2019) "The Indian Dalit man killed for eating in front of upper-caste men," BBC, May 20, https://bbc.com/news/world-asia-india-48265387 (last accessed April 2022).
10. Mari Marcel (2016) "Drowning in Liquid Filth—in 21st Century India," in New Internationalist Magazine, March 25, 2016, https://newint.org/blog/2016/03/24/drowning-in-liquid-filth-india-in-21st-century (last accessed April 2022).
11. Noam Chomsky and Andrew Vltchek (2013) *On Western Terrorism*, Pluto Press, London, p. 86.
12. Apoorvanand (2017) "What is behind India's epidemic of 'mob lynching'?" *Al Jazeera English*, July 6, https://aljazeera.com/opinions/2017/7/6/what-is-behind-indias-epidemic-of-mob-lynching (last accessed September 2021).
13. Akshaya Mukul (2014) "Ancient caste system worked well, ICHR head says," *Times of India*, July 15, https://timesofindia.indiatimes.com/india/ancient-caste-system-worked-well-ichr-head-says/articleshow/38401312.cms (last accessed September 2021).
14. Alex Traub (2018) "India's Dangerous New Curriculum," *New York Review of Books*, November 6, https://nybooks.com/articles/2018/12/06/indias-dangerous-new-curriculum/ (last accessed October 2021).
15. Arundhati Katju (2020) "The Hindu Nationalist Myth of Love Jihad," *Foreign Affairs*, December 23, https://foreignaffairs.com/articles/india/2020-12-23/hindu-nationalist-myth-love-jihad?utm_source=google&utm_medium=cpc&utm_campaign=gap_ds&gclid=CjwKCAiAlrSPBhBaEiwAuLSDUK9riNTPveX7uBpic4awVBvNj-4UF4O7LbeyvMgWah810CR-zaOowxoCogsQAvD_BwE (last accessed January 2022).
16. Gopal B. Kateshiya (2016) "Gujarat: 7 of Dalit family beaten up for skinning dead cow," *Indian Express*, July 20, https://indianexpress.com/article/india/india-news-india/gujarat-7-

of-dalit-family-beaten-up-for-skinning-dead-cow-2910054/ (last accessed October 2021).

17. Justin Jones (2019) "India's triple talaq law has divided even those who oppose the practice," September 16, https://qz.com/india/1709560/will-criminalising-triple-talaq-help-indias-muslim-women/ (last accessed September 2021).
18. For decades, the state has been battling an insurgency in central India, predominantly populated by tribal communities, many of whom have remained unwilling to let their homes, land and forests become fodder for corporations or "state development."
19. Kranti Kumara (2021) "Indian courts continue to sanction open-ended imprisonment without trial," *World Socialist Website*, December 3, https://wsws.org/en/articles/2021/12/04/navl-d04.html (last accessed January 2022).
20. Niha Masih and Joanna Slater (2021) "Evidence found on a second Indian activist's computer was planted, report says," *Washington Post*, July 6, https://washingtonpost.com/world/2021/07/06/bhima-koregaon-case-india/ (last accessed January 2022).
21. The first Dharma Sansad (or a platform at which decisions are made regarding Dharma, or law, duty, or religious principles) was organized by the right-wing Vishva Hindu Parishad (VHP), also known as the Universal Hindu Council) was held in 1984, where the Ram Temple movement was launched. The movement believed that a mediaeval-era Babri Mosque in Ayodhya had been built on top of the birthplace of the God Ram. In 1992, the mosque was razed to the ground by a mob and revitalized the Hindu nationalist movement across India.
22. Lalmani Verma (2022) "Dharma sansad and mahamandaleshwar: who they are, the role they play," *Indian Express*, January 20, https://indianexpress.com/article/explained/explained-dharma-sansad-and-mahamandaleshwar-7715041/ (last accessed March 2022).
23. Al Jazeera (2021) "India: Hindu event calling for genocide of Muslims sparks outrage," *Al Jazeera English*, December 24, https://aljazeera.com/news/2021/12/24/india-hindu-event-calling-for-genocide-of-muslims-sparks-outrage (last accessed August 2022).

24. Dhirendra K Jha (2022) "Unholy Orders," *Caravan*, March 1, https://caravanmagazine.in/commentary/haridwar-dharma-sansad-vhp-rss-hate-speech (last accessed June 2022).
25. Satadru Sen (2015) "Ethnocracy, Israel and India," *History and Sociology of South Asia*, Vol. 9, No. 2, p. 109.
26. Oren Yiftachel (2006) *Ethnocracy: Land and Identity politics in Israel/Palestine*, University of Pennsylvania Press, Philadelphia, p. 100.
27. Ibid.
28. It should be noted that the goal to annex the occupied Palestinian territories predates Benjamin Netanyahu.
29. B'tselem (2021) "A regime of Jewish supremacy from the Jordan River to the Mediterranean Sea: This is apartheid," *B'tselem*, January 12, https://btselem.org/publications/fulltext/202101_this_is_apartheid (last accessed January 2022).
30. Yiftachel, *Ethnocracy: Land and Identity politics in Israel/Palestine*, p. 100.
31. My decision to use Yiftachel's characterization of Israel as an "ethnocracy" as opposed to a liberal Western democracy is not an attempt to valorize democracies in North America, Europe, or Australasia, all of whom as Oren Yiftachel writes, exercised violent means to establish ethnocracies at the time of formation or independence. These Western states remain de facto ethnocracies today, as demonstrated by the resurgence of white supremacy and anti-immigrant rhetoric and policies throughout much of Europe and North America. However, in Israel's case, the ethnocentrism of the Jewish dominance in state apparatus is underwritten by law. And whereas other settler-colonial Western states, like the U.S., Canada, or Australia have been increasingly forced to face-up to their history of genocide, colonization, and ethnic cleansing, Israel still seeks to convince (the world and itself) that the settler Jews are the original inhabitants and that this is their homeland.
32. Yiftachel, *Ethnocracy: Land and Identity politics in Israel/Palestine*, p. 94.
33. M.S. Golwalkar (2006 [1939]) *We or our nationhood defined* Pharos Publishing, Delhi, p. 104.

34. Sen, Satadru (2015) "Fascism without Fascists? A comparative look at Hindutva and Zionism," *South Asia: Journal of South Asian Studies*, Vol. 38, No. 4, pp. 690–711.
35. Kaushik Raj and Alishan Jafri (2022) "As Hindu Extremists Repeatedly Call For Muslim Genocide, The Police Ignore An Obvious Conspiracy," *Article 14*, January 10, https://article-14.com/post/as-hindu-extremists-repeatedly-call-for-muslim-genocide-the-police-ignore-an-obvious-conspiracy-61dba33fa759c?fbclid=IwAR28UN-vALZzFq4DOUxkna6WFe-M8wEQ8SQ3IQCLPWE_i94iUmSDhkd5NSGQ (last accessed January 2022).
36. Satadru, "Fascism without Fascists?" pp. 690–711.
37. Ibid., p. 710.
38. *Hindustan Times* (2020) "Former JNU student Umar Khalid arrested in connection with North-East Delhi riots," *Hindustan Times*, September 14, https://hindustantimes.com/india-news/umar-khalid-/story-lj2XPxkP50PNZ100HIlACI.html (last accessed January 2022).
39. Umar Khalid (2021) "I have not spent a day or night in my cell without extreme anxiety: Umar Khalid from Tihar," *The Print*, May 26, https://theprint.in/opinion/i-have-not-spent-a-day-or-night-in-my-cell-without-extreme-anxiety-umar-khalid-from-tihar/665033/ (last accessed January 2022).
40. Amnesty (2020) "In the pandemic, India's middle class shrinks and poverty spreads while China sees smaller changes," Amnesty International, April 20, https://amnesty.org/en/wp-content/uploads/2021/05/ASA2021742020ENGLISH.pdf (last accessed January 2022).
41. According to the *New York Times*, the only other Amnesty country office to shut down had been in Russia, back in 2016. Sameer Yasir and Hari Kumar (2020) "Amnesty International Shutters Offices in India, Citing Government Attacks," *New York Times*, September 29, https://nytimes.com/2020/09/29/world/asia/india-amnesty-international.html (last accessed January 2022).
42. AB Wire (2016) "Indian Govt. bans 20,000 NGOs from receiving foreign funds, in American Bazaar," December 27, https://americanbazaaronline.com/2016/12/27/indian-govt-bans-20000-ngos-receiving-foreign-funds/ (last accessed March 2022).

43. Express News Service (2022) "Hate speech condemnation must not be selective: 32 ex-diplomats in open letter," *Indian Express*, January 6, https://indianexpress.com/article/india/haridwar-dharam-sansand-diplomats-letter-7708029/ (last accessed April 2022).
44. UN Women (2016) "UN Women Deputy Executive Director Lakshmi Puri receives the Eleanor Roosevelt Human Rights Award," UN Women, October 24, https://unwomen.org/en/news/stories/2016/10/speech-by-deputy-executive-director-lakshmi-puri-receiving-eleanor-roosevelt-award (last accessed January 2022).
45. Raj and Jafri, "As Hindu Extremists Repeatedly Call For Muslim Genocide . . ."
46. The Hindu Bureau (2022) "Focus on rights made India weak, says PM," *The Hindu*, January 22, https://thehindu.com/news/national/system-being-created-where-there-is-no-place-for-any-discrimination-pm-modi/article38296828.ece (last accessed January 2022).
47. PTI (2017) "Hindus should follow 'We two, our eight' policy: Religious guru Swami Prabodhananda Giri," *Economic Times*, May 1, https://economictimes.indiatimes.com/news/politics-and-nation/hindus-should-follow-we-two-our-eight-policy-religious-guru-swami-prabodhananda-giri/articleshow/58460719.cms (last accessed January 2022).
48. Sheikh Saaliq (2022) "Indian scholars, activists criticize school hijab ban ruling," *AP*, April 3, https://apnews.com/article/narendra-modi-india-religion-islam-education-4956a0d0f914587 4993bbbc72939a2f4 (last accessed April 2022).
49. Azad Essa (2022) "For Indian Muslims, the end times have arrived," *Middle East Eye*, April 13, https://middleeasteye.net/opinion/india-muslims-end-times-arrived (last accessed July 2022).
50. Iram Siddique (2022) "In Khargone, bulldozers also leave behind rubble of house built under PM Awas Yojana," in Indian Express, April 13, https://indianexpress.com/article/cities/bhopal/mp-khargone-demolition-communal-violence-houses-pm-awas-yojana-7866760/ (last accessed July 2022).

51. Naveen Tewari and Sandeep Pandey (2022) "Bulldozing houses in UP: India isn't Israel, Muslims living here 'aren't Palestinians,'" *CounterView*, June 26, https://counterview.net/2022/06/bulldozing-houses-in-up-india-isnt.html (last accessed July 2022).
52. Angshuman Choudhury (2022) "Bulldozing Indian Democracy, Israeli-Style," *The India Forum*, June 21, https://theindiaforum.in/article/bulldozing-democracy-israeli-style (last accessed July 2022).
53. Interview with Afreen Fatima, June 17, 2022.
54. Interview with Achin Vnaik, October 8, 2021.
55. Ramzy Baroud (2017) "'Children of the stones': the day Palestine was reborn," *Al Jazeera English*, December 8, https://aljazeera.com/opinions/2017/12/8/children-of-the-stones-the-day-palestine-was-reborn (last accessed April 2022).
56. Abdulla Moaswes (2019) "What's happening in Kashmir looks a lot like Israel's rule over Palestine," *+972 Magazine*, August 12, https://972mag.com/kashmir-india-israel-palestine-occupation/ (last accessed June 2022).
57. Samreen Mushtaq and Mudasir Amin (2021) "'We will memorize our home': exploring settler colonialism as an interpretive framework for Kashmir," *Third World Quarterly*, pp. 3012–29.
58. B'Tselem (2017) "Open-Fire Policy," *B'Tselem*, November 11, https://btselem.org/firearms (last accessed July 2022).
59. Samreen Mushtaq and Mudasir Amin (2020) "India's settler colonialism in Kashmir is not starting now, eliminating the natives is a process long underway," *Polis Project*, https://thepolisproject.com/read/indias-settler-colonialism-in-kashmir-is-not-starting-now-eliminating-the-natives-is-a-process-long-underway/ (last accessed January 2021).
60. Faheem Hamid Lone (2020) "Indian General Bipin Rawat argues for internment camps for Kashmir's children. This is not the first time the general of the colonial state has made such vile comments," *Stand with Kashmir*, January 17, https://standwithkashmir.medium.com/indian-general-bipin-rawat-argues-for-internment-camps-for-kashmirs-children-2b53fb18faab (last accessed January 2022).
61. The Wire Staff (2019) "BJP Workers Excited to Marry Fair Girls From Kashmir, Says UP MLA," *The Wire*, August 7, https://

thewire.in/women/vikram-saini-bjp-kashmir-article-370 (last accessed April 2022).

62. HAF (2019) "FAQs about Kashmir and Articles 370/35A," HAF, https://hinduamerican.org/issues/kashmir-struggle/faq-article-370 (last accessed December 2021).
63. Ather Zia, The Specter of Gender Discrimination in the Removal of Kashmir's Autonomy," *Association for Political and Legal Anthropology*, September 1, https://politicalandlegalanthro.org/2020/09/01/the-specter-of-gender-discrimination-in-the-removal-of-kashmirs-autonomy/ (last accessed January 2021).
64. Anish Gawande (2019) "The False Link Between Article 370 and Queer Rights," *The Wire*, September 6, https://thewire.in/lgbtqia/all-you-need-to-know-about-the-false-link-between-article-370-and-queer-rights (last accessed December 2021).
65. SWK (2020) "Pinkwashing and 'Pride Kashmir,'" *Stand with Kashmir*, July 7, https://standwithkashmir.org/pinkwashing-and-pride-kashmir/ (last accessed January 2022).
66. Ram Madhav (2019) "Kashmir is ours also means every Kashmiri is ours," *Indian Express*, February 26, https://indianexpress.com/article/opinion/columns/pakistan-terrorism-pulwama-attack-india-kashmir-unsc-5600564 (last accessed August 2022).
67. Mushtaq and Amin, "India's settler colonialism in Kashmir is not starting now . . ."
68. Mushtaq and Amin, "'We will memorise our home.'"
69. Ibid.
70. Azad Essa (2019) "India consul general in United States calls for 'Israeli model' in Kashmir," *Middle East Eye*, November 26, https://middleeasteye.net/news/india-consul-general-united-states-calls-israeli-solution-kashmir (last accessed July 2022).
71. Al Jazeera (2019) "Anger over India's diplomat calling for 'Israel model' in Kashmir," *Al Jazeera English*, November 28, https://aljazeera.com/news/2019/11/28/anger-over-indias-diplomat-calling-for-israel-model-in-kashmir (last accessed December 2021).
72. Ibid.
73. Al Jazeera (2019) "India's BJP to revive Hindu settlement plan in Kashmir: Report," *Al Jazeera English*, July 12, https://aljazeera.

com/news/2019/7/12/indias-bjp-to-revive-hindu-settlement-plan-in-kashmir-report (last accessed August 2022).

74. Zainab Ramahi and Azadeh Shahshahani (2020) "Destroying to Replace: Settler Colonialism from Kashmir to Palestine," Verso Blog, August 10, https://versobooks.com/blogs/4817-destroying-to-replace-settler-colonialism-from-kashmir-to-palestine (last accessed January 2022).
75. SWK (2019) "Why is Rutgers University hosting an Islamophobe and a sexual predator to talk about Kashmir?" *Stand With Kashmir*, https://standwithkashmir.org/why-is-rutgers-university-hosting-an-islamophobe-and-a-sexual-predator-to-talk-about-kashmir/ (last accessed January 2022).
76. Gowhar Geelani (2019) "Right-wing exaggerates the number of Kashmiri Pandits killed. Militants targeted Muslims more," *The Print*, https://theprint.in/pageturner/excerpt/right-wing-exaggerates-number-of-kashmiri-pandits-killed-militants-targeted-muslims-more/271666/ (last accessed January 2022).
77. Mihir Sharma (2019) "The Politics of Life Itself," *Jamhoor*, September 13, https://jamhoor.org/read/2019/09/13/the-politics-of-life-itself (last accessed January 2022).
78. Deepti Misri and Mona Bhan (2019) "Kashmiri Pandits must reimagine the idea of return to Kashmir," *Al Jazeera English*, August 10, https://aljazeera.com/opinions/2019/8/10/kashmiri-pandits-must-reimagine-the-idea-of-return-to-kashmir (last accessed April 2022).
79. Hafsa Kanjwal (2020), "India accelerates its nationalist transformation of Kashmir as world remains silent," *Washington Post*, August 4, https://washingtonpost.com/opinions/2020/08/04/india-accelarates-its-nationalist-transformation-kashmir-world-remains-silent/ (last accessed January 2022).
80. Mushtaq and Amin, "'We will memorise our home.'"
81. Ibid.
82. Ramahi and Shahshahani, "Destroying to Replace: Settler Colonialism from Kashmir to Palestine."
83. Mushtaq and Amin, "'We will memorise our home,'" p. 3023.
84. Times Now Digital (2022) "Now anyone can buy land in Jammu and Kashmir, Ladakh," *Times Now*, October 27, https://timesnownews.com/india/article/centre-notifies-land-law-anyone-can-now-

buy-land-in-jammu-and-kashmir-ladakh/673317 (last accessed July 2022).

85. Shrimoyee Nandini Ghosh (2019) "One nation, One flag, one constitution," *Raiot*, September 16, https://raiot.in/dismantling-370-in-kashmir-part-1/ (last accessed January 2022).
86. Auqib Javed (2020) "Why It's Easier For Army To Take Over Land In J&K," *Article 14*, July 29, https://article-14.com/post/2-legal-tweaks-make-it-easier-for-armed-forces-to-take-over-land-in-j-k (last accessed January 2022).
87. Aakash Hassan (2020) "Why are Kashmiri Muslim nomads being evicted?" *Al Jazeera English*, November 20, https://aljazeera.com/news/2020/11/20/tribal-community-face-eviction-from-forests-in-kashmir (last accessed May 2022).
88. Mahmood Mamdani (2020) *Neither Settler Nor Native: The Making and Unmaking of Permanent Minorities*, Wits University Press, Johannesburg, p. 292.
89. Raja Muzaffar Bhat "With Fresh Order, Jammu & Kashmir Will Lose Its Limited Farmlands," *News Click*, January 10, https://newsclick.in/With-Fresh-Order-Jammu-Kashmir-Lose-Limited-Farmlands (last accessed January 2022).
90. Shinzani Jain (2020) "New Delhi's Twin Agenda in J&K—Control Land Use, Destroy Food Security," *News Click*, October 13, https://newsclick.in/new-delhi-twin-agenda-jammu-kashmir-control-land-destroy-food-security (last accessed January 2022).
91. Mushtaq and Amin, "'We will memorise our home,'" p. 3023.
92. Ishan Kukreti (2019) "With state under lockdown, J&K FAC issues record forest clearances," *Down to Earth*, October 18, https://downtoearth.org.in/news/forests/amp/with-state-under-lockdown-j-k-fac-issues-record-forest-clearances-67322 (last accessed June 2022).
93. Mushtaq and Amin, "'We will memorise our home,'" p. 3024.
94. Evita Das (2020) "Was Kashmir being readied for demographic change even before Article 370 was scrapped?" *News Laundry*, September 7, https://newslaundry.com/2020/09/07/was-kashmir-being-readied-for-demographic-change-even-before-article-370-was-scrapped (last accessed January 2022).
95. Hafsa Kanjwal (2020) "India accelerates its nationalist transformation of Kashmir as the world remains silent,"

Washington Post, August 4, https://washingtonpost.com/opinions/2020/08/04/india-accelarates-its-nationalist-transformation-kashmir-world-remains-silent/ (last accessed January 2022).

96. Mushtaq and Amin, "'We will memorise our home,'" p. 3024.
97. Alexander Cornwell (2022) Dubai's DP World to build dry port in India's Jammu and Kashmir, regional leader says," *Reuters*, January 6, https://reuters.com/markets/commodities/dubais-dp-world-build-dry-port-indias-jammu-kashmir-regional-leader-says-2022-01-06/ (last accessed August 2022).
98. Siddhartha Deb (2019) "India's Looming Ethno-Nationalist Catastrophe," *New Republic*, August 7, https://newrepublic.com/article/154682/india-looming-ethno-nationalist-catastrophe (last accessed January 2022).
99. Hafsa Kanjwal (2021) "Kashmir's Already Vulnerable Civil Society is Being Crushed," *Washington Post*, December 8, https://washingtonpost.com/opinions/2021/12/08/kashmir-civil-society-khurram-parvez-democracy-summit-india/ (last accessed January 2022).
100. SWK (2021) "India is arresting Kashmiris for anything & everything under the "UAPA law," in Stand With Kashmir, December 20, https://standwithkashmir.org/india-is-arresting-kashmiri-for-anything-everything-under-the-uapa-law/ (last accessed January 2022).
101. Riffat Fareed (2021) "UN calls for release of Kashmir rights defender Khurram Parvez," *Al Jazeera English*, December 1, https://aljazeera.com/news/2021/12/1/un-calls-for-release-of-kashmir-rights-defender-khurram-parvez (last accessed April 2022).
102. Several Kashmiri journalists told me they would rather not speak publicly about the visits from the intelligence services in order to avoid further harassment.
103. OHCHR (2021) "Israel's 'terrorism' designation an unjustified attack on Palestinian civil society—Bachelet," OHCHR, October 26, https://ohchr.org/EN/NewsEvents/Pages/DisplayNews.aspx?NewsID=27708&LangID=E (last accessed January 2022).
104. Irfan Amin Malik (2020) "Why Journalists Are Worried About the New Media Policy in Jammu and Kashmir," *The Wire*, July

17, https://thewire.in/media/kashmir-new-media-policy-press-freedom, (last accessed January 2022).
105. Auqib Javeed (2020) "Kashmir's New Media Policy Menaces Its Media," *Article 14*, July 6, https://article-14.com/post/kashmir-s-new-media-policy-menaces-its-media (last accessed January 2022).
106. Safwat Zargar (2020) "'We're being watched': Kashmir decision to vet social media feeds of new employees sparks alarm," *Scroll*, https://scroll.in/article/989089/were-being-watched-kashmir-decision-to-check-social-media-feeds-of-new-employees-sparks-alarm (last accessed January 2022).
107. https://thebaffler.com/latest/a-culture-of-resistance-asokan (last accessed July 2022).
108. Muzamil Jaleel (2021) "Kashmir Meet After Two Years of Ruin: A Reckoning or a New Tack?" *Inverse Journal*, June 24, https://inversejournal.com/2021/06/24/kashmir-meet-after-two-years-of-ruin-a-reckoning-or-a-new-tack-by-muzamil-jaleel/ (last accessed January 2022).
109. BDS India, the Indian news site News Click and the People's Dispatch (2020) "Israel-India Military Relations: Ideological Paradigms of Security," January, p. 7, https://peoplesdispatch.org/wp-content/uploads/2020/01/India-Israel-Military-Relations-2020_compressed.pdf (last accessed July 2022).
110. Shir Hever (2022) "Elbit Systems: The Israeli arms company under fire from activists," *Middle East Eye*, January 14, https://middleeasteye.net/news/israel-uk-elbit-systems-arms-company-under-fire-activists (last accessed July 2022).
111. MEMO (2020) "Israel's largest arms manufacturer targeted in London by Palestine Action activists," *Middle East Monitor*, August 21, https://middleeastmonitor.com/20200821-israels-largest-arms-manufacturer-targeted-in-london-by-palestine-action-activists/ (last accessed July 2022).

Index

Thanks to our Patreon subscriber:

Ciaran Kane

Who has shown generosity and comradeship in support of our publishing.

Check out the other perks you get by subscribing to our Patreon – visit patreon.com/plutopress. Subscriptions start from £3 a month.